FIRST EDITION

Library of Congress Cataloging-in-Publication Data has been applied for.

ISBN 978-0-06-288444-2

23 24 25 26 27 LBC 8 7 6 5 4

This book is dedicated to all women who are feeling the hunger to embody their truth, to break the cycles of trauma in their families, and to more fully express their power and potential. As we heal our personal and collective trauma, we clear the way for more female power to manifest in the world. May you feel the support of all the brave women across time and space, with you, cheering you on.

One day you finally knew

what you had to do, and began,

though the voices around you

kept shouting

their bad advice—

though the whole house

began to tremble

and you felt the old tug

at your ankles.

"Mend my life!"

each voice cried.

But you didn't stop.

You knew what you had to do,

though the wind pried

with its stiff fingers

at the very foundations—

though their melancholy

was terrible.

It was already late

enough, and a wild night,

and the road full of fallen

branches and stones.

But little by little,

as you left their voices behind,

the stars began to burn

through the sheets of clouds,

and there was a new voice,

which you slowly

recognized as your own,

that kept you company

as you strode deeper and deeper

into the world,

determined to do

the only thing you could do—

determined to save

the only life you could save.

"THE JOURNEY" BY MARY OLIVER

CONTENTS

AUTHOR'S NOTE

The nature of memory and perception is subjective, inherently rooted in the observer's own experience.

The personal examples in this book are based on my own perceptions of people and events that took place in my childhood and how I feel they have impacted my life as an adult.

I've done my best to be accurate and fair when describing my recollections of people and events throughout this book and want to be clear that these perspectives are not statements of fact but of my own personal opinions and perceptions.

INTRODUCTION

From a young age, I felt that something was wrong in my relationship with my mother, but instinctively I coped by keeping silent and obedient in the role of the "good girl." Around nineteen, my symptoms became so intense that I sought professional help, and was fortunate to embark on a rare decades-long journey with a therapist specializing in in-depth, corrective, relational-based therapy, a journey that continues to this day. In the beginning, I avoided examining my relationship with my mother, but I felt determined to understand the root cause of my despair, which for years felt like a mystery to me. Week after week, year after year, decade after decade, I've continued to discover insights, connections, and breakthroughs that I haven't seen reflected in accessible works of personal development, psychology, or self-help.

In 2013 I started a blog, hungry to share all that I was discovering about the Mother Wound. No one seemed to be talking about this phenomenon, and I wanted to help other women who, like me, were struggling to identify the root cause of their symptoms. Almost immediately after I started my blog, my articles began to go viral and word spread quickly across the world. A steady stream of emails began pouring in from women telling me their stories and thanking me for articulating the experiences they didn't have the words or the courage to speak about.

Synchronicities began to unfold all around me. Several months later, I had just booked a trip to Barcelona, Spain, for a rare vacation when I got an email the next day from a teacher in Barcelona asking if she could translate one of my articles for a women's workshop. I replied, saying that I'd actually be there at that time and would be happy to give a talk while I'm there about the article. One thing led to another and I ended up teaching two sold-out workshops during a single weekend of that trip. By introducing me to her network of collaborators in Europe, I came back to Spain to do a teaching tour of cities from Barcelona to Bilbao, Madrid, Valladolid, and more. Women traveled from all over Europe to these workshops. Before I knew it, I was taking a train across the UK, teaching workshops in London, Totnes, Frome, Nottingham, and others. Then the invitations started coming in from Budapest, Berlin, Italy, Vienna, Croatia, Belgium, Poland, the Netherlands, and Austria, and from further afield in India, Bali, Japan, and Thailand.

In every city I went to, I would enter a room packed to the gills with women, curious, nervous, and eager to connect with other women and heal this issue. These women ran the gamut from business executives, therapists, academics, and stay-at-home moms, to college students, grandmothers, entrepreneurs, and millennials. By the end of each workshop, an initial heaviness in the room opened into immense lightness, spaciousness, and electricity in the air. I was amazed at the deep bonds that were quickly created as we explored this taboo issue together.

Later that year, I returned home from a women's conference frustrated by what I saw as a lack of depth in our discussion of women's issues. I saw how even at the highest levels of success the Mother Wound was hiding in plain sight but still being avoided. From this sense of urgency, I penned an essay called "Why It's Crucial for Women to Heal the Mother Wound." This particular article appeared to rapidly increase awareness about the Mother Wound to a whole new level, with women starting to use the term more widely in news articles, podcasts, workshops, and on social media.

I knew that I wanted to write a book about the Mother Wound, but it stayed on the backburner as my business kept expanding as I continued writing, traveling, and teaching. Eventually I was able to leave my job as a university administrator and focus on this work full time. Over time, I noticed that one of the markers of women healing the Mother Wound is an increased willingness to disrupt and transform business as usual, a powerful desire to be true, authentic, and to live life on one's own terms. I saw women walking away from marriages, jobs, and relationships that didn't serve them, or begin transforming them from within, and in both cases, inspiring and galvanizing the people around them, moving things to a higher level.

When Trump was elected, I felt an increased urgency to write a book so that I could reach more women and teach them about the Mother Wound, how it relates to dismantling patriarchy, and why it's important we heal it. One morning I woke up with a clear feeling it was time to get the book out as soon as possible; the world was changing and this message was needed more than ever. I had planned to reply to one of the publishers who had reached out to me, even without an agent. But it seems the universe had other plans as the very next day I received an unsolicited email from an agent interested in representing me. The result is the book you are holding in your hands.

In short, writing a book about the Mother Wound has been an organic outcome of over two decades of research and painstaking inner work. This is the book that I wish I'd had at the time when I began my own journey. This is also a book *for this* time, a time when a global awakening of women is essential to our collective survival.

In this book I will share with you my own journey of how I discovered the Mother Wound and the tools I use to continue to work through it myself and with thousands of women. I will also discuss the profound breakthroughs that emerged from finding my own Inner Mother, and the resulting insights I've gained about feminism, intergenerational trauma, and human potential.

The Mother Wound Is a Form of Cultural and Familial Trauma Specific to Those Living in a Patriarchy

Both men and women have the Mother Wound. Manifestations of this wound are personal, cultural, spiritual, and planetary. This topic is so endemic in our culture that it could and should fill several volumes: this book is only an introduction, and its focus is mostly on the personal level. I have focused here on what the Mother Wound looks like where you will first encounter it: in your own experience. I believe once we have each healed the Mother Wound sufficiently on an individual level, we will be better prepared to meet the demands of transforming it as a society. This work isn't about blaming our mothers but about generational and intergenerational responsibility. It's about owning our power as women and, consequently, creating a new balance and harmony between healthy masculine and feminine energies in our world.

Through the years writers such as Adrienne Rich and Christiane Northrup have mentioned the term "Mother Wound," but no one has ever fleshed out exactly what the Mother Wound is and why it remains a universal experience of women the world over. In this book, I aim to fill a crucial gap in our understanding of women's psychology and empowerment by comprehensively defining the Mother Wound, explaining how it manifests in women's lives, and providing an overarching vision along with practical guidance for the healing journey.

Although I have bachelor's and master's degrees in psychology, I am a coach, not a psychotherapist or a trauma specialist. An appendix with more technical terms elaborated on by my therapist, Nicole Ditz, has been provided on page 257 for those who want to learn more, as this book will touch on topics like brain functioning and complex developmental trauma.

Discovering the Inner Mother will brush up against topics of intersectionality, gender, sexuality, race, religion, and other vectors of our culture laced intrinsically with the Mother Wound. Likewise, the relationship of sons and the Mother Wound, as well as the patterns for fathers interacting with daughters, are incredibly important areas adjacent to the material in this book. The ways in which these topics intersect with the Mother Wound are deserving of quality and in-depth analysis, which the constraints of a single volume do not allow. I look forward to addressing them at length in future works.

To that end, I would also like to acknowledge that my experiences are informed by the privilege of who I am and where I come from as an educated, white, middle-class woman. We are all limited by the scope of our own lives, and my experiences do not speak for everyone. I am aware that my own experiences and identities limit my perspectives and understanding. I offer my story as one example and a doorway into discussion, in hopes that it will help you shine a light on your own unique situation.

I have written this book as a white woman who has benefited from unearned skin-based privileges, who has benefited from the painful legacies left by my ancestors, and who is committed to my own internal and external work toward dismantling racism and systems of oppression, and to the highest standards of accountability. While my research and conversations with thousands of women reveal a resonance with the phenomenon of the Mother Wound across many races and cultures, factors of systemic, institutionalized racism, race-based oppression and trauma, and others compound and intersect with the Mother Wound for many women.

When I speak of the Mother Wound in the context of patriarchal cultures, I am referring to the pervasive, patriarchal, capitalist cultures rooted in colonization and destruction of the earth that have come to dominate much of the world. This book, describing my own personal story and observations, is intended to serve as merely an opening for a loud chorus of women's voices from a wide variety of backgrounds, races, and cultures to emerge and share their lived experiences of the Mother Wound.

While this book is focused on women, I think that anyone who reads it will gain something of value. For those women who are mothers, I invite you to read this book from the perspective of yourself *as a daughter*, as that is the perspective from which the Mother Wound is healed. As you gain insights about how you were raised and the impact this had on you, how you show up as a mother is likely to shift in positive ways as a result, enabling stronger, healthier bonds with your children.

This book moves from the personal to the cultural, beginning with a discussion of what the Mother Wound is, how it manifests, and the kind of power dynamics it feeds on. From there, we delve into the process of addressing the trauma within your own family, the inner work this requires, and finally the changes you can expect to see as you make your way to the other side. At the conclusion of each chapter is a set of questions for reflection, offered to assist you in exploring the material in the context of your own experience. For those who read the book and feel ready to dive deeper into the healing process, I recommend checking out my website for more resources and information.

Ultimately, healing the Mother Wound is not about our mothers. It's about women embracing ourselves and our gifts without shame. It's about expanding our capacity for holding and transforming emotional pain into consciousness. It's about restoring an ancient imbalance created by patriarchy. No longer do we unconsciously feel ourselves to be abandoned children in despair, projecting our unconscious pain all around us. Healing our Mother Wounds allows us to become the loving witness to the beloved child within, and to embody the benevolent feminine consciousness that has been lying dormant within many of us. Intergenerational healing requires that we learn how to embody the very things we never received, to be the loving presence that we longed for ourselves, the unconditional, benevolent presence that's there no matter what. To realize that within us we have an untapped reservoir of support with which we can link at any time. We become not only the holder but the held, the longing and the longed-for, a collective vessel for something new and unprecedented to be born into this world.

Here's a brief sample of what we gain through healing the Mother Wound:

Resensitize Yourself to Life: Life gets reanimated. Instead of seeing things through a lens of deadening labels and an overlay of traumatic projections, we can more easily perceive the visceral beauty, depth, and preciousness of life all around us.

Integrate Instead of Compartmentalize: We are better able to see life as an integrated whole, and our self-awareness increases. We see connections more than differences. The differences we do see feel less threatening. We are more open to feedback.

Redefine Triggers as Opportunities: Our reactivity is a pointer showing us what is next for us to heal from our past. Each trigger is an opportunity to make new choices that we couldn't as kids.

Reclaim Embodied Ways of Knowing: Felt experience becomes a source of wisdom and information. We act on our own self-knowledge and learn to trust it. We reclaim ourselves as the authority of our experience. We learn to trust our own observations and intuitions.

Anoint Being over Doing: We trust our need for rest, for silence, for space, for time without feeling like something terrible is going to happen if we aren't productive.

De-objectify the World Around You: As we become emotionally available for the traumatized child within us, we become emotionally available for other people, we feel empathy more deeply, and we feel more connected to nonhuman species and the earth itself.

Value the Vulnerable: As we get in touch with the scope and magnitude of how much we suffered emotionally as children, we see value in things like anger and grief, welcoming them rather than judging or shaming ourselves for them. We look forward to the renewal and regeneration they offer and the clarity that always follows in their wake.

Healing the Mother Wound is not a quick, glamorous, or easy path. But it is the true path to intergenerational healing and transformation that we must undertake to create lasting change for generations of the future. Through this work, we create a better world for ourselves, our families, our children, and the earth.

Chapter 1

WHAT IS THE MOTHER WOUND?

All great truths begin as blasphemy.
—*George Bernard Shaw*

WE WERE A MIDDLE-CLASS family in New England. My parents had stable jobs, and we lived in a nice neighborhood. I had a roof over my head, food on the table, and summer vacations. I received new school clothes and was thrown graduation parties. But as well-intentioned as my parents were, to me our home felt like an emotional war zone, with me at the center. My parents married young and, I believe, unconsciously replayed the dysfunctional patterns they had been subjected to growing up within their own families.

I was as young as six when my mother told me I was her best friend, and that she loved me more than anyone else. Around the same time, I noticed that my father had begun to stay out late drinking at bars; I would comfort my mother as she cried and join her in being mad at my father when he would finally come home.

I was her ally, her warrior, and, in an emotional context, her surrogate spouse. I sensed that my safety depended upon providing her with emotional support. When my dad was out late, we'd watch TV in her bed and talk. Her reliance on me made me feel needed and important, but I also felt imprisoned by her pain. I held out hope that one day my needs would be met, too.

As the years passed, I increasingly played family mediator—yelling at my dad on behalf of my mom; cushioning my dad from my mother's rage; stepping in to protect my brother when my father was violent. I was the family sponge for unwanted feelings, the shock absorber for crises, the problem-solver, and the emotional dumping ground. As a result, I continuously buried my needs, observations, feelings, and authentic responses deep within, sacrificing myself while overfunctioning for the family system. I was calm on the outside, but privately hypervigilant for impending catastrophes.

Around age seven, my repeating dreams were of finding a real baby, a baby who was mine and whom I could care for. I longed to be a real girl, not a doll, not an object, but a real girl deserving of emotional care and sustained, loving attention from a healthy adult. From elementary school through middle school, I developed a deep devotion to the Virgin Mary. My parents were not religious, so my devotion felt like my own special world apart from them, a lifeline amid the chaos. I would stay over at my great-grandmother's house on occasion, and she taught me how to pray. I was ten when she died, and I was given all her religious paraphernalia—statues, prayer cards, rosary beads, and books. I created an altar in my room and used to pray that Mary would appear to me on my walk home from school or in my backyard, as she did to the children in Fatima. I would do good deeds secretly, like helping other students at school or being generous with my brother, and offer them to her. I would try to go entire days without committing a single sin.

At eleven years old, I remember the silence of the house on a late afternoon when no one else was home. I pulled a large serrated knife out of a drawer in the kitchen and lifted up my shirt. I put the tip of the knife to the center of my chest and closed my eyes. I thought, this would make everything better, everyone would be happier without me. With me erased, I felt their pain and my pain would be finished. Ultimately, I was too scared to go through with it. Looking back I can see how clearly I had perceived my existence as the problem due to how dismissively I felt I was treated throughout my childhood.

All the way through college, I remained the "good girl" while feeling stalked by my mother's needs, which began to feel like an ominous shadow always at my back. From as early as I can remember, she would confide in me about various situations that were troubling her, whether that involved her dysfunctional relationship with my dad or something she was dealing with at work. As I got older, she seemed to expect me to be her sounding board, and with time, my resentment and anger grew about what I perceived as an imbalance in the relationship, which required my needs to be invisible. She appeared to expect me to relieve her from her worries. Often, a mention of my own troubles would seem to cause her to withdraw or be outright hostile. My role as emotional servant seemed to function as a lid on her rage. I felt I could not deviate from this role without some degree of punishment.

When I was successful as a student or in the arts, her pride in me always felt laced with the sharp, unspoken demands of "Don't leave me. Don't surpass me. Don't threaten me." I could acutely sense what felt like a ravenous abyss that she revealed only to me, which seemed to be kept at bay only by my "staying inside the lines" of what I perceived as her expectations that I be her pet, her personal cheerleader, and her best friend. When I expressed opinions that contrasted with hers, set boundaries, demonstrated a moment of confidence, or exerted my independence from her, she treated it as a betrayal. She would respond with a harsh take-down, an exasperated huff, or a swift dismissal of what I had said. Sometimes her response was just an angry, incredulous look, as though my capacity to express a separate reality to hers was causing her an abrupt physical pain. I had recurring dreams of being a prisoner, with my mother as my prison guard, making me sit and watch her eat food as I stood by, starving.

In college, I was adrift. I was beginning to live my mother's life, finding myself in relationships similar to the one she had with my father, and on the same career path, training to be a schoolteacher. I felt increasingly lost, depressed, and empty—and was less able to hide it. My own pain began to emerge, but I had no model for self-care. At nineteen, when I became unexpectedly pregnant, I had to stop and reevaluate who I was and who I wanted to be.

I remember the day I was in a health food store and went to the bulletin board looking at the flyers and business cards, quietly searching for information on local therapists. My eyes landed on a card that had the symbol of the goddess on it. I called the number on the card. I went to my first therapy session a week after my abortion. I embarked on what was to become twenty-two-plus years of in-depth, intensive, comprehensive, relationally based developmental trauma therapy. This therapy has continued regularly through all these years, up until the present day, and continues to be a lifeline on my journey.

Compared to conventional therapy, which typically includes a short-term relief of symptoms, a short duration of therapy with a focus on quick results, and a top-down approach, my therapist, Nicole, offered an intensive trauma-based therapy focused on a deeply reparative, relational process that has helped me profoundly change my wounded internal landscape, heal my inner child parts, and grow the capacity to mother myself. The heart of my work with Nicole has been the formation of a corrective, secure, and healing primary attachment bond, based on a variety of theories and practices from many other schools of psychotherapy.

The therapy style has been collaborative, with a high level of respect for my individuality, a deep empathic attunement and regard for me, even in moments of hostile countertransference that arose from unconsciously projecting my Mother Wound onto Nicole. In short, because I consistently received precisely the opposite of what I had experienced in my family for so many years, I was able to rework my Mother Wound to a profound degree, culminating in a capacity to support other women in their healing journeys as well.

After the abortion, I took a semester off and decided to change my major from education to psychology. I applied to graduate school and moved back in with my parents, continuing to support myself by waiting tables. All this time, I intentionally approached my relationship with my parents in a way that was measured and civil. By the time I had earned my master's in psychology and been accepted into a doctoral program, I'd fallen in love with David, a coworker and longtime acquaintance, whose sister-in-law was looking for tenants for her apartment in Manhattan. I chose not to pursue a PhD and instead moved with David to New York City, eventually getting a job as a writer/editor at an Ivy League medical school. I'll never forget riding in the U-Haul as David drove down I-95 South to Hell's Kitchen on that gray September morning, and opening a greeting card from my mother that read, "I love you like no other." I abruptly put the card in my purse, took a deep breath, and felt happy to have my own home ahead of me. At this point, I navigated the relationship with my mother through calculated distance to maintain a baseline level of superficial harmony. Even after years in therapy, *it wasn't until I'd had some time and physical distance from my mother that I really began to feel the magnitude of her impact on me. Around this time, I discovered a deep pool of rage and enormous grief over how my mother had treated me and how my father had failed to protect me.*

In consciously exploring my deepest levels of pain in a psychologically skillful, deeply attuned, and corrective therapeutic relationship, I slowly, almost imperceptibly in moments, began to form a new sense of self, feeling increasingly solid ground forming within me. Bit by bit, session by session, year after year, I experienced the joy and relief of becoming free. This was a slow, arduous, and liberating process.

Difficulty and challenges between mothers and daughters are rampant and widespread but not openly spoken about. It's generally considered taboo to acknowledge and discuss painful dynamics with our mothers. This silence about the truth of mother-daughter relationships is part of what keeps the Mother Wound in place, keeping it hidden in shadow, festering, and out of view. In recent years women are now increasingly willing to break our silence in order to share our truth, heal, and break the cycle for future generations, a crucial step for the healing and empowerment of women as a whole. Let's dive now into defining exactly what the Mother Wound is and how it manifests in our lives. The Mother Wound, a social condition rooted in patriarchy, exists on four levels: personal, cultural, spiritual, and planetary.

Personal Mother Wound: A set of internalized limiting beliefs and patterns that originates from the early dynamics with our mothers that causes problems in many areas of our adult lives, impacting how we see ourselves, one another, and our potential.

Cultural Mother Wound: The systemic devaluation of women in most aspects of patriarchal cultures, rooted in colonization, that have come to dominate much of the world, and the dysfunctional imbalance in the world as a result.

Spiritual Mother Wound: The feeling of being disconnected and alienated from a higher power and life itself.

Planetary Mother Wound: The harm caused to the earth (e.g., deforestation, mass extinction of species, climate crisis, etc.) that is threatening life on this planet.

It all starts on the personal level. As we heal the personal level of the Mother Wound, we increase our connection to ourselves, to each other, and to the earth.

The Mother Wound Is Healed at the Level of One's Daughterhood

Not every woman is a mother, but *all* women are daughters. Healing the Mother Wound is not about pitting mothers and daughters against each other; rather, it's about women collectively stepping into their power. The best thing that a mother can do for her daughter is to commit to healing her own Mother Wound. Through this healing process, she will expand her capacity for self-empathy and thus her empathy and emotional availability for her daughter. Their relationship can then shift from that of "either/or" ("only one of us can be fully lovable and fully powerful") to one with abundant space for both mother and daughter to each be equally loved and powerful. There is space for belonging as well as space to be a separate individual for both the mother and daughter. This process breaks the enmeshment, or "merging," that patriarchal cultures foster in the mother-daughter relationship and opens up new possibilities and expressions for authentic connection.

It is not necessary to be in a relationship with your mother to heal your Mother Wound. Because the Mother Wound is within *ourselves*, we can heal even if our mothers are absent, deceased, or refuse to engage with us in a healthy way. For some women, healing the Mother Wound will bring them closer to their mothers, and for others, it will create more distance. One cannot know at the outset which way it will go. But in either case, the healing and empowerment of the daughter is the primary result. This requires us to have faith that whatever the outcome, we will develop a healthier and more solid connection with ourselves, which is essential for our ability to thrive.

The Cost of Avoiding the Mother Wound

The Mother Wound keeps women separated from themselves, from one another, and from their true empowerment. Our collective trauma has been allowed to fester unimpeded through generations, distorting the mother-daughter relationship into a power struggle that is impossible to win. The cost of avoiding the Mother Wound is simply too great. It ensures that the disowned pain of the Mother Wound will continue to be passed down to future generations.

The cost to our personal lives means living our lives indefinitely:

- With a vague, persistent sense that "There's something wrong with me."
- Never actualizing our potential out of fear of failure or disapproval.

- Having weak boundaries and an unclear sense of self.
- Not feeling worthy or capable of creating what we truly desire.
- Not feeling safe enough to take up space and voice our truth.
- Arranging our lives around "not rocking the boat."
- Self-sabotaging when we get close to a breakthrough.
- Unconsciously waiting for our mother's permission or approval before claiming our own lives.

The cost to society and the world is that generations of women keep themselves small so as not to offend, are compelled to blame themselves, and bypass the chance to fulfill their potential. Thus, the genius, power, love, and gifts of countless women are lost to the world. This is a tragedy we cannot allow to continue.

The cost to the earth is best summed up by Eckhart Tolle: "The pollution of the planet is only an outward reflection of an inner psychic pollution: millions of unconscious individuals not taking responsibility for their inner space."

What We Gain by Healing the Mother Wound

Until we get to the root of the causes of our inner suffering, which are the foundational patterns put in place in the earliest days of our lives, and mourn the situations that caused us to internalize them, the personal development or spiritual work we do can only reach a superficial level at best. Many of the surface issues that continue to play out in our everyday lives, including struggles in our relationships, careers, and health, all point back to a common core: the pain related to our mothers and the beliefs about ourselves that originated from that primary relationship. I believe healing the Mother Wound is the most important thing a woman can focus on, because of the incredible potential that lies on the other side of it and the magnitude of transformation possible through healing it. No other relationship has the power to limit us or liberate us as our relationship with our mother does.

Benefits of healing the Mother Wound include:

- Being more fluent and skilled in handling our emotions; seeing them as a source of wisdom and information.
- Having healthy boundaries that support self-actualization.
- Developing a solid "inner mother" that provides unconditional love, support, and comfort.
- Knowing ourselves as competent; feeling that anything is possible and being open to miracles and all good things.
- Being in constant contact with our inner goodness and our ability to bring it into everything we do.
- Having deep compassion for ourselves and other people.
- Not taking ourselves too seriously—not needing external validation to feel OK.
- Trusting life to bring us what we need in every moment.
- Feeling safe in our own skin and feeling the freedom to be ourselves.
- Seeing ourselves and our mothers accurately; not taking our mother's limitations personally.
- Arriving at gratitude for what our mothers *could* give us . . . and compassion and acceptance for what they could *not* give us.

Anger, Shame, and Guilt

The Mother Wound exists because there is not a safe place for mothers to process their rage about the sacrifices society has demanded of them. In an essay published in *Teen Vogue* called "Most Women You Know Are Angry. And That's All Right," Laurie Penny writes,

> Female anger is taboo, and with good reason—if we ever spoke about it directly, in numbers too big to dismiss, one or two things might have to change. How many times have men in power—including Donald Trump—tried to push back and put down women who criticize them by implying that our opinions are nothing more than a mess of dirty, bloody hormones, none of it rational, none of it real? These jokes are never just jokes. They're a control strategy. The patriarchy is so scared of women's anger that eventually we learn to fear it, too.

Many adult daughters still unconsciously fear rejection for choosing not to make the same sacrifices as previous generations did, and this fear often comes out, unconsciously, to one's own children. A young daughter is a potent target for a mother's rage, because the daughter has not yet had to give up her personhood for motherhood. The young daughter may remind her mother of her own unlived potential. And if the daughter feels worthy enough to reject some of the patriarchal mandates her mother has had to swallow, then she can easily trigger that underground rage for the mother.

Healing the Mother Wound Is Not About Blaming Your Mother

Mother-blame is avoiding responsibility, and healing the Mother Wound is a form of taking personal responsibility.

Mother-blame is characterized by:

- Complacency and a sense of victimhood.
- Hiding from our own power and responsibility.
- Projecting unprocessed anger onto others.
- Avoiding underlying grief about your childhood.

Healing the Mother Wound involves:

- Examining the mother-daughter relationship with the intention to gain clarity and insight in order to create positive change in our lives.
- Transforming limiting beliefs we've inherited with the intention of adopting new beliefs that fully support our self-actualization.
- Taking responsibility for our own paths by becoming conscious of previously unconscious patterns and making new choices that reflect our true desires.

There's a lot of talk these days about feminism and being an awakened, conscious woman. But the reality is that we cannot be truly empowered if we have not yet addressed within us the very places that have felt banished and in exile from the feminine. Our first and most formative encounter with female power was with our mothers. Until we have the courage to break the taboo and face the pain we have experienced in relation to our mothers, images of female power are another form of fairy tale, a fantasy of rescue by a mother who isn't coming. Waiting for a savior keeps us, to some degree, in immaturity. We have to separate the human mother from the archetypal mother in order to be true carriers of conscious female power. We have to deconstruct the patriarchal lies, distortions, and faulty structures within us before we can truly build a new foundation within ourselves to hold this energy. Until we do this, we remain stuck in a kind of limbo where our empowerment is short-lived and the only explanation that seems to make sense is to blame ourselves.

Patriarchy as the Root Cause
of the Mother Wound

Patriarchy gives rise to the Mother Wound. In male-dominated cultures, women are conditioned to think of themselves as "less-than," not deserving or worthy. This feeling of less-than has been internalized and passed down through countless generations of women.

The corrosive principles of patriarchy that give rise to the Mother Wound include:

- Prioritizing men over women.
- Domination, holding power over.
- Normalizing the suppression of feelings.
- Viewing the expression of feelings as inherently weak or bad.
- Feeling shame for having needs.
- Feeling shame for resting or slowing down.
- Needing to produce to feel valued.
- Violation of boundaries.
- Sense of scarcity of money, time, love, energy.
- Feelings of isolation and disconnection.
- Objectification; not seeing people as people.
- Obedience and compliance are demanded.
- Viewing violence as powerful.
- Admiring a lack of empathy.
- Romanticizing/eroticizing the dynamics of domination and submission.
- Looking down upon whatever is perceived as feminine.
- Considering men as the default human being.
- Holding the racist belief that "white is right."
- Holding the belief that heterosexuality is the norm and ideal.

Motherhood and the Mother Wound

Historically, patriarchal cultures have not only treated motherhood as a mandate for women, they've also made it oppressive, holding mothers to unreasonable standards, such as requiring them to:

- Relinquish personal ambitions to care for their families.
- Deplete themselves to support their families and raise children.
- Be the primary caretakers of the household.
- Constantly serve others and others' needs, while not attending to their own.
- Handle everything with ease 100 percent of the time; have well-behaved children and maintain a high standard of beauty, a sex drive, a successful career, and a solid marriage.

Our society's unspoken messages to mothers include:

- "If motherhood is difficult, then it's your own fault."
- "Shame on you if you're not superhuman."
- "There are 'natural mothers' for whom motherhood is easy. If you are not one of these, there is something deeply wrong with you."

As a result of these limiting beliefs and superhuman standards, women forgo their dreams, bottle up their desires, and suppress their needs in favor of meeting the cultural ideal of what womanhood should be. This pressure is suffocating for most women, engendering rage, depression, anxiety, and overall emotional pain, which—when not addressed, as is often the case in patriarchal cultures—is then unconsciously passed on to daughters through subtle or even aggressive forms of emotional abandonment (mothers can't be emotionally present when stressed), manipulation (shame, guilt, and obligation), or rejection. Children interpret these moments of maternal abandonment, rejection, or manipulation as, "There is something wrong with me," "I'm responsible for my mother's pain," or "I can make my mother happy if I'm a good girl." This makes sense when one considers the limited cognitive development of a child, who sees herself as the cause of all things. Left unaddressed, these unconscious and untrue beliefs at the very core of the Mother Wound can negatively affect every area of our lives.

For mothers who have indeed sacrificed so much to have children in our culture, it can truly feel like a rejection when your daughter surpasses or exceeds the dreams you thought possible for yourself. There may be a sense of feeling owed, or entitled to, or needing to be validated by your children, which can be a very subtle but powerful manipulation. This dynamic can cause the next generation of daughters to keep themselves small so that their mothers can continue to feel validated and affirmed in their identities as "mother," an identity that many have sacrificed so much for, but received so little support in and recognition for in return.

Mothers may unconsciously project deep rage toward their children in subtle ways. However, the rage isn't really toward the children. The rage is toward the patriarchal culture that requires women to sacrifice and utterly deplete themselves in order to mother a child. For a child who needs her mother, sacrificing herself in an effort to somehow ease her mother's pain is often a subconscious decision made very early in life and usually not discovered as the cause of underlying issues until much later, when the daughter herself is an adult.

Much of this goes underground because of the many taboos and stereotypes about motherhood in this culture, which say:

- Mothers are always nurturing and loving.
- Mothers should never feel angry or resentful toward their daughters.
- Mothers and daughters are supposed to be best friends.

While the generational stereotypes have changed across the decades, the underlying message of unrelenting criticism has been the same: in the '50s, mothers were too put together; in the '70s, mothers were too lax; in the '80s, too ambitious; in the '90s it was all about the participation trophies; in the '00s, it was the tiger moms. The stereotype of "All mothers should be loving all the time" strips women of their full humanity. Because women are not given permission to be full human beings, society feels justified in not providing full respect, support, and resources to mothers.

The truth is that mothers are human beings and all mothers have unloving moments. And it's true that there are mothers who are simply unloving most of the time, whether because of addiction or mental illness or some other struggle. Until we are willing to face these uncomfortable realities, the Mother Wound will remain in shadow and continue to be passed down through the generations.

Of course, most mothers want what is best for their daughters.

However, if a mother has not dealt with her own pain or come to terms with the sacrifices she has had to make, then her support for her daughter may be laced with messages that subtly instill shame, guilt, or obligation. These messages can seep into the most benign of situations, usually in some form of criticism or of bringing praise back to the mother. It's not usually the content of the statement, but rather the energy with which it is conveyed that can carry hidden resentment.

Patriarchal cultures not only distort the mother-daughter relationship into this power dynamic, they also put daughters in a double bind. If a daughter internalizes her mother's unconscious beliefs (some form of "I'm not good enough"), then she will have her mother's approval, but she will also have betrayed herself and her own potential. However, if the daughter doesn't internalize her mother's unconscious beliefs as her own limitations but rather affirms her own power and potential, she is aware that her mother may unconsciously see this as a personal rejection.

The daughter doesn't want to risk losing her mother's love and approval, so internalizing these limiting, unconscious beliefs is a form of loyalty and emotional survival. It may feel dangerous for the daughter to actualize her full potential because this may mean risking some form of rejection by her mother. The daughter may unconsciously sense that her full empowerment may trigger her mother's sadness or rage at having had to give up parts of herself in her own life. Her compassion for her mother, a desire to please her, and a fear of conflict may cause her to convince herself that it's safer to shrink and remain small. Hence, daughters grow up in patriarchal cultures having to choose between being empowered and being loved.

The Mother Wound Belongs to All Women

The Mother Wound exists on a spectrum, with healthy, supportive mother-daughter relationships on one end and abusive, traumatic mother-daughter relationships on the other end. There are many factors influencing where we fall on this spectrum, such as the extent to which the mother has addressed her own Mother Wound and whether there was domestic violence, addiction, or financial hardship in the family.

A daughter who has a healthy, loving bond with her own mother may not have much of a Mother Wound on the personal level, but she must still contend with the cultural Mother Wound. Because patriarchal cultures devalue women and all things feminine, this cultural Mother Wound affects how she sees her own body, her potential, and her relationships. However, having a solid, healthy, loving relationship with our mother—one in which we are valued and celebrated for our individual, separate selves while still deeply connected with our mother—protects or buffers us from some of the virulent impacts of cultural patriarchal beliefs about women.

As author and psychologist Mario Martinez has said, mothers function as "significant cultural editors," defining the limits of what is possible through their own beliefs and behaviors, which we, their children, unconsciously internalize as our own as we develop in early life. The limiting messages that we inherit from our mothers have been deeply fused with our deepest human needs for love, safety, and belonging. Letting go of those beliefs that hold us back can feel like letting go of "mother" herself. Our task is to decouple those inherited beliefs from our need for love, safety, and belonging so that we can effectively dispose of them. Because they come from the one person that we as daughters must bond with to survive, disempowering beliefs that are passed down through mothers are more damaging than any of the cultural messages combined.

The severity of our Mother Wound depends most powerfully on how harshly our mothers were wounded in relation to their own mothers. In the best of situations, mothers unintentionally project feelings of inferiority and vulnerability in an innocent effort to protect their daughters from potential rejection or shaming ("Don't be too big, visible, or powerful. If you are, you'll end up rejected or alone"). In the worst of situations, mothers who have deep Mother Wounds of their own will scapegoat their daughters, projecting their disowned pain onto them and unleashing abuse or neglect with impunity.

Unconscious, Unacknowledged, and Taboo

The unconscious mind is responsible for protecting us from our unprocessed pain. In the introduction to his book *Before You Know*

It: The Unconscious Reasons We Do What We Do, John Bargh writes: "Once we acquire the right frame for understanding the interplay between the conscious and the unconscious operations of our mind, new opportunities open up to us. We can learn to heal wounds, break habits, overcome prejudices, rebuild relationships, and unearth dormant capabilities." He goes on to write that "after decades of research, experiment after experiment has shown that the unconscious isn't an impenetrable wall, but a door that can be opened." My favorite line from this section of the book points out the biggest ramification of such findings: "Just think how much more control you can gain by recognizing and taking account of these [unconscious] influences, instead of pretending they don't exist (and so allowing them to control you)."

One of the main cultural messages we receive is that feelings are inherently weak and are to be suppressed. Some emotions are actually labeled "negative" and are viewed with judgment as weak, unattractive, inconvenient, and "bad." At one time or another, we've all experienced negative feelings toward our mother when she did not or could not meet our needs. Despite the fact that numerous studies in the psychology of human development reinforce such feelings as normal, natural, and to be expected, children are shamed for acknowledging negative feelings toward their mothers, which causes these emotions to fester into painful dynamics that affect their self-concept and ability to thrive in the world.

In *My Mother/My Self*, Nancy Friday's classic book on the mother-daughter relationship, Friday observes how our tendency to polarize mothers into either idealization ("Mothers are to be revered") or denigration ("It must be the mother's fault") is, on an individual level, "one of our most primitive mechanisms of defense." As daughters, we don't want to be in alliance with the patriarchal culture that perpetrates harm toward our mothers, so we turn away from the opportunity to examine the relationship for insight and healing. We're taught to think of this willful ignorance as beneficial and protective to her and to ourselves. As Friday writes, "We will wait for [the good mother's] return for years, always convinced that the woman before us, who makes us feel guilty, inadequate, and angry, is not mother."

Through the cultural mandate that we see all mothers as loving all the time, we may unconsciously avoid any reflection on the pain we may feel in relation to our mothers, for fear of being seen as mother-blaming.

If we avoid acknowledging the full impact of our mother's pain on our lives, we still remain, to some degree, children.

Coming into full empowerment requires looking at our relationship with our mothers and having the courage to separate out our own individual beliefs, values, and thoughts from hers. It requires feeling the grief of having to witness the pain our mothers endured and processing our own legitimate pain we endured as a result. This is challenging, but it is the birth of real freedom. As we embrace the pain, it can be transformed into self-knowledge, integrity, and increasing self-confidence.

As we heal the Mother Wound, the distorted power dynamic among women is increasingly resolved because women are no longer asking one another to stay small to ease their own pain. The pain of living in patriarchy ceases to be a taboo topic of conversation. We don't have to pretend and hide behind false masks that bury our pain under a facade of effortlessly holding it together. The pain can then be seen as legitimate, embraced, processed, and integrated, and ultimately transformed into wisdom and power.

As women increasingly process the pain of the Mother Wound, we can create more safe places for women to express the truth of their pain and receive much-needed support. Mothers and daughters can communicate with one another without fear that the truth of their feelings will break their relationship. The pain no longer needs to go underground and into shadow, where it manifests as manipulation, competition, and self-hatred. Our pain can be grieved fully so that it can then turn into love, a love that manifests as fierce support of one another and deep self-acceptance, freeing us to be boldly authentic, creative, and truly fulfilled.

As we heal the Mother Wound, we begin to grasp the stunning degree of impact a mother's well-being has on the life of her child, especially in early childhood when the child and mother are still a single unit. Our mothers form the very basis of who we become: our beliefs start out as her beliefs, our habits start out as her habits. Some of this is so unconscious and fundamental, it is barely perceptible.

We address the Mother Wound because it is a critical part of self-actualization and saying YES to being the powerful and potent women we are being called to become. Healing the Mother Wound is ultimately about acknowledging and honoring the foundation our mothers provided for our lives so that we can then fully focus on creating the unique lives we authentically desire and know we are capable of creating.

As we engage in this healing process, we slowly remove the thick fog of projection that keeps us stuck so that we can more clearly see, appreciate, and love ourselves. We no longer carry the burden of our mother's pain or keep ourselves small as a result of that pain. We can confidently emerge into our own lives with the energy and vitality to create what we desire without shame or guilt, but with passion, power, joy, and love.

The Mother Wound serves as a veil, creating a sense of disconnection and separation from ourselves, from each other, and from life itself. In the earliest days of our lives, our experience of our mothers was synonymous with life itself. To an infant, mother is Food, mother is Breath, mother is World, mother is Self. Our very experience of ourselves and of the world was filtered through the body and psyche of this person who was our mother. Healing the Mother Wound is a process of gaining clarity on the predominant dynamics with our mothers that impacted our early development and continue to impact our choices now as adults. It also involves processing the challenging emotions that accompany those dynamics for the purpose of healing and self-discovery. Eventually we reach a place of insight, wisdom, acceptance, and gratitude.

For every human being, the very first wound of the heart was at the site of the mother, the feminine. And through the process of healing that wound, our hearts graduate from a compromised state of defensiveness and fear to a whole new level of love and power, which connects us to the divine heart of life itself. We are from then on connected to the archetypal, collective heart that lives in all beings, and are carriers and transmitters of true compassion and love that the world needs right now. In this way, healing the Mother Wound is actually an opportunity to be initiated into our true female power. This is why it's so crucial for women to heal the Mother Wound: our personal healing and reconnection to the heart of life, by way of the feminine, affect the whole and support our collective evolution.

Questions for Reflection

1. In the context of the principles of patriarchy as described on page 13, in what ways do you see patriarchy influencing your life at the moment? How have you been coping with this?

2. As an extension of patriarchy's devaluation of women, our culture has a wounded relationship with mothers, seeing them as either all-loving all the time or to be blamed for everything. How did your own mother cope with this? How has this cultural distortion impacted your relationship with your mother? To what degree did you feel you had to carry or absorb your mother's pain as part of the role of being a good daughter?

Chapter 2

HOW DOES THE MOTHER WOUND MANIFEST?

AS A LITTLE GIRL, *I developed into the role of the "good girl," the overachiever, and the meditator of family scuffles. I was my mother's confidante and best friend, someone she confided in about issues with my dad, her troubles at work, conflicts with friends, and gossip about other family members. Playing this role made me feel important, but also empty and hollow inside in a way that I wouldn't recognize until much later.*

I remember once sitting with my mother and aunts and one of them saying to me, "Oh, I didn't even know you were here, you're such a good girl." On the surface, I was invisible and helpful; underneath, I was fearful and hypervigilant, always on the look-out for the first sign of trouble. I learned I was a good girl when I seemed to cease to exist to the adults around me.

In my teen years, as I began to expand beyond my family unit, I was able to find a vibrant community of friends and received support in ways that I wasn't receiving in my home life, giving me the opportunity to rebel in a safe way. With my friends, I felt valued for my presence, not for being invisible. Yet the "good girl" role was still operating in me, and I made sure to be the one who was always extra-accommodating and available to whoever needed support.

At the age of nineteen, I became accidentally pregnant. This was a crossroads, the moment I realized that I couldn't give birth to anyone until I gave birth to myself. I had an abortion and got myself into therapy. I became determined to figure out who I was and what I wanted out of life.

At this time, I took a year off from college, waitressed, and rented my own apartment. In those first therapy sessions, I talked about how great my family was, and how I admired my mother. But I cried nonstop. I couldn't figure out why I was such a mess. All I knew was that I felt completely empty. I threw myself into learning about spirituality and Eastern religions, an avoidance technique that I would later learn is called "spiritual bypassing"— unconsciously trying to use spiritual concepts as a way to avoid looking at my childhood trauma.

In therapy, I worked on figuring out my career path and the issues I had with food and my body image, and navigating strings of failed relationships. But I didn't go near my relationship with my mother. I avoided looking at it because it seemed too scary, too threatening. I didn't want to be an ungrateful daughter. I didn't want to rock the boat in my family, as I always felt responsible for our fragile equilibrium. After all, I thought I had saved my mother from depression, protected my father from my mother's emotions, and shielded my brother from my dad's violence. I believed they needed me. What I didn't realize was that I had been exposed from birth to all the toxicity I'd felt and it lived in me already, just waiting to become conscious. It was eventually going to catch up with me.

I realized, through looking at everything but my relationship with my mother, that nearly everything eventually came back to it. The problems I had with relationships, my body image, and my career always eventually came back to the same issues, beliefs, and patterns that originated from that core relationship with my mother, which seemed related to this awful feeling in the background, this sense that there was something horrifyingly wrong with me.

I was so high-functioning that I didn't think of myself as a trauma survivor. But slowly, over time, I learned that I was suffering from complex developmental trauma. It would take me years to realize the breadth and depth of my developmental trauma, how it had fractured my sense of self, leaving me with extremely painful and pervasive symptoms on every level of being. These symptoms included free-floating fear, terror in moments, dread, guilt, self-doubt, shame, perfectionistic striving, and lack of self-worth. They also included attenuation of myself around others for fear of rejection if I appeared too powerful, a vague sense of menace and danger in my environment, dissociative feelings of being in a fog, and nightmares of invasion and persecution. All this had been locked away under the facade of the "good girl" and would gradually come to light in the process of healing.

Eventually, I felt strong enough to look at my relationship with my mother directly, mostly because I saw that not looking at it was precisely what was keeping me stuck. Deep down I knew that to postpone this exploration was to postpone the life I truly wanted.

The mother-child relationship can be seen as the first
relationship violated by patriarchy.
—*Adrienne Rich*

Denial, Martyrdom, and Entitlement

Women's capacity for empathy has been exploited in our culture, distorted into guilt, a sense of obligation, emotional caretaking, codependency, and self-recrimination. These distortions can paralyze us when we feel the desire to express our true power in our lives.

For those of us who have mothers unable to claim their own power in their lives, it can seem very frightening to do it for ourselves. Loving ourselves may feel foreign. It's a skill that we are being called to learn without many models. A common dynamic that many adult daughters experience is the compulsion to rescue, fix, and heal their mothers. This is complicated by the fact that many older mothers frequently present their emotional problems to their daughters, feeling entitled to significant and intensive support.

A mother's pain may show up in various forms:

- An unhappy marriage.
- Addictions.
- Mental illness.
- The dramas that may play out in her own relationships.
- Illness, health problems, or disabilities.
- Loneliness and fears of aging.
- Financial problems.

There are legitimate ways we can support our mothers that do not deplete us emotionally. And then there are other ways that our mothers may ask for support that are not appropriate, that may violate our boundaries and keep us stuck in a cycle of guilt, exhaustion, and self-doubt. We may comply with inappropriate demands or behaviors out of love and compassion, but this is not sustainable if our basic well-being is being increasingly diminished.

In order to express and embody our power, we have to sever any threads of dysfunctional enmeshment we may have with our mothers.

The dysfunctional enmeshment between mothers and daughters can show up in many ways:

- Mother using daughter as a comforter and dumping ground for her unprocessed emotions.
- Daughter needing mother's approval on all aspects of her life before she's able to feel good about herself and her choices.
- Mother finding comfort in having daughter as a "pet" who always agrees with her and conforms to her views and beliefs, and rejecting daughter if she expresses independence.
- Mother using daughter as a narcissistic tool to bring attention and praise back to herself.
- Daughter feeling overwhelmed with mother's needs; spending an inordinate amount of energy worrying about mother's problems and how to solve them.
- Mother feeling she must speak to daughter hourly or several times daily in order to maintain her own emotional stability.
- Mother feeling entitled to access and/or control major aspects of daughter's life, from physical items to personal details and information.
- Mother criticizing daughter out of her own fear that she is not a good mother, and seeing daughter's normal expression of negative emotions as a threat to her control and a sign that she's failing as a mother.

Mothers who do these things usually do them totally unconsciously and unintentionally as a way to relieve their own pain and avoid their own unresolved personal challenges. Yet mothers who use their daughters in these ways are also exploiting their daughters' empathy in a patriarchal fashion.

In order to come into balance and heal the exploitation of our empathy, daughters must refuse to feel guilty for their desire and ability to be powerful and independent. Even if that means rejection from our mothers when we set clear, healthy boundaries in the relationship.

It's important for mothers to recognize and own the ways they may be unconsciously holding their daughters down because of their own unresolved issues. It's important for mothers to own the patriarchy within themselves. If mothers are unwilling to do so, daughters must stand firm and claim their own right to themselves and their own lives.

We can be good daughters and set healthy boundaries with our mothers. But we can't rely solely on our mothers' opinions of us to feel secure in our decisions to do so. We have to feel empowered and secure with the limits we set in the relationship.

Daughters are not responsible for the emotional stability of their mothers. When we are able to face the fact that we are powerless, as daughters, to heal our mothers, we can do the mourning that is necessary to move on and finally step into our power and live authentic, joyful, abundant lives . . . without guilt.

It's a tragedy that some mothers actively manipulate their daughters out of their own unconscious feelings of deprivation and fears of abandonment. And it's a tragedy that some daughters miss the opportunity to step into their empowered selfhood out of a feeling of paralyzing guilt toward their mothers.

The deprived child within a mother may be looking to her daughter for the emotional nourishment that she never received from her own mother. This is one of the ways that the Mother Wound gets passed down. Mothers are not served by their daughters' self-sacrifice and codependency with them. It perpetuates their stuck-ness and denial. And it is detrimental to the daughter; it directly hampers her ability to confidently embrace her own separate self.

In our culture, self-sacrifice is idealized, based on the residues of older generational beliefs that say:

- Martyrdom is admirable.
- Women are naturally happy to serve and take care of others.
- Women are *not* supposed to be vocal, willful, or assertive.
- Women who refuse compliments and are prone to self-deprecation are commendable and praiseworthy.

The Compulsion to Heal Mother

If we look deeper, there may be an unconscious, childlike belief operating that if we as daughters can heal or save our mothers, they will eventually transform into the mothers we always needed—strong, unconditionally loving, happy, nurturing, etc.—and as daughters we can finally get the mothering that we've needed. But this is not possible. It's impossible because our childhood is over, and we can never go back and get what we needed. Grieving this fact is a key to our freedom.

There is a direct relationship between our childlike desire to save our mothers from their pain and our fear of powerfully claiming our own lives.

Each mother-daughter relationship is different. Each adult daughter in this situation must reflect and come to clarity on what she is and is not willing to do and accept in her relationship with her mother and to respectfully communicate that to her mother. It is an individual choice, and it can take time to figure out where your boundaries lie. Ultimately, the daughter has to be loyal and true to herself first and foremost. Ironically, this is what every mother in her healthy state would want for her daughter: to be good to herself and do what is best for her.

But when a mother has unresolved trauma and early unmet developmental needs, her desire to get her own needs met can override her ability to accurately see and love her adult daughter as a sovereign, separate, independent adult who has the right to say no without guilt.

Shame, Guilt, and Isolation

"I can't seem to get ahead in my career. I don't know why I keep sabotaging my success."

"I feel guilty whenever I do things for myself. I'm caught in a loop of guilt and resentment."

"I realized that I basically married my mother!"

"My professional life is soaring but my relationships are in shambles."

"I'm so triggered by my kids. I feel like I can't do anything right."

Because the Mother Wound impacts our core sense of self, its manifestations show up in every area of our adult lives, some areas more intensely than others. From our marriages to our parenting to our careers to our relationship with our bodies, the Mother Wound is there, under the surface, limiting our sense of self, narrowing our sense of possibilities, and keeping us stuck, running in place. We may notice that the same issues come up again and again in different guises. Like an invisible fence, the Mother Wound keeps us unconsciously locked into certain patterns, thought loops, and behaviors. We may misattribute our challenges to other causes on the surface level, not realizing that there's a single core cause lying deep beneath. The pain of that stuck-ness is often what precipitates the necessary motivation and energy to find the deeper cause and make a change.

Manifestations of the Mother Wound include:

- Feeling less-than.
- Comparing ourselves to others.
- Feeling competitive and jealous of other women.

- Double binds ("Be smart but not too smart. Be sexy but not too sexy.").
- Overworking, burnout, exhaustion.
- Feeling like there's something wrong with you.
- A feeling of not being "real"; having to put on a happy face.
- A feeling of being stuck, paralyzed, unable to make changes.
- Loneliness, depression, disconnection.
- Feeling the need to dominate others.
- Rigidity and perfectionism.
- Avoidance of long-term relationships.
- Overfunctioning and emotional caretaking of other people.
- Codependency and "merging" with others.
- Harshness, lack of compassion for yourself.
- Fear of being alone.
- Feeling unable to set boundaries.
- Overfunctioning and doing emotional labor for others.
- Addictions, depression, eating disorders, and more.

Many daughters equate silence about their pain as a form of loyalty to their mothers.

Yes, your mother may have tried her best. Yes, she may have endured incredible suffering and struggles in her life. AND your feelings matter, too. They are of equal importance. It's about making an "either/or" into a "both/and." Our compassion for our mothers should never eclipse compassion for ourselves.

It's very common for women to resist embarking on the process of healing the Mother Wound, especially if their relationship with their mother is riddled with painful tension. However, the more resistance you feel to doing the work, the more important it is for you to do the work. The painful manifestations of the Mother Wound can actually be helpful to us in getting in touch with our trauma and transforming it.

It is precisely when women give themselves permission to *feel* their full anger and outrage on behalf of the little girls they once were that their power, authenticity, clarity, and confidence begin to emerge in full force. The empathy found there births a profound tenderness toward oneself that manifests as a fierce refusal to allow harm to come to that little girl within.

"I'm so afraid I'll turn into my mother."

The fear of turning into our mothers is a healthy fear of not living our own individual lives. It's the legitimate fear of getting sucked down into the riptides of familial and cultural myths that directs us to lead smaller, narrower lives than our souls demand. It's the fear of our lives slipping away while we deplete our energies into patterns of obligation, emotional caretaking, and conformity. It's a sign of the rot of female potential that we sense, to some degree, in our mothers' unlived lives, the bitterness and discontent that may live under their forced smiles and the cloaked aggression that peeks out in the most benign moments. We see the warning signals in our mothers' lives. And we don't want to repeat their mistakes and pass on their wounds. It's important that we make the reasons conscious, by doing some accounting of why we feel that way and what experiences we have had to come to this point.

The Creation of the
False Self as Little Girls

As a way to survive a hostile emotional environment in their families, many little girls learn to suppress their individuality to soothe their mothers. Lindsay C. Gibson, in her book *Adult Children of Emotionally Immature Parents*, explains that "A child's individuality is seen as a threat to emotionally insecure and immature parents because it stirs up fears about possible rejection or abandonment," and "Therefore, their children, in an attempt to prevent their parents from becoming anxious, often suppress any authentic thoughts, feelings or desires that would disturb their parents' sense of security." Some of the painful beliefs these children are taught include: Always think first of what other people want you to do. Don't ask for support. Don't advocate for yourself. It's shameful to want something for yourself. A child may begin to unconsciously see her own existence (with her separate needs and feelings) as a form of disloyalty to her mother. This creates a split in the child, a constant war between loyalty to her mother and the fact of her own separate existence.

There's no place for a "real" girl: the capacity for tension is taken up entirely by the parental situation.

The equilibrium in dysfunctional families is often so tenuous that the natural tension that arises from family members exercising their individuality is not tolerated. In such families, enmeshment and co-dependency are what bond family members together, not emotional intimacy and genuine connection. The tension in the family may be caused by various issues such as addictions, financial troubles, domestic violence, or mental health issues, to name a few. Unclear boundaries in the family and marital problems are the fertile ground in which children become "parentified," playing the role of parents to their parents. Children may see the tension caused by their own needs as the problem, thereby internalizing the belief that they are inherently bad, wrong, and flawed, and need to be improved. This is the creation of a "false self" to please the parent. It's beyond the capacity of a child to see that the painful tension they're responding to is actually not related to them at all, but is a result of their environment, namely their parents and their management of their own lives, factors completely outside the child's control.

The Tragedy of Good Girls and Parentified Daughters

It goes without saying that little girls are totally dependent on their mothers for physical, mental, and emotional support. To this end, the road between a little girl and her mother is meant to be a one-way street with support flowing consistently from the mother to the daughter. However, one of the many faces of the Mother Wound is the common dynamic in which the mother inappropriately depends on the daughter to provide her with mental and emotional support. This role reversal is incredibly damaging to the daughter, having long-range effects on her self-esteem, confidence, and sense of self-worth.

In order to meet these demands, the young daughter must repress her own developmental needs to accommodate the emotional needs of her mother. Instead of the daughter getting mirroring from her mother, she is expected to do the mirroring. Instead of being able to use her mother as a secure emotional base for exploration, she is expected to be her mother's secure emotional base.

The daughter is vulnerable and dependent on her mother for survival, so she has few choices available to her; one is to comply and fill her mother's needs, and the other is some degree of rebellion toward her mother.

A daughter is being exploited when her mother gives her adult roles, such as surrogate spouse, best friend, or therapist. When a daughter is asked to be an emotional prop for her mother, she is unable to rely on her mother enough to get her own developmental needs met.

Parentified daughters may respond to this dynamic in a number of ways:

- "If I'm a really, really, good girl [compliant, quiet, without needs], then Mother will finally see me and take care of me."

- "If I stay strong and protect Mother, she will see me."
- "If I give Mother what she wants, she will stop abusing me."

As adults, we may be projecting this dynamic onto others in our lives. For example, in our relationships: "If I keep trying to be good enough for him, he will commit to me." In our careers: "If I keep working weekends, I'll be good enough to get promoted."

These mothers set up a competition with their daughters for who gets to be mothered.

The message is that there's not enough mothering or love to go around. Girls grow up believing that love, approval, and validation are *very scarce*, and one must work oneself to the bone in order to be worthy of these precious commodities. Then, as adults, they attract situations that replicate this pattern over and over. (Many of these dynamics and effects are also true for male children.)

Parentified daughters are robbed of their childhoods. The daughter does *not* receive affirmation for herself as a *person*; rather, she receives affirmation only as a result of performing a *function* (relieving her mother of her pain).

Mothers may expect their daughters to listen to their problems and ask them to provide comfort and nurturing to calm their adult fears and worries. The daughter may be expected to bail her mother out of her problems or to clean up her mother's messes, whether physical or emotional. She may be regularly called in as a problem-solver or mediator.

What this mother conveys to her daughter is that she, as the mother, is weak, overwhelmed, and unable to handle life. She conveys to her daughter that her daughter's developmental needs are simply "too much" for her as the mother, so the child blames herself for even existing. The young girl gets the message that she does not have a right to have needs, does not have a right to be listened to or validated as her own person.

The role of "good girl" comes with many enticing payoffs. For example, the daughter might only receive praise or validation when she acts as her mother's warrior, savior, or comforter. So the child becomes very comfortable playing that role, and it gives her a sense of control in an otherwise unpredictable environment. Parentified daughters may cling to this role and its awards even into adulthood.

For some, expressing your own needs may mean rejection or abuse from your mother.

As the daughter grows up, she may fear her mother would be too "easily shattered" and so may hide her own truth for fear of what it would do to her mother. The mother may feed into this by playing the victim and causing the daughter to see herself as a perpetrator if she dares to express her own separate reality. This can manifest into the daughter's unconscious belief that "I'm too much. My true self injures others."

While these daughters may carry the projection of the "good mother" for their mothers, they may also carry the projection of the negative mother. For example, this can play out when, as an adult, the daughter is ready to separate emotionally from her mother. The mother may unconsciously see the daughter's separation as a replication of the rejection she felt from her own mother. The mother may react with overt infantile rage, passive sulking, or hostile criticism.

Mothers that exploit their daughters this way are often the same ones that say to them "Don't blame me!" or "Stop being so ungrateful!" if the daughter expresses discontent about or wants to discuss their relationship. Daughters who have been robbed of their childhoods by their mothers' invasive needs are often attacked by their mothers for having the audacity to propose a discussion about the dynamics of their relationship.

These mothers may be unwilling to see their role in the daughters' pain because it's too painful for *them*. And they are likely in denial of how their relationships with their own mothers have impacted them. "Don't blame your mother" can be used as a way to instill shame in daughters and silence them from speaking the truth of the pain they've endured.

If we are to claim our power as women, we must be willing to see the ways in which our mothers truly were responsible for our pain when we were children—and how, as *adult* women, *we* are fully responsible for healing these wounds within ourselves.

Part of being powerful is the capacity to create harm, whether intentionally or unintentionally. Whether mothers are completely ignorant of the harm they have created or shy away from that knowledge, the fact is that as the adults in the relationship, the mothers were responsible. Daughters must own the legitimacy of their pain. If they don't, no true healing can occur. Facing the magnitude of the suffering you experienced as a child is painful and uncomfortable, but it is a necessary part of the liberation process. Daughters will continue to sabotage themselves and limit their ability to thrive and flourish in the world until they can recognize these patterns from their origin point.

Patriarchy has deprived women to such a degree that when they become mothers, women often turn to their young daughters, starving and ravenous for validation, approval, and recognition. This is a hunger that a daughter could never possibly satisfy. Yet generation after generation of innocent daughters have offered themselves up, willingly sacrificed themselves on the altar of their mother's suffering and starvation, with the hope that one day they will finally "be good enough" for her. There is a childlike hope that by "feeding the mother," she will eventually be able to feed the daughter. That meal never comes. You get the meal your soul has been longing for by engaging in the process of healing the Mother Wound and owning your life and your worth.

We have to stop sacrificing ourselves for our mothers, because ultimately, our sacrifices don't feed them. What will feed your mother is the transformation that is on the other side of her own pain and grief, which she must reckon with on her own.

When we refuse to acknowledge the ways our mothers may have been to blame for our suffering as children, we continue through life as adults feeling there is something wrong with us, that we are somehow bad or deficient. This is because it's easier to feel shame than it is to face the pain of realizing the truth of how we may have been abandoned or exploited by our mothers. Thus, shame can function as a protective buffer from the pain of the truth.

The little girl within us would rather feel shame and self-hate because it preserves the illusion of the "good mother."

We hold on to shame as a way of holding on to our mother. In this way, shaming ourselves functions as a way to feel mothered. Thus, shame is one of the biggest manifestations of the Mother Wound.

We must have the courage to release the pain our mothers have asked us to carry for them. We release the pain when we can put responsibility where the responsibility truly lies: with the adult in the situation, the mother, not the child. As children, we were not responsible for the choices and behavior of the adults around us. Once we really take this in, we can then take full responsibility by working through it and acknowledging how it has impacted our lives, so that we can make new choices as adults that are in alignment with our authentic selves.

Many women try to skip this step and go right to forgiveness and empathy, which can keep them stuck. You can't truly move on if you don't recognize what you are moving on from. Forgiveness is not something we can just "do." True forgiveness is the by-product of a process of transformation, in which pain is acknowledged, processed, accepted, and transformed into self-knowledge. Forgiveness then becomes less about the other person and more about our own wholeness. Any time we are being pressured to forgive, either by ourselves or another person, we must not give in to the pressure but instead take the time we need to heal.

As little girls, many of us felt the terror of "no one is at the wheel" in our families. For a variety of reasons, we may have gotten the message that the adults were "checked out" to some degree and we were on our own. Our nervous systems responded with fight, flight, or freeze, laying down early blueprints for how we cope with stress and change.

For women who grew up with the pattern of the "good girl," there is a sense of being used, a sense of having to perform, and an underlying sense of emptiness. The good girl believes something like, "One day Mommy/Daddy will be full and then they will give me what I need." The problem is that that day never comes. These women grow up to be adults who experience high levels of stress and hypervigilance when faced with everyday situations like disappointing someone, receiving compliments, setting boundaries, and taking care of themselves.

We are taught that survival involves performing for the patriarchal male. Many "good girls" or "parentified daughters" watched their mothers condone toxic male behavior, whether embodying it in themselves or tolerating it in the men in their families, or both. We may have learned to internalize damaging beliefs like "I could lose their approval if I don't give myself away" or "To be likable, I have to devalue myself." We may have watched our mothers having to depend on crumbs of approval from ignorant males. We may have watched other older women tolerate ineptitude and abuse in silence. We may have endured as our mothers invaded us or withdrew from us out of their own deprivation.

As recovering "good girls," it's important to see our unconscious complicity in being used, and fiercely claim our self-sovereignty.

The "used child" within us longs to be loved for her real self, not just when she is wearing the mask of the "good girl" and demonstrating patriarchal values (productive, perfect, conforming to expectations, making others look good, sacrificing, suppressing, etc.). The used child longs to be loved when she disappoints you, when she is grumpy, when she is inconvenient, when she is messy, when she is confused, when she produces nothing, when she is inconsistent, when she is empty-handed, when she changes her mind, etc. The real question is, how willing are we to love *ourselves* in these moments? The more we can love ourselves for our real selves, the more we can feel worthy of love from others.

Questions for Reflection

1. How did your mother convey and pass along to you her beliefs, either through her spoken words or covertly through her choices, decisions, and actions?
2. What were your mother's beliefs about the big areas of life, such as money, men, sexuality, career potential, her own body, marriage female friendships, her own mother, family norms, etc.?
3. How are your mother's beliefs showing up in your own life? Are there ways you have unconsciously absorbed her beliefs as my own?
4. What are some simple ways you can act more in alignment with your own authentic beliefs instead? Are there any fears about how your own authentic choices and beliefs would impact your relationship with my mother?

Questions for Moms to Reflect On to Honor Themselves *and* Clear the Way for Their Daughters

1. What did I need from my own mother that I did not get? In what ways may I be unconsciously projecting these needs onto my daughter or other people?
2. Am I getting the mothering and nurturing I need in my daily life? If not, how can I get those needs met (friends, experiences, tools, professional support)?
3. Am I neglecting my daughter's emotional needs? Do her emotional needs make me uncomfortable? If so, which ones? What do they bring up for me?
4. Am I asking my daughter to mother me in any way? If so, what are some ways I can get the support I need from another source so I don't put this burden on my daughter?

5. Do I feel any rage or resentment about being a mom? If so, what are some safe and healthy ways I can process and work through that?

6. Do I feel at all jealous of or threatened by my daughter? If so, why? How does this manifest in my daily interactions with my daughter? How can I find a safe, healthy way to process that?

7. What limitations did I have to accept about myself as a young girl my daughter's age? How did that impact my life? How can I support my daughter in not accepting those same limitations?

8. How can I demonstrate to my daughter that I value myself?

9. What comes up for me when I reflect on my daughter having more opportunities than I did?

10. In what ways might I be passing along that belief in limitations? How might I turn that around?

Chapter 3

POWER DYNAMICS OF THE MOTHER WOUND

AS A CHILD, I IDEALIZED MY MOTHER. It would take me de-cades to question her narrative that we were best friends; only then did I realize that this illusion of best friends had only been possible because I had diligently played the role assigned to me—that of the "good girl," confidante, and family mediator. "Best friends" had worked because I emotionally absented myself and catered to her. Instinctively, I tried my best to hide my true feel-ings and needs, any evidence that I was a child. I basically pre-tended to be an adult. There were moments when my mother's own pain leaked out from her steely exterior, either overtly or covertly, leaving me feeling confused, stunned, and in despair. I automatically interpreted the loss of connection in those mo-ments as my own fault, the result of something I had done wrong. I lived my life in a state of hypervigilance, determined to never make the same mistake twice. For example, any time I would ex-press spontaneous confidence, or a wildly differing opinion or stance from my mother's, I would viscerally feel her begin to with-draw from me, cast a jealous stare, or emit a haughty grunt or a disapproving sigh, and when I felt this it was so painful. I had unconsciously learned to equate the feelings of freedom and joy with an expectation of punishment and abandonment.

But there were other times when the dominance I sensed from my mother was more overt, and in those moments, I felt my mother was making it clear who was in control, who called the shots, and who would not be surpassed under any circumstances. I remember being seven or so, sitting in the back seat of our car and saying in a moment of wishfulness, "Mom, someday I'm going to be rich!" As the light turned red, my mother turned around and, as I recall it, glared at me with daggers in her eyes, her face drawn and depleted. In what felt like a bitter, cutting tone, she said, "That's what I thought, too, Bethany." The message I heard was, Don't you dare think you're capable of that; don't you dare think you're better than I am and that you will succeed where I have not. *That brief interaction made a deep impression in my young psyche.*

If I expressed my own opinions openly, with sincerity and sensitivity, my mother would sometimes say, "You think you're so superior!" and I felt it was as though she couldn't perceive my independence without also feeling personally attacked. As her best friend, these moments were unbearably painful, so I began to voice my opinions less and less until I was a perfect mirror reflecting her. I had no idea, but I was in the process of splitting between the good girl she wanted me to be and the real girl I had buried down beneath.

There were also interactions in which, I came to conclude later, it seemed like her own pain was being projected onto me. At the time I had no concept of projection; I only saw that my mother was hurting me, and the only possible reason she would do that was because I deserved it. I remember one night as a preteen, telling my mother about Laurie, a mean girl in my class who targeted

different girls to pick on and bully. Wanting my mother's vali-
dation, I asked, "Mom, is Laurie prettier than me?" She paused,
pursed her lips, and said, "Yes, she is prettier than you." I was
jarred by this, because up to this point in the conversation she
had been unusually kind, but suddenly her message, as I felt it,
had turned cold, cutting, and uncompassionate. After she said
this, I had a yuck feeling and closed myself in my room, feeling
confused, rejected, and alone. I sensed that being vulnerable with
her was dangerous, and I began to shut down around her even
more than I already did.

All mothers and daughters experience some degree of struggle due to
the influence of patriarchy on the mother-daughter relationship. Power
is always at play, to some extent, due to this cultural atmosphere. For
adult daughters of mothers with a more robust authoritarian parenting style or personality, communication and establishing a relationship
based on mutuality can be almost impossible. What constitutes a "harmonious" relationship with an authoritarian mother will almost always
involve some loss of self. This is because this style is inherently disin-
vested in cooperation and mutual growth. Mutuality is actually seen as
defeat and loss of power for mothers of this style. What makes it even
more confusing is that the mother can unpredictably take on an authoritarian tone when she is triggered and sometimes, when in a more
positive mood, come from a place of mutuality, which the child cannot
predict. This results in an "intermittent reinforcer," the most powerful
form of reinforcement, in which the mother is sometimes empathic and
loving, but when triggered becomes controlling, hostile, or cutting. This
constantly shifting dynamic keeps the child on a never-ending roller
coaster of emotions and fosters a sense of instability within her.

In her landmark book *The Verbally Abusive Relationship*, Patricia
Evans lays out the two kinds of power that pervade our world. For

thousands of years the world has operated under the patriarchal realm of "power-over," domination of other people. Evans describes this in the context of verbally abusive relationships in which men are the controlling partner, but this power dynamic is also present in relationships between mothers and daughters, and can explain a lot of painful dynamics between them. When you feel like you're speaking a different language from your mother, when you feel like nothing ever gets resolved, when you regularly question your own perceptions, getting clarity on the power dynamics at play can explain a lot.

Evans calls power-over "Reality 1," which is characterized by inequality, competition, manipulation, hostility, control, and negation. In this reality, a sense of safety comes from having "one-upped" someone else. There's inherent distrust of mutuality and vulnerability. Often those coming from this reality experienced deep wounding in their own childhoods and became closed off to their own feelings, projecting them onto others. Mutuality is experienced as a threat to their security and identity. They unconsciously experience equality with another human being as inferiority. Those in this reality do not experience personal power because they are so disconnected from their own feelings, and so they avoid feelings of powerlessness by focusing on controlling and dominating others. Power-over is an attempt at manufacturing personal power, the power that comes from within. Being vulnerable, asking for what they want, is too scary because it opens up the possibility of rejection and having to feel the associated feelings of disappointment and humiliation. They base all choices on an unconscious need to avoid facing their feelings and the vulnerable parts of themselves they had to abandon in order to survive their childhood. They are in deep denial of their feelings and can distort and confuse reality, gaslighting other people without knowing what they are doing. This reality makes healthy relationships and communication virtually impossible.

Personal power, which Evans calls "Reality 2," is characterized as coming from a place of equality, partnership, mutuality, goodwill, intimacy, and validation. In this reality, personal power comes from connection with one's own feelings and some level of connection with life itself. There's an assumption that both people are intending to grow, support, and enhance each other's lives. Reality 2 is a shared reality with others. One person alone cannot create this kind of mutual relationship with another. It takes two participants. Women are often frustrated when they are doing everything they can to connect with their mothers and nothing is working. The truth is, we cannot create this kind of mutual relationship with our mothers if they are primarily coming from Reality 1.

Evans explains that the single biggest factor in whether people develop a Reality 1 or Reality 2 is if there was *a compassionate adult witness in their childhood*, a stable, loving adult who was emotionally present and reassuring during moments of emotional distress. By having a compassionate adult witness in moments of suffering, the child becomes able to maintain a connection to herself and develop a trust that she can endure challenging emotions. This sets her up to feel a sense of personal power as an adult. For those who did not have a compassionate witness in childhood and who experienced traumatic emotions with little to no emotional support, their painful feelings were likely pushed into the subconscious as a way to survive, and power-over is adopted, to some degree, as a mechanism of self-defense. Thus, without access to personal power, they are more likely to end up with a Reality 1, power-over, dominant orientation to the world.

The Deadly Assumption

One of the things that keeps the Mother Wound in place is the cultural assumption that all mothers are coming from a place of concern, mutuality, kindness, goodwill, and validation—Reality 2. However, our mothers are human beings who have likely experienced some degree of trauma, both from their own families and the trauma of being a woman in a patriarchy. And unless our mothers had a compassionate witness to the pain they endured as children, helping them maintain access to their feelings as a point of connection and sense of personal power, they may be operating from Reality 1, a place of manipulation, domination, projections, distortions, abuse, and control. When a mother doesn't have access to her own feelings, she may see her daughter as an extension of herself and view her own negative feelings as having come from her daughter rather than from her own pain, which has been deeply suppressed in her unconscious. In this way, she may isolate and abuse her daughter, repeating the same abuse that she herself experienced, all while being in denial or unaware that she is doing this.

Mother Tantrums and "Momipulation"

The patriarchal oppression of women will increasingly lose hold as older women take responsibility for their own pain and younger women refuse to carry wounds that are not their own. This will allow young women to walk confidently in the direction of their dreams without crippling shame or guilt.

As your life changes based on adopting new, expansive beliefs, your family may feel confused, left behind, or betrayed. Moving the framework from "either/or" into "both/and" requires that we risk alienation in favor of being authentic and setting boundaries. The way mothers display the response to their own pain being triggered can range from a minor unsupportive critical response to a full-on explosive episode (e.g., flying into a vicious rage, jealously withdrawing or sulking, calling you every name in the book, or bringing up every mistake you ever made to shame you back into being her emotional crutch).

I call these upsets "mother tantrums," because this is when the unhealed inner child within a mother overtly starts projecting unprocessed pain onto her daughter in response to the daughter not complying with the unspoken mandate to stay nonthreatening to her. A mother tantrum occurs when the daughter steps out of her role of being subservient, deferential, or submissive to her mother and dares to change the dynamic in the relationship by more fully expressing her authentic, true self around her mother. (This could be in the form of the daughter setting boundaries, speaking her truth, limiting contact, making authentic choices that are not necessarily in alignment with her mother's beliefs, etc.)

The following stories from adult daughters are real-life examples of mother tantrums. They are composites of examples I've heard from my students and clients through my online course, and retreats and workshops I've taught. All names have been changed. These examples illustrate what it looks like when mothers who have failed to address their own Mother Wounds are triggered and act out, tragically projecting those wounds onto their daughters. The trigger in itself is not a problem; it's normal to feel triggered by your children at times. The problem is when the mother does not take responsibility for working through that trigger and instead projects her own wounds onto the child.

> **Shawna:** "My mother went through all my journals that were in storage in her attic after I said I needed a couple of weeks of no contact while I worked on a major assignment at work. She said over email that she couldn't understand why I would abandon my mother and she didn't know what else to do because I wouldn't talk to her. She began to criticize things I had written in my journals and said she was worried about me. I knew she was comfortable disrespecting my boundaries but I never thought she would go so far."

Talia: "My mother bought gifts for people at my rehearsal dinner even though I specifically asked her not to until I'd had a chance to take a look at them online. She yelled at me at the top of her lungs, 'The gifts are from me to them, so I had every right to do it!'"

A.J.: "The more successful my career becomes, the more my mother wants to talk to me on the phone about superficial stuff. I recall once when I was busy during exams in law school, she demanded I speak to her on the phone for three hours to give her advice about planning a vacation to Mexico, just about every night that week. It wasn't until years later that I realized she was, on some level, trying to distract me so that I wouldn't surpass her. On the day of my graduation, she went into the ER with claims of chest pain. I missed my graduation as I sat in the waiting room with my siblings. She turned out to be fine."

Tanesha: "My mom becomes distant from me every time I share something positive that I'm doing. She changes the subject immediately, as though she can't stand giving me a positive focus. Sometimes she'll even start talking about something similar that friends' children are experiencing, almost to say I pale in comparison to them. It feels so hurtful, although I know she is totally unconscious of it."

Olivia: "My mother has to make a harsh comment about my appearance every time I see her. 'Are you still doing Weight Watchers?' or 'Did you iron that blouse?' or 'Your hair looks really messy. Here, use my comb.' These infantilizing comments make me feel like I'm five. The irony is that my mother was an alcoholic and I helped her get ready for work, ironing her clothes, handing her lipstick and socks. It totally negates my experience of having to support her. My presence must remind her on some level of how much she failed me. I'm not even sure she would remember. I wonder if she is even capable of truly caring about me. Avoidance of her own pain seems to be the organizing principle of her life."

Jordyn: "After my father left my mother when I was a teen, it was like she and I became best friends. She would complain to me about her life and how alone she was. She told me I was the only person in the world who understood her. I lived at home in college and when I would bring a boyfriend home, she would get really passive-aggressive with me. She would do things like 'accidentally' bleach a favorite piece of my clothing. Or my phone would disappear for hours and she would suddenly find it. One time when I was getting really serious about a guy, she actually did something to my car engine so the car wouldn't start when I tried to leave. Growing up, I thought she did these things because she loved me. Now I see that on some level she felt like she owned me."

Finn: "My whole family revolved around the mantra 'Don't upset your mother.' She was incredibly anxious and had little tolerance for us kids. She also had a strong preoccupation with 'what the neighbors might think.' I recall spending hours on the weekends doing gymnastics in the front yard while she cooked in the kitchen, hoping that she would notice me. There were other times I watched her drop everything to spend hours chatting with the very friends she complained about. I would sit there listening to their conversations, feeling emotionally starved for her attention. Any time I did express sadness or anger, it was met with a sarcastic 'What's wrong with her now?'

I feel like most of my childhood, I was standing there looking out the window waiting for her to come home. When she was present, there was no connection. I think she saw my emotional needs as a total drain on her."

Brooke: "My mom always needed to be prettier than I was. When someone would compliment me in her presence, she had to saunter up to the person and get their attention. Sometimes it was so subtle that no one else would notice; other times it was painfully obvious to everyone that she was competing with me. I'll never forget her antics during my wedding; several people were commenting on my dress and my mother busted into the conversation and loudly asked someone to help her clasp her bracelet. Everyone turned to her, eyes rolling, as she proceeded to tell a banal, irrelevant story. Ever since I was a teenager, it's made her skin crawl to see me as the center of attention."

Destiny: "My mother loves to get my husband to side with her and pit us against each other. Without fail, at family gatherings, she finds a way to flirt with him in an almost undetectable way, and he falls for it. Before I know it, I feel ganged up on by both of them. For so long, my husband didn't see that he was being manipulated. But now he's learning how to navigate this so that no matter how hard she tries to isolate me and make me feel like I'm not good enough, we stick together. It could be about my meal being too salty, my washer being too loud, or questioning why I still haven't bought a new car. She'll find something to criticize me about and enlist others in questioning my decisions. It drives me crazy."

Elizabeth: "My mother sends emails to me that are terse and seemingly benevolent. But there's a tone of disapproval that sends me off balance. The message is that she's a better mother than I am, and that I am inherently deficient. 'When are the kids off from school? Did you check their school calendar???' When I answer the question, there's always a second clarifying question, as though she doesn't trust me: 'They have FOUR days off???' I am so sick of defending myself to her for the simplest of things. It's wearing me down."

Mich: "My mother would humiliate me in front of my children and allow them to do things against my wishes. One time she told my daughter that she was worried about my sanity. It felt like she was trying to create alliances with my children to put me down. My daughters told me that they don't want to hang out with Granny alone anymore. I can see why. I thought I would be depriving them of a grandmother; instead, I was putting them in harm's way by allowing her to babysit. I had hoped that becoming a grandmother would lessen her narcissistic tendencies, but I was wrong."

Claire: "Both my parents were scientists. Our house was full of activists, writers, and academics. I would stay up late listening to them talk. My mother was so passionate and engrossed in the 'cause' that she would often forget to feed or bathe me. As an only child, I learned how to blend in and do everything for myself at a young age. I've struggled majorly with depression for all of my adult life. Every time we get together, I begin the visit hoping that we can somehow connect. But it always ends with her asking me, 'Why can't you pull it together?' 'What's wrong with you?' and 'I don't know why you can't have a normal life like all my friends' children.' After each visit I go into a slump for days."

Abbie: "My mother was a single parent from the time I was two. She came close to a breakdown when I was ten, and I was her main emotional support. My younger brother has struggled with drugs and goes from job to job. Being my mother's 'angel,' I was a good student and got a PhD. Every time she calls me, which is most days of the week, she gets defensive about my brother. He recently moved into her house. It's like they've ganged up on me, even though all I want to do is connect with her. I've strived for all this success so she would finally see me and feel proud of me, but instead she's intimidated. She's constantly pushing me away or, conversely, pulling me toward her in order to hurt or drop me in some way. I just want her to love me."

Dawn: "I told my mother I didn't like the tone she used when she spoke to my child. She was harshly critical when he made a spelling mistake in his homework. Initially, she apologized. But the next day, she sent me an email saying she will no longer help me pay my student loans. This was two weeks after I asked her to please allow me to have the login info for my student loans, as I'd like to take those on, and she said no, that it was something she wanted to do for me. It was like she needed to find some way to 'get back' at me for setting a boundary."

In the moment of a mother tantrum, your mother is not seeing you accurately (as her daughter), but rather is seeing you as *her own rejecting mother*. That's why it may feel like the interaction, though benign on the surface, may have an aggressive undertone—you're witnessing the regressive energy of the angry child that your mother has yet to integrate and heal within herself. Understanding this may help you to not take your mother's behavior personally. Her behavior is really not about you at all.

It's normal to want to ignore or prevent the mother tantrum at all costs; no one wants to witness or be subject to these hurtful and disturbing interactions. And the child within you is terrified of this situation as it likely replays painful dynamics of your childhood. The point is to support your inner child and highlight to yourself that although you may not have felt emotionally safe as a child (rejection by mother meant death), you are now, as an adult capable of supporting your inner child through this experience. You will survive the tantrum, and being emotionally prepared for the consequences while your mother has her upset will liberate you. We best serve both ourselves *and* our mothers when we refuse to present versions of ourselves that distract our mothers from their pain; playing small only prolongs their suffering and postpones their healing.

Recognizing "Momipulation" in Action

Contrary to the more overt dynamics of mother tantrums, which are typically more explosive and conflict-ridden, are the quieter, more covert dynamics I call "momipulation." Momipulation is a form of subtle manipulation from one's mother that can easily fly under the radar because the judgment or hostility is cloaked in language or behaviors that seem "motherly" (i.e., nurturing, concerned, adoring, or supportive). Momipulation can be difficult to recognize, and often its main symptom for the daughter is a sense of dread, despair, or rage that can't be pinned on any one interaction, causing the daughter to blame herself, as her response feels disproportionate to the interaction. An exchange can appear one way on the surface—kind, benign, benevolent—but the energy and undertone of the interaction is very different: harsh, hostile, aggressive. Like any form of bullying, the best way to recognize momipulation is to notice how *you feel* in your body during an interaction. Look deeper if all seems well on the surface, but you find yourself feeling low or down after an encounter with your mother. It's very possible that momipulation is at play.

How you respond in the face of a mother tantrum or momipulation will be specific to the particular dynamics between you and your mother. The challenge is to not get pulled into the drama of victim, perpetrator, or rescuer, but to stand in your truth. For some, that means speaking out; for others, it means remaining silent. Reflecting on what would be the most empowering and appropriate response to momipulation or a mother tantrum is a powerful process of discovery in itself.

Feelings of Being Owed

One of the most problematic and common beliefs daughters can have is "My mother gave me life. I owe her _____." Of course, there's nothing wrong with having genuine love and respect for one's mother and genuine appreciation for all that she may have done for you. However, the feeling of "owing" your mother is something very different and a painful illusion that can bear an enormous price. Many women use this rationale to hold themselves back from what they desire, as a cause for feeling guilt or self-doubt, as a reason to tolerate poor treatment or to stay in a stuck place.

Children don't "owe" their mothers, yet this illusion of indebtedness keeps generations of women stuck. I once saw a video on Facebook that was geared toward mothers who are feeling stressed, sleep-deprived, and unappreciated. At the end it said, "Look into the eyes of your child and know that you matter." Line after line expounded upon how the mother is elevated in the eyes of the child, implying that that should be enough to get you through. The entire point of the video was that a mother need only look into her children's eyes for validation. I found it odd that it didn't mention the support of friends, partners, or communities to help women through tough times as mothers. It didn't mention self-care. It didn't help women to see themselves as inherently valid and important. It simply told mothers to look to one place for a sense of value and meaning: the eyes of their children.

At first glance, this can seem like a harmless video, with the intention of honoring the ceaseless work mothers do. It was "liked" by thousands of people. But I found this video disturbing for many reasons. For mothers, it perpetuates the illusion that the approval of one's children should be compensation enough for the brutally unending, thankless, isolating work of motherhood in the modern world. And it sets up the child for bearing the emotional burden of a mother's struggles and learning how to overfunction as an emotional caretaker. It sets up the child to feel that she "owes" her mother a version of herself that protects her mother from pain. That belief is like a poison that can damage the daughter's self-concept, self-esteem, and ability to form lasting, healthy relationships with others.

Unfortunately, one of the most common manifestations of the Mother Wound is a codependent, enmeshed relationship between mother and daughter. Portrayals like the one in the video I described perpetuate and reinforce this unhealthy enmeshment as normal "mother love." A child should not be expected to be her mother's savior, mirror, therapist, or sole reason for living. It's a mother's responsibility, as an adult, to get the support she needs from other adults including therapists, spouses, partners, community, institutions, etc.

A mother's well-being is not a child's responsibility. A mother expecting emotional labor from her child makes her child a hostage to her own pain. Often if this pattern starts in childhood, it continues until the daughter is an adult, causing her to experience self-doubt, guilt, suppressed rage, impostor syndrome, and problematic relationships, among other symptoms. Our culture, with its hostility toward women as expressed in diminishing access to reproductive healthcare, the wage gap, lack of ample maternity leave, and male violence against women, as well as other systemic barriers like institutional racism, all combine to isolate the mother and coerce the child into carrying the burden of emotionally validating her mother in the absence of support from partners, adults, institutions, and society in general. That is a void that a child can never fill. Children are asked to pick up the slack for the lack of respect and emotional support mothers are given in this culture. Society tells mothers that their children should be enough of a reward and shames them when they feel anything less than total satisfaction.

Pain from our mothers gets passed down to us from two main sources:

- The degree of inherited trauma or abuse that she experienced in her family of origin, which she may unconsciously pass down to some degree.
- The cultural Mother Wound: the pain of being a woman in this culture and how that pain gets passed down through the generations.

The culmination of many factors may result in a child feeling like she "owes" her mother:

- That natural loyalty that all children feel to their mothers.
- Seeing her mother suffer without support while knowing her mother is necessary for her survival.
- The mother reinforcing the idea that the child is responsible for her mother's well-being.
- The mother's belief that her child is indebted to her due to her own history (she may have felt she owed her mother).
- The mother's lack of support from her spouse/partner, family, friends, etc.

In generations past, and still for some people today, being a parent meant providing your child or children with food, shelter, clothing, and education. Emotional needs were seen as less important than physical needs. Like objects or pets, children were "to be seen and not heard." Issues like addictions, mental illness, financial struggles, and abuse were simply not talked about. People believed that if you pretended these problems didn't exist, kept them secret, then everything would be OK. We are beginning to realize that this is not true. These issues don't go away when you pretend they're not real or try to forget them. They are present in our everyday struggles.

A child's natural development includes growing up and having their own separate, independent life.

For a daughter enmeshed with her mother, attempts at individuation can be a brutal battlefield for ownership over herself. It's crucial that the daughter get support in debunking the distorted patriarchal logic that states that having your own separate life makes you a perpetrator of harm against your mother, that separateness is equivalent to aggression, or that your boundaries are an attack. One must resist these distortions and get support from multiple sources to set in motion new, healthy patterns instead. I learned early in my own journey as a recovering "parentified daughter" the painful belief that "I'm depriving my mother when I take care of myself."

It has been a long journey of learning to:

- Decouple what I perceived as my mother's sense of entitlement from my own self-care.
- Take up space without fearing abandonment.
- Attract a romantic partner with a capacity for equal reciprocity.
- Voice a clear "no" to people who appear to expect silent complicity with my own subjugation, however subtle.
- No longer equate empowerment with loneliness.

This work takes time, step-by-step, to build trust with the inner child and help her learn a new paradigm in which it's safe to be real, safe to have needs, safe to say "no," safe to have emotions, safe to celebrate herself, and safe to be seen. It takes getting professional support (such as some form of relational psychotherapy), setting boundaries, practicing radical self-care, and allowing yourself to grieve. So many of us have witnessed our mothers struggle, sacrifice themselves, and suffer under all manner of oppressions. Children are naturally loyal to their mothers out of necessity for survival. But true respect is not possible when it is commanded or based on obligation, shame, or emotional debt. "Owing" is not about respect. It's about control.

Mothers can get the idea that their children "owe" them if they as mothers:

- Feel deprived or not valued in other areas of their adult lives.
- Have a lack of insight about their own childhood history.
- Have a childhood history that involved abuse, neglect, or trauma with little or no therapy.
- Show signs of possible mental illness.
- Believe that mothers hold the power over their children absolutely.
- Have an authoritarian parenting style.

Mothers who reinforce this are often unaware that they are doing so. It's important for daughters to get support and set healthy boundaries with their mothers. The staggering amount of love and physical and emotional output that a mother has to offer needs to be given its due respect, awe, and sacred place in our society. But it will remain devalued and relatively invisible as long as mothers play out the damaging dynamic of expecting their children to be their mirrors, saviors, and reasons for living. And motherhood will remain devalued as long as society devalues women and induces children to pick up the tab.

We must become conscious of the ways in which patriarchy deprives mothers and how that deprivation is delivered upon their children, ultimately crippling us all collectively, to some degree.

So much has been *permitted* under the belief that "I owe my mother." Emotional abuse, physical abuse, neglect, painful silence, other traumas. So much has been *repressed* under the ache of "I owe my mother." True desires, potential, dreams, inspiration, abundance, wealth, and more have been bypassed and suppressed by women who were taught that their true expression injures those they love. Emotionally deprived mothers who feed into this dynamic steal their daughters' life force and feed on it as though it were their own.

The following are some examples of unspoken messages of mothers in a patriarchal mind-set (which comes from feeling powerless and out of control in her own life):

- "You're being ungrateful when you're being your full, big, authentic self."
- "You're honoring me when you're suffering because look how much suffering I endured to bring you into the world."
- "I'm your mother and I deserve your respect no matter how much I denigrate or abuse you."
- "You make me feel inadequate when you reach your goals."

Soon, there begins to be an association between being safe and being nonthreatening.

For many women, one of *THE* hardest things is allowing your mother to have her own painful lessons and her own healing process. This is about releasing the need to display a false self to please your mother and instead being your authentic self in her presence, even if she expresses disapproval. It involves allowing your mother to express displeasure about your truth without allowing it to disorient you and without getting pulled into a battle with her.

You are not a "bad daughter" for allowing your mother to have her own lessons and challenges without rushing to solve them for her.

In the best of situations, letting your mother handle her own painful lessons and problems may stimulate the grief that is necessary to bring true healing within her, but only if your mother is open and willing to grow. The unfortunate truth is that some mothers are patently unwilling to do the hard work of healing their own wounds and would rather make their daughters feel responsible for them.

As a daughter, if your mother has a pattern of reacting with hostility when you express your own separate selfhood, individuality, realness, and power, it may be because your authentic expression has stimulated the seeds of the potential that never came to blossom in your mother herself. She may experience your true, vital, authentic self as a painful mirror showing her the ways she had to forsake herself in order to survive her own family. It may trigger deep grief over her loss of self. If she's unable or unwilling to feel the full grief and process it, she may react with anger, manipulation, competition, jealousy, or withdrawal.

The deprivation that your mother feels cannot be solved by anything that *you* do.

Her pain cannot be filled by you staying small and unhappy. Walking on eggshells and "not rocking the boat" may accomplish short-term "peace," but in the long term, you are handing your life force over to the Mother Wound. It's a form of giving your power away. You do not owe your mother anything. Your unhappiness and dissatisfaction will never compensate for her unhealed wounds and struggles. She is the only one who can take the necessary actions to change her situation.

When we emotionally caretake our mother in the form of self-sabotage, we actually inhibit our mother's healing because we become complicit in maintaining her illusions. And we put our lives indefinitely on hold waiting for her approval, which will never come.

The experience that breaks this pattern is realizing that you can survive your mother's rejection of you. This may seem obvious to your intellectual adult mind, but to your inner child or the primitive, emotional parts of your brain, rejection from your mother still feels very dangerous and way too risky. That's why we get so far and then *BOOM*—we unconsciously feel unsafe and revert to old patterns of guilt, emotional caretaking, shrinking to please others, apologizing for existing, and being addicted to approval and external validation.

Feeling small and stuck doesn't feel good, but to our inner child, it feels SAFE.

In order to heal self-sabotage, we need to break the link between being authentic and some form of loss of mother, such as the feeling of being abandoned or rejected by her. And we must create a *new* link between being authentic and being safe, loved, cherished.

Healthy emotional separation between mother and daughter needs to happen for both to flourish as individuals and to have an authentic, nourishing heart connection between them.

Anything obligatory is forced and not free. It's not about true connection. It's a transaction. There is a whole new world beyond the illusion of "owing" where your life is your own, and where your needs and feelings are embraced, not shamed. Your life belongs to you. You don't owe your mother. Discouraging our ability to be confident in our separateness has been a tactic of the patriarchy to oppress women. I'm not talking about being separate in a cold, defensive way but as being singular, whole, and one unto yourself.

Our separate personhood is a place of power we must cultivate and support each other in developing. It doesn't have to be either/or. Being separate is not equivalent to being exclusive or disconnected. The more we feel entitled to our own love and support, the stronger we can become and the more positive change we can bring about together.

It's time to reclaim the holy impulse to be separate. The taboo of the Mother Wound has long stalled the process of healing women individually and collectively. It's important that we see the truth, however uncomfortable, that healing the Mother Wound is *not* mother blame. It is an essential part of being a conscious, mature adult. In fact, healing the Mother Wound (and not passing it on to the next generation) is the ultimate expression of maturity and personal responsibility.

When Sympathy for Your Mother Keeps You Stuck

The impacts of a mother's patriarchal beliefs are especially devastating to a daughter's personal development and individuation process. A mother's denial of her own pain is part of what keeps the Mother Wound in place. Daughters are more likely than sons to see their mothers as victims of their own unlived dreams, of lack of opportunity, or of having been devalued by men. Because of the daughter's sympathy for her mother's plight, she is more likely to absorb her mother's pain as her own, creating a toxic enmeshment that directly prevents her ability to flourish in her own life. The more unconscious and intense the mother's own unhealed wounds are, the more threatened she will feel by her daughter's separateness and individuality. Thus, the mother-daughter bond may be forged in an environment of pain that keeps both stuck.

The more spacious and loving a woman is toward herself, the more she can offer that to her daughter. A mother cannot give her daughter the support, love, guidance, and empowerment that she herself does not have. If a woman does not have that healthy model of self-love in her mother, she has to seek those models elsewhere.

The patriarchal bind is that women are told that they should be successful but not too successful; sexy but not too sexy; strong but not too strong; smart but not too smart; etc. A mother may unintentionally perpetuate this out of an unconscious need to avoid getting triggered by her daughter. If her daughter remains disempowered, small, and

always a bit doubtful of herself, then the mother eliminates the possibility that her daughter will trigger the unacknowledged pain within
herself that she'd rather ignore. For mothers unwilling to do their own
inner work, this is an unconscious form of emotional self-preservation
at the daughter's expense.

For an unconscious, deeply wounded mother, a disempowered
daughter is the perfect antidote to her misery because she allows the
mother to maintain an illusion of personal power without having to
do the hard work of self-growth and healing. If the daughter is empowered, flourishing, happy, and fulfilled, the wounded mother would
more likely be faced with the task of confronting her unhealed pain.

A mother may outwardly display a facade of calm and pleasantness,
but underneath there may lurk a sense of emotional impoverishment
that expresses itself primarily in relation to her daughter, who may
carry the projection of her mother's disowned wounds.

The unspoken message to the daughter in both instances is: "Your
empowerment is unacceptable." The daughter's empowerment is unacceptable because it reminds the mother of her ungrieved losses or
the unexpressed rage she may feel toward the patriarchy in her family
and culture. A mother may experience her daughter's empowerment
as a betrayal, a personal rejection, or a slight. She may unconsciously
pressure the daughter to attenuate her voice, downplay her suffering,
narrow her ambitions, or settle for less, just as she may have felt pressured to do herself as a young woman.

An empowered daughter is a stimulus for the unhealed parts within
the mother to come forward and be healed. A wounded mother may
confuse the pain she feels in her daughter's presence as being her
daughter's fault and responsibility, not seeing that the pain was there
all along and belongs solely to her—the mother. In this way, the daughter is actually giving her mother a gift. Her own light reveals her mother's shadow and the next step in her healing. If the mother is healthy

and open, she will more easily see the gift. But if the mother is unconscious, deeply wounded, and stuck, she will probably see it as a reason to lash out at her daughter (covertly or overtly).

Examples of patriarchal power plays from mothers include:

- Daughter is used as her emotional dumping ground.
- Mother is neglectful but uses daughter as narcissistic tool to bring her mother attention.
- Mother has no use for daughter if she doesn't conform to her mother's views. It's her way or the highway.
- Mother tantrums: overt hostility, bullying, explosive rages, storming off, physical violence.
- Momipulation: cold withdrawal, competition, jealousy, triangulating daughter against other family members, thinly veiled threats or put-downs, criticism veiled as innocent feedback, sarcastic humor, etc.

(Note: All these dynamics could be played out with a son as well. And they could also be features of mental illness in the mother.)

You'll notice that all of the dynamics listed above have to do with one thing: gaining power and control. The mother who has given her power away will seek it out in other ways. This is true of all of us. When we give our power away, it creates a vacuum, and we are compelled to fill it somehow, usually by processing it or projecting it. For a mother, the easiest target of projection is her daughter. It gives the relationship a vampiric quality: the daughter stays weak and the mother feels strong. However, it benefits neither mother nor daughter.

Patriarchy prevents a major human function from happening, which is to feel the truth of all our feelings. To some degree, both men and women (boys and girls) are shamed away from feelings, whether through violence, abuse, or neglect, whether in our families or in our culture at large. The shame is due to the patriarchal belief that feelings are inherently weak and must be suppressed.

The task of healing is for each of us to metabolize and process our own pain fully. As we do this, owning our wounds, feeling our pain, and grieving to completion, the energy of the Mother Wound transforms into wisdom, love, and power. For mothers and daughters, this means there needs to be a healthy emotional distance in which both can engage fully with their healing process and each can experience her own personal power and freedom. Both need support and resources to successfully navigate their journey.

As we metabolize the truth of what we endured as children, we are then capable of finally decoupling how our mothers treated us from our own worth as human beings. We begin to see our mothers as individuals, with their own paths and journeys and lessons. And we can stop making our mother's dysfunction, pain, or limitations mean something about *us*. This necessary process of decoupling is essential for true individuation and self-actualization, of giving birth to the true self and embodying it in the world. This is an act of great courage, fortitude, and endurance.

Patriarchy is about power at all costs. One way that power has been gathered is through rigid ideas of what is right and what is wrong. But in truth, there is no absolute right or wrong, just a multitude of preferences and consequences. By increasingly dissolving the charge of polarizing concepts such as right/wrong and good/bad, infinite possibilities begin to open up and individuals can make choices that are truly authentic and right for them, without fear and shame.

All around us, we are seeing patriarchal institutions fail and crumble from within: religions, governments, media, etc. The family is also a patriarchal institution, and families will increasingly feel the pressure to shift and accommodate a new consciousness that is emerging. In the dominator mode of patriarchy, a dysfunctional family is threatened by the individuality of its members. In this way, patriarchal mothers may be threatened by their daughter's individuality and may unconsciously sabotage it. As a new form of the family emerges, I sense that families will be more flexible, inclusive, and welcoming of individuality. Perhaps the very definition of "family" will change and expand. People who call themselves family may not be linked by blood but by soulful connections that mutually nourish their journey to discover and live their authentic truth. This cultural shift starts at the level of individuals who choose to do the work of healing and recovery.

For mothers, the journey of healing their own Mother Wound is precisely what frees their daughters from this painful legacy.

To be whole, empowered women, we have to be disloyal to the patriarch in our mothers. We have to say no. We must refuse to give up our power to feed the pain body of our mothers, which, ultimately, is a great gift to them and to the world. It's time for us to honor ourselves. It's time for women to heal the Mother Wound. We have to do the hard and holy thing, which is to focus on our own healing so that we can finally experience ourselves as whole and model this new level of wholeness for our daughters and the women of the future.

In the next chapter, we'll explore in detail the underlying personal and cultural elements that keep the Mother Wound in place.

Questions for Reflection

1. How do you see power dynamics playing out in your life? In your interpersonal relationships, communities, organizations?
2. In what ways do you see the "patriarchal bind" play out in your life and the lives of women around you? (Patriarchal bind is the sense of needing to be successful but not too successful, pretty but not too pretty, etc.)

3. Looking back at your childhood, how did your family approach difficult emotions? How were they addressed or avoided? How do those coping mechanisms impact you now?
4. In reflecting on the relationship with your mother, what was the power dynamic like between you? Did any of these dynamics resonate with you (mompathy, momipulation, mother tantrums)?

Chapter 4

WHAT KEEPS THE MOTHER WOUND IN PLACE, AND WHY DOES IT ENDURE?

MY RESISTANCE TO LOOKING at my relationship with my mother was strong. How could I possibly question my family? They had put a roof over my head, taken me on vacations, paid for piano and sewing lessons. They'd bought me Christmas gifts and Easter baskets. From the outside, nothing seemed wrong. We were a normal, even fortunate, family. But my symptoms were telling an entirely different story. I was starting to have anxiety attacks on a regular basis. I had some triggers that put me in low places for days.

Over time I found I was tired of being a false self, a good girl, a compliant caretaker. I wanted to be authentic, to be REAL. This hunger continued to grow. I studied female-centric spirituality. I discovered feminism. My idealization of my mother began to show cracks. I longed for wisdom from her, for encouragement of some kind as I struggled to give my life meaning and direction. I felt rudderless. But strangely, my mother seemed to become *even more silent or distant. I knew my mother had gone through significant trauma herself, but she never talked about it. She continued to cater to her own aging mother as an adult while complaining about her incessantly, and I could sense the tension she carried about it. My mother's mantra seemed to be always "Suppress and move on." Never show weakness. As I struggled in my twenties, I could feel her jealousy and contempt for me around the edges, but I couldn't fully acknowledge it, even to myself. I needed to believe that she wanted the best for me, that she supported me. I needed to believe that all the support I had offered her for all these years would be someday reciprocated. She was my mother, after all.*

The Mother Wound is held in place by a complex web of factors, including personal (within us as personally due to our own histories), cultural (the atmosphere that we grow up in), and spiritual (feeling disconnected from life as a whole) and on a planetary level (unrooted from a sense of a safe place in our environment), and in the interaction between all four of these. Once we understand these factors and how they interact, we are more capable of seeing the Mother Wound at play and more equipped to transform it in our daily lives, loosening its hold over us to limit our choices and dictate our behaviors. With this greater clarity, we are less susceptible to guilt, shame, and isolation, which can paralyze us in our pain. We become more empowered and creative, more inspired and energized to be cultural change agents, clearing the way for future generations.

Since the Mother Wound is a product of patriarchy, I'm going to start there and explain the larger cultural forces that give rise to the personal dynamics and manifestations of the Mother Wound.

Denial, "Toughness," and Disdain for Feelings

In previous generations, there seemed to be a collective belief in a place called "away." The thinking goes that if we don't talk about emotions and our real feelings, they go away—they cease to exist and their influence on us dissolves. For example, if we have a fight and never discuss it afterward, then we believe the conflict no longer exists.

Developmental psychologists discuss the developmental stage of "object permanence," in which a child learns that even though objects do not appear, they continue to exist. For example, if a caregiver hides a stuffed animal under a blanket, there's a developmental point when a child knows that the stuffed animal is still there even though it's out of view. Like object permanence, this cultural form of denial seems like a failed cultural developmental step of *emotion* permanence." Emotion permanence means taking responsibility for our emotions and their inevitable impact on others. In a way, it's not surprising that there's such widespread fear of strong emotions because we've had so few models of what it means to process strong emotions in a healthy way. Collectively, we've been emotionally stunted.

What we fail to accept, we will project.

Nowadays, people young and old are waking up to the fact that there is no such place as "away" and that suppressed pain does not cease to exist if it is ignored or pushed under the rug. In fact, not only does it continue to exist, it becomes a virulent, unconscious force, negatively influencing our behavior, with toxic consequences for those around us. Pain repressed is pain passed on. Whatever we refuse to process about how we have suffered will influence us, limiting our choices, narrowing our life energy, and creating bitterness, resentment, and misery. Thus, "toughness" or denial is not noble. It's actually weakness.

The tide is turning, and today, having the courage to get support to *process our pain* and harvest the resulting insights that change our behavior, clearing the way for others, is increasingly being seen as the noble choice.

Shame is the main cultural enforcer of patriarchy. It is the primary emotion of the oppressed and the intended emotion of the oppressor because it paralyzes its victim. Shame makes us easy to control. It makes us compliant. Western civilization sees the expression of emotions, particularly "negative" emotions, as shameful and weak. This view keeps us paralyzed individually and collectively.

In older generations, there was a belief that there would be a payoff for pretending. Many are discovering that that payoff never comes. Subsequent generations of parents would say "I don't want to screw up my kids the way I was screwed up by my parents," and thought just saying it was enough to prevent that from happening. But just knowing that you don't want to pass along generational pain is not enough. It takes many, many years of focused inner work to stop cycles of intergenerational pain. And yet nothing is more important or fulfilling than this journey. We can support each other and provide the courage, support, and tools it takes to make it to the other side. Emotion permanence is acknowledging the reality that our emotions will impact our relationships and circumstances whether we like it or not.

The Lie of Female Inferiority

There is a lie of staggering proportions that sits at the center of our lives. This lie is so pervasive that it is rendered virtually invisible. This lie is that female inferiority *is the natural order,* implying that all that is feminine has a natural defect. This is the lie that causes rot in the mother-daughter relationship, crippling women collectively. The crippling can only continue as long as we remain unconscious of the myriad manifestations of this rot, the Mother Wound. At this time in history, we have to make the manifestations as conscious as possible so that we can move beyond it.

The patriarchal lie of female inferiority situates the daughter in conflict between her natural desire to live her full potential and the truth of her mother's deprivation at the hands of patriarchal institutions including the family, the church, the school, the media, and the state. The mother-daughter bond may have a background tension fostered by the inherent scarcity of personal power they are permitted in society and also an enmeshment between them due to their plight. Their bond is colored to some degree by how each of them copes with the lie about their inferiority.

This belief in a "female defect" keeps women on a never-ending wheel of self-improvement, constantly working to meet an impossible standard of what a "desirable woman" ought to be. The mother is often the first to impart these standards to the daughter, often in an unconscious effort to keep the female child safe in a world hostile to women. The problem lies in the fact that those standards actually harm the daughter as they harmed her mother, and her mother's mother before her.

Every new child comes with a healthy demand to live life on his or her own terms.

When a daughter attempts to go beyond the mother's standards into a life lived on her own terms, it can feel like a betrayal of the mother. However, that impulse to go beyond the ideals of the mother is a healthy, life-giving impulse. To individuate and live as the real self, not the false self that patriarchy requires, is the natural impulse. To fight that healthy impulse is to keep the daughter in a kind of emotional immaturity, always a bit distrustful and doubting of herself and never fully living her own life.

"I Endured and You Can, Too.
Why Should I Make It Easier for You?"

This attitude can be seen in families, teams, and organizations of all kinds. Here's how it generally plays out: Some form of pain is experienced by people of a certain generation or a certain level in an organization. There is resentment felt about what this group experienced, a legitimate sense of unfairness and unresolved anger. But since they haven't accounted for or made an effort to or been successfully able to process the pain they went through, that resentment stagnates and gets redirected into a sense of pleasure in seeing others go through it as well. Rather than make it easier for those who follow, they feel a sense of justice in watching them inherit the same pain. The true source of the pain is not acknowledged or addressed. This is a tragedy because, as a result, the oppressor is protected and the oppressed just keep oppressing each other. For some, over time the ability to endure pain and dysfunction becomes part of one's identity, and so when new generations are seeking to transform or change, whether themselves or an organization or a tradition, some from older generations may perceive that desire for change as a threat to their identity and actively sabotage, dismiss, or push against it. This often prevents the very communication and connection that both are craving.

Idealization of Mothers That Shames Children

All humans have the capacity for human emotions, yet we're shamed for having those emotions considered "negative"—feelings like anger, sadness, jealousy, disappointment, rage, longing, etc. Further, all humans have the capacity to feel these negative emotions toward our mothers; this type of negative feeling is the most taboo.

All of the following very common platitudes give the illusion of elevating the mother and disparaging the child for having a normal range of feelings:

"Don't blame your mother."

"Your mother gave you life."

"How dare you question your mother."

"Your mother is trying her best."

"You only have one mother."

Stereotype of Women as the "Emotional Laborers"

Patriarchy not only makes emotions seem frivolous, weak, and shameful, it projects the entire emotional domain onto women. Individuation requires that the daughter withdraw from any overfunctioning (emotional labor) for the mother, whether as her scapegoat, her emotional confidante, her problem-solver, her pet, her target for rage, or her distraction. It also requires that the daughter stop waiting for the mother to do things that she may simply lack the capacity to do, such as celebrating the daughter, accurately seeing her, acknowledging their differences with love, etc. There's often a lot of grief to work through here.

Some degree of emotional differentiation from your mother is essential to feeling in charge of your own life.

Unfortunately, our culture dismisses daughters who examine their relationships with their mothers as simply "mother-blaming." Though the swift dismissal appears to protect the mother's "elevated status" in the culture, it actually exploits her by protecting her ability to pass on damaging patriarchal norms, keeping her ignorant of the true magnitude of her own suffering. Conscious reflection on this relationship is the basis of true adult responsibility, yet many still believe the opposite.

The unlived life of a mother can be experienced by her daughter as a powerful burden, consciously or unconsciously. Important factors include how much the mother had conflict with her own mother, how deeply she internalized the lie of her own inferiority, and whatever unhealed trauma is in her own history. In other words, whatever a mother refuses to confront in her own life will present some kind of challenge in her relationship with her daughter and, additionally, may contribute to some kind of challenge for her daughter in her own life.

Mothers may feel jealous of their daughters, putting daughters in a tough situation. A daughter may assume that she is responsible for her mother's deprivation. As one woman told me, "I always felt like the implication was that I was bad when good things happened easily for me. The unspoken question was 'How do you think that makes Mommy feel?' causing me to associate guilt with feeling good."

Healthy differentiation from your mother is about ceasing to live in the shadow of your mother's dysfunction as if it is your own.

Another woman explained, "I felt this awful helplessness of not being able to make my mother see that I'm not trying to be cruel to her when I'm happy. No matter how much I tried, she could never see it that way. I gradually learned that doubting myself was a form of loyalty to her. Not being fully successful, not fully ambitious, was a way to love her. If she felt me crossing the line, even *approaching* that line, into a state of sustained contentedness or confidence, I would feel her energetically pull away from me. She'd begin to mock, criticize, or punish me, mostly in subtle, underhanded ways. I don't think she was conscious of any of this. The one time I didn't acquiesce to her demand to attenuate myself for her, she dropped me completely. I realized later that my willingness to curb my potential for her was a kind of nourishment she depended upon in her life that was otherwise bereft of validation."

A scarcity dynamic arises: a sense of not enough love, space, or power between them. Comparison, competition, jealousy are manifestations of this background sense of scarcity.

For daughters of jealous mothers, it can feel like having to choose between the love of your mother and your own potential. Because a child depends on her mother, she will, of course, have to choose her mother and forsake herself. Left unhealed and unexamined, this dynamic will create a festering sense of deprivation and resentment that she could likely pass on to her own daughter. And this is one of the ways the wound is perpetuated in another generation.

I'm increasingly convinced that the world will be healed by women's ability to feel the full scope of our own feelings.

The paradox is that feeling the truth of our own feelings involves refusing to feel other people's feelings for them. In other words, it involves refraining from overfunctioning and taking responsibility for those who are unwilling to *do their own inner work.*

It's up to us to see the ways we emotionally overfunction and refrain from doing so.

Traditionally, women's work has not only been the cooking, cleaning, and caring for children, but also involved bearing the emotional labor of relationships: cleaning up emotional messes, starting the uncomfortable conversations, feeling the burden of silences, living with things unsaid, burying unspoken needs, being the projection screen of disowned pain, wading silently through passive-aggressive slights, etc. The problem is that men have traditionally been taught to devalue emotional labor and see it as purely women's work, when in reality, both partners should shoulder equal responsibility for emotional intelligence and communication skills.

Women have historically been the "cleaning ladies" of the culture, the proverbial trash bin of unwanted emotions, expected to feel them for others and then blamed for expressing the very emotions that others refuse to feel. It's time to put down this role. We are clogging ourselves with material that blocks us from our own power and clarity. And we are protecting people from their own painful truths—the very truths that will free them.

It's time to dismantle the false ethics of patriarchy that keep women stuck in the role of emotional laborers.

For women, patriarchy conflates emotional labor with a false sense of ethics. It's this false ethics that causes us to perpetuate our own internalized oppression. We are taught in various ways that emotional labor is an innate skill of women, and if we don't do it, the implication is that we're not a "good person" or a "desirable woman." This leads us to feeling suspicious of ourselves if we feel fed up with it. There is a tendency to feel shame when we approach our thresholds for carrying the emotional weight for others.

You're not being a "bad person" when you refuse to carry the emotional weight for others.

We've been taught to pride ourselves on our ability to endure the imbalanced responsibility for the emotional aspects of our relationships. The willingness to put up with this burden is rooted in a sense of scarcity; the notion that the crumbs we're receiving are the best we can get. In many ways, healing the Mother Wound is about the fundamental movement from scarcity to abundance.

Often our most potent resistance is to dropping the emotional labor we do for our mothers.

One of the most heartbreaking conversations I frequently have with women is when they tell me they're completely exhausted by feeling responsible for their mothers' happiness. And when they consider ceasing to play that role, they question their value as a person, they feel "bad" for even acknowledging their exhaustion with it. Playing this role grinds you down to the core. Nothing you do for your mother will be enough, because what she is seeking is impossible to get from anywhere but within herself. It's a dead end. Refuse to absorb the guilt. Your impulse to throw off this weight is a trustworthy impulse. The weight was never yours to carry in the first place.

We are usually trained for emotional labor by our mothers, either through cleaning up our mother's emotional messes or observing her carrying out emotional labor for others.

Recently I was speaking to a client who summed up her relationship with her mother this way: "I protect her from herself and I end up paying the biggest price." I hear variations on this theme all the time. Many of us who had mothers who were emotionally absent have swung the other way, becoming emotional caretakers, giving to others what we desperately needed from our own mothers.

Ways you may be protecting your mother from herself:

- Showing her a mask; displaying only the emotions she prefers.
- Not confronting her when her behavior is insulting, demeaning, or manipulative.
- Allowing her to use you as a dumping ground for toxic negativity.
- Absorbing her projections without speaking out (walking on eggshells).
- Molding yourself to cater to her insecurities and appear nonthreatening.
- Not setting boundaries with "mother tantrums" that arise when you express your individuality.

Ways this harms you:

- Reinforces the idea that your rightful role is as the emotional dumping ground.
- Fosters feelings of shame for your own separate, legitimate opinions, thoughts, observations.

- Keeps you stuck in unconscious patterns that reflect childhood fears and beliefs.
- How you attenuate yourself around your mother will show up in other contexts and relationships (career, parenting, romantic relationships).

Healing the Mother Wound is essential to detoxing from the role of emotional laborer. It dissolves the dysfunctional enmeshment with our mothers and creates the necessary emotional separation for us to feel our power as individuals. This emotional separation comes in the form of setting healthy boundaries that honor our personal sovereignty.

The women of the future will not perform the "feeling" function for others.

When we hand back our mothers the responsibility to process their own pain, it creates the space for us to take responsibility for *our* own pain. *The two go together.* Carrying your mother's pain and taking responsibility for her happiness may appear kind and altruistic on the surface, but we must see it for what it really is: avoidance of our own power.

Know that whatever you deprive yourself of in the name of your mother is a "check" that you will present to someone else to pay back to you in the future, whether it be your partner, your child, or your female friends. That imbalance will seek to right itself eventually. Don't perpetuate the debt in your mother line to the next generation. Claim your own life now. Free yourself and the generations to come.

No relationship is worth losing yourself for, including your relationship with your mother. If your mother (or anyone else) refuses to interact with you unless you play the role of emotional caretaker or emotional dumping ground, you are not being loved—you are being used. Facing this can be really hard, but face it we must if we want to truly claim our lives as our own.

In addition to speaking out in ways that we've been silent, we must also remain silent where we once spoke in ways that gave our power away. We have to be able to endure that silence and hold our tongues where we used to fill the empty space for others who refuse to do their own inner work, speak with their own voices, and process their own pain.

This is one of the greatest services we can offer to others in our lives, even if they rail against it.

When we refuse to toil emotionally for others and cease to ask others to emotionally labor for us, we are correcting an ancient imbalance. This imbalance is responsible for so much human suffering.

I invite you to courageously see yourself as a pioneer in righting an imbalance that women have been enduring for centuries. Take the long-term view and honor yourself as a powerful piece in the collective puzzle of a new era of women's empowerment. You are helping to build a new mother line not just for your lineage, but for all women. Don't underestimate how small actions you take every day to honor yourself contribute to opening up new ways of being for all.

Our Physiological Makeup

Our physiological system is designed to ensure our physical survival, whatever it takes. *Our system prefers the familiar.* It's set up to see change and novel ways of doing things as a threat. Our system is not set up to ensure that we thrive, only that we survive. This means that the very adaptations and coping mechanisms that we developed to survive dysfunctional environments in our childhood later become barriers to our true health and fulfillment as adults. Our brains are wired with three main responses to perceived threat: flight, fight, and freeze. If we haven't processed or worked through our trauma, every-day situations that have similar flavors or features to those from our childhood can cause us to have emotional flashbacks. These emotional flashbacks, or "triggers," are potent opportunities to heal the past and make different choices than we could as children, opening us up to new possibilities for our future. But without that level of awareness, we mistake the trigger (the out-of-proportion emotional response) as having come from the surface-level situation, which is really just a tip of the very large iceberg of the past. We cycle through the same problems and issues without any resolution, feeling bewildered about the cause, trying every workshop, book, and healing modality we can find but only experiencing superficial, short-lived results.

The "inner child," a concept introduced in the 1970s, is a living energy within us, trapped at a younger level of development when some original trauma occurred. Emotional flashbacks or triggers come from this part of us, our inner child. The good news is that we can form a bond with this very young part of ourselves and rework the early attachment traumas we experienced to become healthier and more liberated adults. We can learn to transfer the primary attachment from our mothers to ourselves, and to meet those needs from within.

The conversation about the inner child raises the important question of how we mother this inner child, because if we just mother the inner child the way we were mothered, we actually perpetuate our trauma again within ourselves. That is why the work of "inner mothering" is central to healing the Mother Wound. (More on that later.)

Prioritizing "Traditions" Despite the Suffering They May Cause

Different cultures value different things and have different traditions. In regards to the Mother Wound, the question is: To what extent do we "tolerate" cultural traditions that are oppressive to women, no matter how "precious" those traditions are to the culture? It's true that older generations may *not* see some traditions as harmful—after all, they endured them, they say. But each new generation in its youth sees the traditions with fresh eyes and, if aware enough, has the opportunity to change the culture for the better, to make it freer and more supportive to women. It's about the people inside the culture changing it from within, by being brave, willing to question the status quo and offer a new vision for how women can be treated and positioned in a culture.

It's a valid question for every culture: How are women treated in the culture, how is this treatment perpetuated, and why? There's really no strong right or wrong answer; it comes down to the experience of the women in the culture. Do we have to suppress ourselves to belong, to survive, to be approved of? At what cost? In what situations are we confusing tradition with abuse? Or loyalty with abuse?

The most insidious forms of patriarchy pass through the mother.

Most of us learn patriarchal thinking in our families, and it is usually taught unconsciously by mothers, often as a way to try to keep their daughters safe from harm. The messages are some version of "Don't rock the boat. Put others before yourself. Be quiet. Be pleasing to others." Yet these are the very beliefs that we must overcome in order to heal the Mother Wound and move the culture forward. While these beliefs may have kept us alive or out of harm's way in a hostile, male-centered world, they also narrowed our potential and ability to find fulfillment as adult women. This can be particularly damaging for daughters and their ability to flourish as empowered women, because a mother's treatment of her daughter gets internalized by the daughter as her own sense of self. The patriarchal messages daughters receive from their mothers are more insidious and damaging than any combination of cultural messages. Why? Because they come from the one person the daughter must bond with in order to survive.

The patriarchal thread that runs through all dysfunctional dynamics between mothers and daughters is the demand for obedience in exchange for love.

The dynamics between mothers and daughters that cause pain all have one similarity. Whether a mother is neglectful or, at the other end of the spectrum, invasive, the same patriarchal message is conveyed: compliance is required in order to be accepted. One could say that that is the core message of patriarchy to both men *and* women—you will not be loved unless you obey. This message permeates and emanates from all facets of society: education, religions, governments, and media.

In order to be fully empowered, actualized, and fulfilled, we as women must be disloyal to the patriarch within our mothers and, consequently, the patriarch within ourselves.

The "Mother Ceiling": We may feel we have to return the sacrifice by not stepping into our power fully because our mothers did not have that chance.

Daughters in this situation often hold these beliefs:

- "I have to 'shrink' to be loved."
- "If I give to myself, I deprive others."
- "If I'm seen as powerful, no one will love me."

As daughters, we must refuse to be the food for "starving mothers." We cannot let them feed on our dreams through covert competition and guilt. This is not the true nourishment they seek, but in their pain, it may seem like there is no other way. We have to let our mothers have their own healing journey, for in mourning their wounds lies the gift of their own transformation.

Our mothers can only be fed by the relief of their own grieving.

As painful as it is, mothers must mourn the ways they have been deprived, and not put the onus to compensate for their losses on their daughters. Mothers have to deal with their difficult feelings on their own time, not make it their daughters' responsibility.

It's totally natural for an older woman to seek solace in other women, even her daughter. But there is a line between honestly sharing how you're doing and dumping your wounds onto the younger woman, particularly a child. Sometimes a mother may unconsciously look to her daughter for the mothering and nurturing that she did not receive from her own mother. This happens because the older woman is unaware that she has an "inner mother" she can cultivate and turn to for support. To prevent the Mother Wound from being passed to them, younger women must feel empowered to set a firm boundary when older women seek to make them the dumping ground for their wounds.

Mothers may unconsciously hold their daughters back due to their own ungrieved wounds, unknowingly crippling their daughters. We have to stop equating being a loyal daughter with carrying the unresolved pain of the women who went before us.

As daughters, our starvation serves no one; it only keeps the Mother Wound alive, passing it down over and over again through the generations. When we offer ourselves up as food to the "starving mother," the pain is passed on to us and we then become starving ourselves.

We have to gain a sense of entitlement to ourselves and to living our greatness on our own terms.

We have to be willing to examine and reevaluate relationships that benefit from our smallness. We have to see the futility of expecting true comfort from those who are threatened by our potential, even if those people are women we love. Women who cut other women down, either consciously or unconsciously, are coming from a place of woundedness. We can show them there is a different way.

We can model to each other that it is possible to be powerful and to be loved.

We must change the "either/or" framework into "both/and." We have to take the risk of being authentic and setting boundaries. We may be pioneers, blazing a new trail without many models and with few leaders. We must step forward, step up to this challenge, and find other women who are mutually supportive as we embrace this new paradigm that supports the greatness in all of us.

One of the most powerful things we can embody is: "I don't owe you a version of me that distracts you from your responsibility to face your own pain."

The many women around the world I speak to about the Mother Wound tell me of mothers who display disturbing behavior that reflects the patriarchal mind-set: intolerance for differing views, contempt for autonomy, demanding "my way or the highway," mocking and showing cruelty for expressing feelings, etc. These mothers are typically women who have been brutally wounded by patriarchy and who are threatened by women who don't buy into it.

Disruption: Moving from Female Attenuation to Female Individuation

Families are systems, and all systems seek equilibrium by maintaining a status quo. Often daughters look at their families and wonder why they can't fit in or can't make relationships work. They may be scapegoated or deemed the black sheep. Often the healthiest person in the system is the first one to recognize a problem, to see that something is wrong or isn't working. As adult daughters become more healthy, aware, and conscious of toxic family dynamics, it challenges the family system because it threatens the status quo, that comfortable equilibrium, which is in some degree compliant with toxic, misogynist, heteropatriarchal standards and norms. By questioning these familial and cultural norms, we may be ostracized, defamed, or attacked, but it's not because there's something wrong with us; it's because we're upsetting the toxic equilibrium, which is a necessary step to move any system to a higher level. As women healing the Mother Wound, we are disruptors, pioneers living a new world into being. As we refuse to attenuate ourselves, lower our voices, narrow our dreams, or truncate our ambitions, we are claiming our own personal power and enlarging the potential for humanity as a whole.

Questions for Reflection

1. Growing up, did you ever feel obligated to uplift, protect, or nurture your mother? If so, under what circumstances, and how often did they occur? How did this impact you as a child, and how does it impact you now as an adult woman?
2. How was loyalty defined in your family, both explicitly and implicitly?
3. As a female child, how often did you feel obligated to hide or sugar-coat your true feelings? What views about yourself do you think you internalized as a result?

Chapter 5

THE MOTHER GAP

BECAUSE I FELT THAT my mother's emotional needs took up such a large amount of space in the home and in our relationship, I found my safety in soothing her first, in the hope that I would eventually get the support and reassurance I was wanting from her. I found safety in how deeply I could lose myself and blend with her, absorbing her frustrations, mirroring back her opinions, assuaging her fears, boosting her hopes, and bolstering her, always finding the bright side, all while hiding my own needs and difficulties. I was praised by my mother when I was a good mirror, a caring witness, a confidante; and she often withdrew from or mocked me when I expressed needs or feelings of my own. Any time I was going through something I couldn't hide well, which was rare and only happened if I was really struggling, she always seemed to respond with a deep, labored sigh and say "What's wrong?!" in a gruff, frustrated tone. The implication, in my mind, was that I shouldn't be upset, that I shouldn't be feeling what I was feeling. Through tears, I would say "Nothing," and try not to let my guard down in front of her, going into my room alone. Eventually, I stopped going to her at all. When I took a break from college and waited tables, I got my own apartment in a neighboring town. It was a dream come true, an affordable third-floor apartment with a second bedroom that I used for meditation and writing. I recall my mother raging at me for wanting to move out, but I knew it was essential for my mental health to have space from her.

This distance from my mother felt like a huge relief. But at the same time, more pronounced symptoms of my "mother gap" began to emerge in full force. Living alone for the first time, I found myself suddenly unable to prepare or cook food for myself. Up until that point, I had eaten on campus or cooked with friends. But now that I was living alone, it felt impossible to summon the will to feed myself. There was an emotional block that I couldn't seem to put my finger on. I either ate out, ordered in, or ate at the restaurant where I worked, often consuming nothing but coffee before four p.m., when I had to report to work. It was as though I preferred to pretend I didn't have needs, even the basic need for food.

My mother always cooked for us growing up, mostly delicious food. But I always sensed that the food was inseparable from an unspoken emotional agenda. It was as if her feeding us was the tip of an iceberg that led down to the dark depths of her own unconscious emotional deprivation: "Eat to please Mother. Eat to please me. Please validate me." Growing up, she rarely ate with my brother and me; she would eat by herself after my brother and I had finished. Most nights, she ate alone in front of the television at the kitchen table. Before she went to bed, she would leave a plate of food, covered with plastic wrap, on the counter for my dad for whenever he would return home. Most nights during the week, he was down at the local bar with friends and didn't return until after the rest of us were asleep. Those wrapped meals were rarely eaten.

So much went unspoken in that house: the unspoken pain I sensed between my parents, the suppressed pain of my own I felt but couldn't name. There was a constant numbing and disassociating through what I believe was my parents' functional alcoholism *and thinly veiled contempt for one another, which seemed to over-ride any parental recognition of my brother's and my emotional needs. Needing my parents for survival meant continuing to ide-alize them, but under the surface I felt like a zombie, partially dis-associated so I could make it through. A good girl with a happy face who felt dead inside.*

My difficulties with food were symbolic of how the dynamics with my mother had created an unwinnable inner struggle: to think well enough of myself to feed myself consistently felt very foreign, uncomfortable, and vaguely disloyal. I felt like a little girl, unable to betray my mother, who in my mind had taught me that my needs were always to be secondary. Simultaneously, another part of me was resisting in a kind of protest, not wanting to feed myself the way I believed my mother fed herself, to mask her own pain, and the way I felt she had fed me, seemingly using food as a weapon of codependency, guilt, and shame. For me, eating my mother's food had, on some level, always symbolized a loss of self.

In therapy, Nicole's unconditional positive regard toward me functioned like a reliably safe "external womb" that I would over time begin to internalize. My therapy at this time entered a strange new world of learning how to be a separate self. My sessions ex-plored many aspects of this, including cognitive behavioral work to learn to organize my days so I was less overwhelmed, changing my negative self-appraisals, and navigating stronger boundaries in romantic relationships and friendships.

One of my assignments from therapy involved going to the store, washing and cutting vegetables, and making salads for myself after my day shifts at the restaurant. Salads were the healthiest and easiest thing I could think to make. I can recall how delicious those salads were, with Green Goddess dressing, and how I felt a completeness and joy in discovering how eating could be a form of self-definition and self-ownership, not subordination.

Often during this period, my mother would stop by my apartment unannounced with bags of food that I had not asked her to buy. If I stopped by my parents' house, she would give me bags of food, often frozen or processed food that I would never buy myself. Whenever she did this, I'd go into a slump for days afterward. I didn't want the food to go to waste, but many times I left the bags in the back seat of my car for up to a week, finding myself paralyzed, unable to do anything with them. While I felt strong enough to rebel against my mother by not eating the food, I didn't feel strong enough to actually set a verbal boundary with her. Deep down I felt that to accept or consume that food symbolized being dominated and infantilized by her. Under a veneer of warm generosity, what I felt instead was a cold, transactional assertion of "I still own you."

The codependency and role reversal I experienced with my mother proved a template for other disastrous relationships. I had a deep hunger for connection, an "urge to merge" that was laced with my own unmet childhood longings to be truly seen, cherished, celebrated, and honored. With low self-esteem, I was unaware of my own value or worth. I had learned that my true self hurt others and to hide it was a way to ensure my bond with them. It never occurred to me that I could be a fully separate, independent person with differing needs and opinions from someone and still be seen as desirable or lovable by them.

Not surprisingly, my romantic relationships most reflected the deeper roots of this conditioning. I went for men who were exciting or artistic in some way but were also experiencing some degree of turmoil or stagnation in their lives. These men were incapable of meeting me halfway emotionally. The dynamics here mirrored my relationship with my mother, mostly one-way, with me providing the support, cheerleading, overfunctioning, and mentoring to them, while they were well-meaning but incapable of reciprocating. I felt used and unseen, just like in my childhood. I unconsciously picked men who mirrored back to me what I'd learned to see as normal.

What Is the Mother Gap?

The mother gap is the gap between what you needed from your mother and what you received from her. This gap can cause pain and diminish your ability to love yourself (causing low self-esteem), to trust that you are safe and that life is good (causing anxiety), and to be truly fulfilled (causing depression). If we haven't addressed our mother gap, we may be unconsciously projecting our need for mothering onto other people, things, situations, and events, which can create problems within our relationships, our jobs, and our very self-concepts.

What Does a Child Actually Need from Her Mother?

For many of us who have a big mother gap, it can be hard to know what we missed. The list that follows is a powerful resource for what a child needs from her mother to develop optimally. This list, paraphrased from Jasmin Lee Cori's book *The Emotionally Absent Mother*, can help you get clarity on what a child's developmental needs are and what areas you may have missed. It's not necessary that all these needs are met all the time, but enough of the time for the child to develop optimally. Again, this is not to blame mothers or hold them to unrealistic standards, but to take responsibility for how we are suffering as adults due to the mother gap and, as part of healing the Mother Wound, are taking steps to fill that gap from within ourselves.

The Ten Faces of Mother

Mother as source: She provides a sense of coming from goodness and love. Being like mother and coming from mother feel safe and positive. Allows the child to feel a sense of belonging and part of something larger, more powerful than herself.

Mother as place of attachment: Mother is consistently responsive to child's needs. Child feels securely held and safe. Confers a sense of belonging and identity to the child.

Mother as first responder: Mother is present to the child and available when needs or emergencies arise. She responds with love, empathy, and care.

Mother as modulator: Mother helps the child learn how to modulate her own emotions by first empathizing with the child's feelings and then gently leading the child into more comfortable territory. Mother may do this by helping the child to name emotions, providing mirroring, holding, empathic listening, or calm reassurance. It's important that mother's emotions are not extreme and dysregulated. Mother may also adjust the environment as needed to ensure the child's safety, health, and well-being.

Mother as nurturer: Mother is affectionate with the child. Soothes, reassures, and calms the child. Is accepting and understanding.

Mother as mirror: Mother reflects the child's emotional state back to the child, providing the child with a sense that she exists, is real, and is valued. Positive mirroring builds self-respect in the child.

Mother as cheerleader: Mother enthusiastically celebrates the child's progress and achievements. Mother allows the child to express herself as a separate person and celebrates her unique expression of herself. Encourages the child to reach for her best and reassures her that she is capable of doing what she desires. Confers a sense of deservingness and self-worth.

Mother as mentor: Mother is supportive of the child while she is learning and trying new things. Gives encouragement and feedback and honors the child's limitations in a way that feels comforting. Mother is patiently attuned to the learning level of the child and provides support according to the child's understanding.

Mother as protector: Mother provides support in a way that communicates "I'll keep you safe," and models boundaries and self-protection to the child.

Mother as home base: The sense that mother is a stable place you can always come home to for encouragement, support, and comfort.

An unaddressed mother gap is like a smoke screen between ourselves and our adult lives. Through addressing the mother gap directly, this smoke dissolves so that we can see life clearly, without the defenses, fears, and anxieties that previously kept us stuck. The goals of addressing the mother gap are to address the needs and burdens of your childhood directly so that you don't have to project them outwardly (and suffer needlessly as a result). If we don't address the mother gap, we re-create it in different forms. The process of unveiling it helps us to pull back the projections of childhood so that we can see life as it is, loving ourselves and others from an authentic and undefended place.

Patriarchy and Our Collective Legacy of Emotional Abuse and Neglect

It's important to pause and look at how the mother gap came to be. Parenting strategies of old were focused on discipline and obedience. In the past, physical beatings were considered normal and were condoned both at home and at school. Food, shelter, clothing, and education were commonly seen as the key aspects of supporting a child's development; the child's emotional needs and development were barely even considered. Letting a child cry herself to sleep was recommended. Common phrases spoken in homes included "Don't cry or I'll give you something to cry about." The emotional lives of children were seen as frivolous and not to be indulged with much sympathy or attention, lest the child become spoiled or learn to manipulate the parent. A child's emotional security was not considered important, nor was respect for the child's individuality. Thus, children in these generations were punished, withdrawn from, humiliated, or beaten in response to the natural expression of their emotions. This approach to parenting caused many children to become emotionally shut down from an early age, stunting their emotional development as adults, and setting them up for difficult or impossible communication with their own adult children later in life.

If our mothers were raised with this patriarchal parenting style (focused on obedience and neglect of emotions), this legacy was present to some degree as we were raised, leading to a fundamental disconnect with our mothers and consequently within ourselves. Taking this cultural and intergenerational perspective, it's easy to see how mothers' capacity to offer their children the necessary emotional availability was greatly diminished because they themselves were so shamed and deprived, to some degree. Much of this is unconscious and unintentional. However, for a mother operating in this paradigm, her emotional needs will always trump the child's, and an unconscious focus on self-preservation may prevent the mutuality needed for healthy adult-to-adult relationships.

Lindsay C. Gibson, in her book *Adult Children of Emotionally Immature Parents*, explains that because emotionally immature parents had to shut down their own feelings so early in life, they weren't allowed to explore their own emotions enough to develop a strong sense of self and individual identity, which limits their capacity for self-awareness, clear communication, and emotional intimacy.

Gibson identifies a number of common personality traits demonstrated by these parents:

- Rigid and single-minded.
- Low stress tolerance.
- Impulsive decision-making.
- Subjective-oriented rather than objective.
- Little respect for differences.
- Egocentric tendencies.
- Self-preoccupied and self-involved.
- Prefer to be center of attention.
- Promote role reversal.
- Low-empathy and emotionally insensitive.
- Often inconsistent and contradictory.
- Strong defenses that take the place of the self.
- Fear of feelings.
- Focus on the physical instead of the emotional.
- Can be killjoys.
- Intense but shallow emotions.

- Don't experience mixed emotions (sees black or white).
- Difficulties with conceptual thinking.
- Proneness to literal thinking.
- Intellectualizing obsessively.

In response to the mother gap, the mask of a "false self," a term coined by psychotherapist D. W. Winnicott, is formed. The false self is originally developed in childhood as a way to compensate for some level of rejection you may have experienced for being your real self. It's an unconscious attempt to change oneself to be acceptable to the external world. The problem is that as adults, when we confuse our false self for our real self, we end up receiving approval from others for our false self, while deep inside, we want to be loved for who we really are, for our authentic self. Wearing a mask to cover up our vulnerability and shame leads to feelings of being a fraud, emptiness, and depression. As we grow into adults, tension between the real self and the false self increases. Accessing our real self becomes a process of dismantling the limiting beliefs and patterns we internalized from our culture and our families.

Three Parts to Addressing the Mother Gap

There are three main aspects to addressing the mother gap: mental clarity, emotional processing, and bodily integration. All three support one another, happen incrementally, and don't necessarily occur in linear order.

1. Mental Clarity

When we get mental clarity on interactions with our mothers that cause us to feel stressed, angry, or anxious, we become equipped to process those emotions rather than be ruled by them. Mental clarity means articulating the patterns and dynamics between you and your mother.

- What did you need from your mother that you didn't get?
- How did you cope with not receiving her love in the ways you needed it?
- How has it affected your life?
- In what ways have you compensated? What coping mechanisms and strategies have you used to fill this gap in motherly love—both as a child and as an adult?

As we clarify the dynamics and beliefs we inherited from our mothers, either covertly or overtly, we can more easily recognize them in our adult lives. Rather than unconsciously following them or becoming triggered by them, we can interrupt them in the moment and be more adaptable in everyday situations. This knowledge empowers us to disrupt old patterns more easily as they repeat, and make conscious, empowered choices instead.

2. Emotional Processing: Contacting the Original Pain We Could Not Feel as Children

This is about allowing the full range of our emotions, including rage and grief, to come forward and be expressed in a safe way. We avoid uncomfortable, negative feelings because of how vulnerable they made us feel as children and because we may have been shamed for them as well. This avoidance usually creates more suffering than the actual emotions themselves. When emotions are felt in a genuine way, they transform. This discomfort is temporary, and the relief we feel after embracing our emotions is lasting. With practice and support, we can learn on a visceral level that our emotions are important allies in our lives, not intruders we need to defend against.

Author John Bradshaw calls this emotional processing "original pain work." Original pain work involves actually experiencing the original repressed emotions that felt unsafe to feel when we were children. He says it's the only thing that will bring true, lasting change—the kind of change that resolves feelings. If we don't process the original pain we felt as children in its true context of our childhood, the pain usually leaks out in problematic ways through emotional triggers or flashbacks. For example, if a situation resembles a painful experience we had as a child but haven't fully processed, intense emotions, out of proportion to the current matter, can arise. This can cause us to either lash out in anger or feel sadness, anxiety, or any other past emotion that still needs to be processed. In this way, emotional triggers are immense opportunities for healing the past in our everyday lives. As we learn to soothe and tend to the distressed inner child in these moments, we can increasingly make new choices that open up new futures.

3. Bodily Integration

Even if our minds wander, our bodies are always in the present moment, and they always tell the truth. Connecting with and being present in our bodies is an important form of mothering ourselves. As we get more mental clarity and process our emotions, our insights integrate deeply on a physical level. Conceptual truths become living realities as we heal and transform.

Roles, Fantasies, and Masks: How We Compensate for the Mother Gap

All of us have been shaped by the degree to which our parents were emotionally available to us. Getting insight into how this affects us on a daily basis requires looking at our mother gap and seeing how we adapted to fill that gap to survive our childhood environments. A key place to look is at your repeating behaviors or dynamics you've always had. We can mistake these for "who we are," but they may have their roots in survival mechanisms that once helped us cope with some degree of emotional abuse or neglect. The good news is that these coping mechanisms can be transformed.

Family Roles

In addition to the "good girl" role, there are many other roles that one can play in a family. The strong older sister, the family clown, the quiet one, the rebel, the brainy one, the free spirit, the queen bee, the shy one, the baby, the life of the party, the loner, the rock of the family, etc. Many of these roles can function as cloaks around our pain. They give us predictability, stability, and an identity within the family; they can also prove confining in our adulthood, and our potential can wither inside these old constrictions.

While I played the role of the good girl there are many other possible roles we may have played, based on how family dynamics shaped our behavior as children. Many women go the other way and rebel from their mothers right from the beginning; rather than absorb or merge with their mothers' beliefs and choices, some daughters push back and rebel from mother as a form of self-protection and maintaining a separate self. However, whether we played the role of rebel girls or good girls, or something else entirely, the point is that those roles have deep hurting and pain underneath, and are masking that pain in different ways.

Different children in a family can have very different experiences of their parents, though they may live in the same home. For a variety of reasons, mothers may relate to children differently. Siblings may feel emotionally close as they lived the same experiences, and yet because their roles may be different in the family system, there may be tension about how their perceptions differ or contrast with one another. Whatever the behavioral patterns may be, the ones that feel most compulsive, defensive, and emotionally charged are often the behavioral patterns that were created in response to childhood pain as a way to cope. They stay in place as a way to protect ourselves from further harm, even long after that harm is no longer present in our environment.

Cover Stories: "Everything Is OK"

In addition to the false self, we may have told ourselves a story that is some version of "everything is OK" when it wasn't. We did this to defend against the painful emotions of our situation. This is a form of minimizing or downplaying the severity of our mother gap, and a normal part of human survival. Part of healing involves taking in the truth of how unbearable it really was. "It really was that bad" is part of coming to consciousness about our pain and living more reality-based lives. It's the beginning of cracking our denial, welcoming our grief, having compassion for the child we were, and stepping into a clearer vision of the world. Getting support with processing this is important.

Below are some examples of the mother gap. These are in the words of students in my course. These are used with permission and the names have been changed.

An Example of the Mother Gap: Karen

"I am fifty-three, and during my whole life I was just angry and look-ing down on my mother because she never gave me the support and emotional care I needed. Her main focus was on looking good to oth-ers. Recently I realized that many of my own qualities that I like actually come from her: creativity, generous, social, caring (not for me, though), curious, likes travel, books, culture, etc., etc. My mother was never able to support me in all my ambitions and plans because I can see she was jealous and afraid of losing control (I am a trophy child who had to earn esteem for my mother in my father's family). What I always wanted from her was being adventurers, ambitious, courageous, empowered women together (even as a young child I felt this ambitious energy for growth and empowerment so strongly). But I was completely let down by her and often ridiculed. So I am grieving that we will never be the companions I wanted us to be. I can also see that her wound is so much bigger than mine and I am angry that she never addressed it for herself. Feeling and releasing all those emotions of the mother gap has been so powerful. Before starting this work, they had been sabotaging me in every way and in all my business plans and projects; I'd hold back and feel resentful, paralyzed to begin. But now, just this week, I got a business proposal from a company to run monthly retreats for women. The business model is great and the content is everything I ever dreamed of and have been preparing for the past few years. I don't believe this is a coincidence, and I am so excited and grateful I can almost cry. I don't see my mother often, but I make a point, every time we mail or we have a lunch (maybe three times a year), to tell her about my plans, my projects, as a kind of exercise for myself to show her who I really am and the woman I've become. To be able to do that feels wonderful after a full life spent hiding myself and lying to her and just pretending I had a nine-to-five life (which I did not)."

An Example of the Mother Gap: Jennifer

"I have just come in from watching a live theater show of very lively music from the '60s through to the '80s. At the finale, the audience was encouraged to stand up, dance, and join in with the singing. My husband is in pain with a bad hip and didn't stand up and for a while neither did I, when all around me were joyous. I just felt sad—then I saw the Mother Wound so clearly, making myself small from a misplaced sense of loyalty to another's pain. Loyalty to my mother's pain was how I compensated for the way she ignored my pain and saw my needs as selfish. So, I stood up, joined in the singing, but not wholeheartedly, still felt a bit sad. Then I noticed a bit of my energy field was attached to my husband and it was restraining me, keeping me tethered to his suffering exactly as my mum used to do. Any other behavior would have been labeled 'selfish' by her. I somehow let go of the tether, strengthened my sense of boundary. I felt a lot of joy and was able to join in wholeheartedly with the dancing and singing. I suddenly realized I had a right to feel my own feelings and live by them, not someone else's. The threat of being called selfish has hung over me all my life. I suddenly saw how false and manipulative that was, rather than feeling resentment. This felt like a glimpse of freedom, as I've been processing the loneliness and shame I felt as the little girl I was who didn't get validation for my own separate feelings and needs. Now, instead of seeing them as shameful as I used to, I'm feeling safety in being separate and myself. It feels amazing each time I take an action step like this."

An Example of the Mother Gap: Alix

"I was going through a custody battle with my ex-husband. My mother comes from a traditional family who believes that you should stay married no matter what. The divorce process was very contentious and my mother never asked me how I was doing. It was like she ignored it entirely, until one day she called and asked me to tell her everything. I was relieved at first to see her expressing interest in what I was going through, but when I got off the phone, I realized I felt worse. Days later, I realized I felt worse after the call with her because there was no empathy, care, or compassion for the emotional pain that I was going through. She just wanted the facts and then got off the phone without saying much. I realized this is a continuation of what I went through with her as a child. She was constantly trying to talk me out of my feelings as a way to keep 'peace' in the household. The appearance of no conflict was necessary for her, and it guided all her interactions in our household. My dad was constantly stressed about money, and the only control she seemed to have was to keep us silent, obedient, and looking good to others so as not to make it worse. I believe this is part of why I chose partners who seemed to always keep me a little off balance. At first they would shower me with love and affection, but then there was always a 'turn' and they would minimize, downplay, and mock my emotions, and I would question myself, feel less-than, and put their opinion of me before my own. I can finally see how I was set up for this by learning from an early age that my feelings don't matter. This clarity has given me the energy to disrupt this pattern when I see it in myself. It's amazing to see that the more empathy and space I create for my own emotions, the more I can do that for my two daughters as well."

Support Is Essential

As you explore the mother gap, be patient and compassionate with yourself. It's natural to feel emotional pain as we address the mother gap and look beneath the roles, masks, or stories that we've used to avoid it. Feelings like anger and sadness are to be expected as you examine the patterns, events, situations, and emotions of your early childhood.

Support is an essential part of original pain work. There are many ways to get support. It's ideal to get support from several different sources. Sources of support may include:

- Individual long-term therapy.
- Group therapy.
- Art therapy.
- Support groups.
- Workshops.
- Loving relationships.
- Bodywork, massage, energy work.
- Regular time for solitude and reflection.
- Exercise, stretching, and moving the body.
- Getting enough rest and sleep.

Questions for Reflection

1. What is your mother gap (the gap between what you needed and what you received from your mother)?

2. How have you sought to fill the mother gap up to this point? What were the masks you wore or roles you unconsciously played to compensate for the gap?

3. What actions can you take now to fill the mother gap from within yourself?

Chapter 6

SIGNS YOU NEED TO MAKE A CHANGE

AS TIME WENT BY, *increasing grief and frustration had surfaced in therapy as I began to see more clearly the dysfunction of my family. Even though I saw how dynamics with my mother had shown up in different parts of my life, I didn't feel ready to look directly at my relationship with her. It felt like a dark path I didn't want to walk, even though I knew eventually I'd have to. More symptoms had begun to accrue. I wanted to differentiate myself from her, and at the time, that took the form of my being hyper-vigilant about exercise, health, and body image.*

Connecting with my friends and dancing on a regular basis kept me feeling positive and inspired. My main focus had been drawn into spirituality and meditation. I often attended workshops at a small retreat center in a nearby town. I was longing for a sense of purpose and wondering how I could help the world. I wanted to be able to look to my mother for inspiration and support on think-ing big and doing something meaningful with my life, but she was quiet and distant. Around this time, I met a woman named Mi-randa, a psychic, teacher, and healer who taught workshops, and she took an interest in me. I was always the youngest person in her class, and I played the role of good girl and perfect student. I had a session with her in which I confessed I felt the need to devote myself to something bigger for the world, but I didn't know what.

Not long after, Miranda offered to let me be her apprentice and invited me to help her open a retreat center halfway across the country. I accepted—despite many red flags and my therapist's grave reservations. The retreat center was not spiritual or evolved as I had assumed; I came to realize it was a toxic environment and that I was there to be used as a free cleaning lady and administrative assistant. Even knowing this, it took me six months to overcome the misguided notion that things would get better and leave.

I wasn't able to see at the time that my attachment to this instructor was me craving mothering and approval: a loving, empowered mother figure who could value me for the individual I was. My relationship with Miranda was actually a replication of the dynamics and trauma I had experienced with my mother. Realizing this left me disillusioned but ultimately helped me to idealize authority figures much less than I previously had.

When I returned, I threw myself into graduate school. My good girl and overachiever self were in full force. I got an A in every class. I was a teaching assistant in the department, and then became fixated on getting accepted into a doctoral program (which I later decided not to do). I realized much later that I had believed that if I was successful enough to impress my family, they would finally be able to see me, and I would feel worthy and in control of my life. I didn't know yet that nothing in the actual outer world could ever fill this void, that it needed to come from within me.

Around this time, I started a new relationship with a man named David, an acquaintance I had worked with for six years at the restaurant, and within a year, we moved to New York City. Moving was crucial for getting distance from my family and more insight into my childhood and its impact on my current life. Because my bond with David was stronger than any relationship

I had previously had, my Mother Wound started emerging in powerful ways. I started having dreams of "triangulation," of David choosing another woman over me; some included my mother, with her separating David from me or turning him against me.

One night, we were at a club in the East Village and a female friend of ours started flirting openly with David right in front of me, and he didn't set a boundary with her or say anything to stop it. I totally lost it as we walked home and started screaming at him at the top of my lungs; I was furious that he had said nothing, as though I wasn't even there. David had no idea how his lack of boundaries with our friend had triggered intense feelings of abandonment in me. I hadn't yet connected it to my mother. That night, we talked it out, and I told him, "I just want to be THE most important person to you." It was really hard to get the words out. It felt like life or death. He looked at me and said, "You ARE the most important person to me." Something clicked inside, and I was able to take it in. I felt incredible relief, and also a bone-deep grief. Later that night after David fell asleep, I got up and looked at myself intensely in the bathroom mirror, searching my face in the dim light, wondering what was going on with me. What was this intense feeling of devastation really about?

What Are the Signs of the Mother Wound? Why Are They Hard to See? And Why, Once We See Them, Do We Resist Them?

Because the Mother Wound underpins every area of our lives to some degree, recognizing the signs in one area can lead to breakthroughs and awareness in many other areas. Generations of women have long misattributed the signs of the Mother Wound to sources that seemed less threatening, never truly getting to the root of their suffering. The problem is that when we don't get to the root, our issues keep replicating themselves over and over, following us into new jobs, new relationships, and more.

Common Themes to Recognize

These are symptoms that, on the surface, may seem unrelated to your mother. You can have these experiences and still feel like you have a harmonious relationship with your mother.

- Avoidance of difficult emotions. The need to stay positive at all times.
- Numbing out (through substances, social media, shopping, etc.).
- Intense emotions out of proportion with the current situation.
- Repeating patterns that don't ever feel like they get resolved.
- Feeling suddenly like a little girl, powerless, or ridden with panic.
- Large contrast between the outer life you portray and the reality of your inner life.
- Extremes of any kind; for example, cycles of bingeing and deprivation (whether on food, exercise, substances, diets, sex, etc.).
- Fears of abandonment (in friendships, romantic relationships, as a parent).
- Fears of invasion (the need to keep people at a distance).
- Having a hard time with endings, fear of saying goodbye.
- Fears of being destabilized by emotions if you allow yourself to feel them.
- Self-sabotage when you get close to a breakthrough.
- Repeating mental loops of negative self-talk.
- Feeling selfish for putting yourself first.

- Never feeling good enough.
- Constantly comparing yourself to others.
- People-pleasing.
- Approval-seeking; any kind of rejection feels crushing and destabilizing.
- Addictions (shopping, substances, internet, etc.).
- Depression (feeling low, hopeless, empty).
- Anxiety.
- Eating disorders (some level of conflict surrounding food, body, and image).
- Shame about your sexuality.
- Equating being a "good person" with putting yourself last.
- People constantly pushing your boundaries or disrespecting your time.
- Continually attracting the same type of partner, friend, who ends up mistreating you.
- Feeling like you're being a good person based on your choice to endure poor treatment from other people.
- Some level of obsession or fixation: "THIS is the thing that's going to make everything OK!"
- Playing the role of the "female peacekeeper," one who mediates and prevents conflicts, for whom the absence of conflict is paramount.
- Analysis paralysis when you need to take action.

Symptoms that may be more clearly related to your mother include:

- Fear of surpassing your mother: This is a common fear that if you go beyond what your mother has done with her life (what I call the "Maternal Horizon"), then your relationship will somehow be irrevocably damaged. It seems safer to minimize your ambitions out of loyalty and to preserve the harmony of the relationship.

- Feeling low after visits with your mother: This is a sign that toxic dynamics are playing out that you're not yet conscious of.
- Feeling the need to please your mother, but it never feels good enough: Your mother feels unpleasable but there's a sense that in the future, you'll eventually "get it right." Hope springs eternal.
- Self-attenuating around your mother: Staying small to not offend, threaten, or upset her. This can manifest as not expressing your own opinions around her and just agreeing with her to avoid conflict.
- Feeling anger toward your mother but not doing anything about it.
- Moving far away from your mother as a means to cope.
- Feeling like "it will be easier after she's dead" or "I can do what I want once she's passed away."
- Putting excessive emotional labor into the relationship: You feel exhausted by your mother's needs but also feel it would be a betrayal to speak up about your own limits and boundaries.
- A sense that being honest about your own feelings would end the relationship.
- Fear of feeling like an "ungrateful daughter" if you acknowledge painful feelings toward your mother.
- Your mother seems helpless and constantly in need of support.
- Avoidance of your mother.
- Your mother doesn't reach out to you unless she needs something.
- Your mother gossips or has an excessive focus on people she doesn't know very well.
- Feeling responsible for your mother's well-being. If she's struggling financially or in relationships, it feels like your problem to solve.
- Your mother tells you that you're her best friend, favorite child, or the one she loves best, *or* the opposite: you're never good enough.
- Criticism, mocking, or sarcasm is common from your mother.
- Your feelings or experiences are minimized, devalued, or laughed at.

- The expression of your feelings or needs or opinions is met with cold hostility, withdrawal, bitterness, or jealousy.
- You have a sense your mother is jealous of you.
- You have a sense that there will be some kind of "payback" if you stray outside your role as the "dutiful daughter."
- You have a sense that your mother is role focused, meaning her role as your mother is a weapon she can wield over you if you don't act or speak as she wants.
- Your mother communicates through "emotional contagion": she keeps people guessing and walking on eggshells around her instead of communicating respectfully and directly.
- Your mother is unpredictable: you don't know from one day to the next how her mood will be, and this puts you constantly on edge.
- You find yourself "romanticizing" your mother's bad behavior as "That's just the way she is."

Mother Wound Mechanics

These are common experiences and patterns that come up, but their content may vary widely. You may not know why they're happening at all.

- **Triggers or Emotional Flashbacks:** Situations with others can cause strong emotional reactions with an intensity that is out of proportion to the situation.
- **Negative Mental Narrative:** A strong inner critic that is an internalization of your mother's voice.
- **Exhaustion and Depletion:** Not just physical exhaustion, but a deep emotional exhaustion.

- **The Three F's: Fight, Flight, or Freeze:** These are responses that have a strong physiological component, such as heart beating fast, sweaty palms.
- **Sense of Overwhelm:** Everything feels "too much" and there's not enough time or space to rest and recover from the "hustle" of life.
- **Sense of Burden:** Feeling like it's all up to you and you're the only one who can get it all done, which keeps your life feeling narrow and limited.
- **Sense of Bondage:** Feeling trapped by your circumstances and/or relationships and that nothing can get you out of it.
- **"Striving to Survive":** A sense that mental hypervigilance is necessary to be safe and in control of your life. A feeling that if you truly relax, something bad could happen.

There's a strong connection between self-sabotage and the Mother Wound.

Self-sabotage is when we have a goal or desire, but we unconsciously create obstacles that directly prevent the achievement of that goal or fulfillment of that desire.

The pattern of self-sabotage may *not* seem connected to dynamics with your mother at all.

Much self-sabotage comes down to safety, comfort, and what feels familiar. If we were at all withdrawn from, punished, or made to feel bad about our individuality or our own needs and desires, as adults, we will halt our progress to prevent those same outcomes from recurring. Much of this happens outside our conscious awareness, emanating from unresolved fears of the inner child, that split-off aspect of our consciousness for whom the threat of emotional abandonment is very real and to be prevented at all costs.

For some women, being big, visible, and powerful may unconsciously feel like a *betrayal of their mothers*, and to relieve this unconscious guilt, they self-sabotage.

The connection between the Mother Wound and self-sabotage is rather complex. This pattern starts very early in our development, and that's why it can be so insidious. To ensure their survival, children are biologically hardwired to seek their mother's approval at all costs.

As adult women, this pattern may still be unconsciously operating. We may still feel like our happiness rests on the happiness of our mothers. You may observe your mother's unhappiness and begin to feel guilty for your own success. This is particularly common in women who were parentified daughters as children (the daughter being used as a surrogate parent to the unhealed child within their mother).

Self-sabotage may have served as a survival mechanism to prevent abandonment and rejection by our mothers. And it's reinforced by patriarchal culture.

We may unconsciously think, I can't possibly be fully happy or successful if my mother is lonely, sad, uncomfortable, bitter, jealous, etc. This is the viewpoint of the child within us, who still thinks her survival depends on the well-being of her mother.

Learning about the signs, symptoms, and dynamics of the Mother Wound is the first step and a key part of creating and cultivating the inner safety necessary to heal and transform ourselves.

Our growing awareness and emerging clarity on these dynamics within ourselves and in our relationships liberate us to be less caught and stuck in them. Becoming conscious of things that were previously unconscious is a profound part of claiming our personal power.

Questions for Reflection

1. When you were a little girl, what were the specific situations in which your mother responded to you with praise, recognition, rewards, validation, and love?

2. What were the specific situations in which you were met with some degree of rejection, aggressive hostility, cold withdrawal, animosity, jealousy, or bitterness?

3. What is a big challenge that you're having right now in your life that has been a challenge for a long time? How does this relate to dynamics in your early childhood? What painful emotion is coming up for you now that you also felt as a child?

Chapter 7

THE RUPTURE OF THE MOTHER LINE AND THE COST OF BECOMING REAL

DURING MY FIRST YEAR *living in New York City, I started observing traits in my mother that I had never noticed before. Thanks to the physical distance from her and my deepening intimacy with David, I slowly began to see how I had idealized her for most of my life, seeing her as generous, kind, and selfless, while in actuality, many of our conversations I was able to recall consisted of her gossiping or complaining about my father and other family members. I would cringe on the other end of the line, and began to dread the calls. Our conversations were always under ten minutes long and superficial. I'd listen to whatever news or gossip she had to convey, then without fail, after I shared a sentence or two about my life, she'd end the call by saying she had to go. I felt grief as it sunk in that she had always been this way, and I just hadn't been able to see it. My consistent and deepening work in therapy (which had been going on for almost a decade at this point) had steadily been strengthening my sense of self, giving me more confidence in my own perceptions and an expanded awareness of how truly dysfunctional the dynamics in my family were.*

As is true for many survivors of childhood trauma, I had a protracted avoidance and even denial of the extent of the painful events and distressing memories of my childhood experiences. I was becoming aware of my family's dysfunction, but remained quietly tolerant of it all, being much more comfortable working on my current life issues. I wasn't ready to disrupt the positive narrative that had kept me safe as a child, even as part of me realized this disruption would be an inevitable part of my journey.

As I evolved into more of my true self in other areas of my life, I wanted to be able to have a similar level of authenticity and connection with my mother as well. There was growing contrast between our relationship, which felt painfully confining and toxic, and the new standards I was setting for myself in other areas of my life, modeled by the ways my therapist, Nicole, treated and related to me. I was learning what care for my separate personhood felt like from the inside out. Nicole demonstrated consistent respect for my separate individual perspectives and always encouraged and listened with great interest to my ideas and insights, even when they were markedly different from her own. She celebrated with keen excitement my every success, every act of self-empowerment and self-valuing, because she delighted in my well-being separate from her own.

After about nine months of waitressing in New York City, I finally got a dream job at a research office in an Ivy League medical school. I was thrilled that I would finally have health insurance and a regular paycheck. I couldn't wait to call my mother and tell her. On the phone, I was so excited, I could barely get the words out. There was a long pause on the other end, and then my mother said in a flat, unemotive tone, "Oh, that's great, good for you," and within seconds excused herself and hung up. I felt deflated, hurt, and angry that it seemed she couldn't even be happy for me for a few minutes.

I reached a breaking point about a month later. On another call, my mother asked how my new job was going. I said it was going great, and began to describe some workplace politics. In response, she said in a haughty tone, "You're just like me, so you're going to be just fine." The next morning, as I came out of the subway at Fifty-Sixth and Lexington, I felt this surge of energy and outrage flowing through me as her comment resounded in my ears: You're just like me, so you're going to be just fine.

Over the next two weeks, I developed a whole new level of clarity about the toxic nature of my relationship with my mother, and I realized I had had enough. I wanted to confront her directly and shift the dynamic to one in which we could both be connected and seen. I no longer wanted to be her "good girl," her pet, or her security blanket. I wanted a relationship that also nourished me.

I'll never forget the moment before I made that phone call. I was sitting on the bed in my tiny apartment, cell phone in hand, staring at written notes I had prepared of what I was going to say. Before I dialed home, I prayed aloud to the universe for help, because I knew that what I was about to do was akin to detonating a bomb in my family, but it was absolutely what I needed to do for my own integrity. When my mother picked up the phone, I asked if it was a good time to talk, as I wanted to speak to her about a comment she had made in our previous conversation that had been bothering me: You're just like me, so you're going to be just fine. *I told her this comment had made me angry because it represented a lifetime of me feeling unseen by her as a separate person. It symbolized a long-standing pattern in which I felt seen by her only in relation to herself, not as an individual.*

"I've felt that you steal my successes by always tracing them back to you and how I am 'like you,'" I told her. "I want to be proud of who I am because of who I am, not because I mirror who

you are. I know you don't mean to do this, and that's why I've never spoken up before. But I want you to know how painful this pattern has been for me. I want to be close to you, but things need to shift so that we can have a better relationship."

After I said all this, she was very quiet for a moment, then said, "I think you're reading too much into it. I do see you as a separate person. I'll watch what I say from now on." Then there was an awkward silence, followed by, "Well, I gotta go, it's been a long day and I'm tired."

The next morning, I received an apologetic email from her, explaining how she celebrates my individuality and was sorry for unintentionally hurting me. I was stunned. Perhaps I had assessed her incorrectly! However, after that first email, others quickly followed, more defensive and blaming in tone, shifting any responsibility from her back onto me and devising what I saw as increasingly bizarre theories as to what was truly upsetting me.

Months of intense email correspondence followed, in which she continually expressed her feelings of persecution and how much she loved me. There was no curiosity about why I felt the way I did. My presentation of my own feelings had been perceived as baseless attacks and blame. I kept affirming that I loved her and wanted a better relationship, that I wasn't trying to blame her, that I knew she didn't mean to do things she was doing. I tried to keep a balance of being empathetic with her sadness about what I was saying while remaining assertive in my right to my own perceptions and feelings. I didn't back down into guilt or silence as I would have in the past. As time wore on and I continued to stay with my own experience rather than collapse into her narrative, her sulking turned into rage. She expressed anger that no matter what she said or did, she was always wrong. She pointed to my failed relationships and other ventures that hadn't worked out in my life as evidence that I'm not perfect.

The entire period of this correspondence was an emotional roller coaster the likes of which I had never imagined. It felt like we were speaking two completely different languages. No matter how much I tried to explain my good intentions, no matter how much I couched my expression of my own feelings inside lots of empathy and nonthreatening language, it didn't seem to matter. I spent painstaking hours in therapy carefully and thoughtfully discussing the most respectful, empathetic, honest, and considerate ways of communicating, and it still made no difference. Instead, her reprisal was a fully dismissive "Goodbye, Bethany."

Her rage steadily increased. It shocked me to the core to discover there was no "mother" in her energy, no willingness to take any responsibility, no curiosity or interest in understanding my point of view, no desire for mutuality. After that initial apologetic email, she drew her guns, and it felt like she was fighting me to the death, as if her life depended on extinguishing my differing perceptions and my very separateness. She seemed outraged that I would not get back in line and be her "good girl," that I felt free enough to call her out on the ways she had failed me without prioritizing her feelings over my own, but rather advocating for myself as equal to her. She began to end her emails by saying, "I have no daughter."

Living through this felt like my body was on fire twenty-four hours a day, with steep peaks of adrenaline and low days of collapsing into paralyzing grief. Her responses were so beyond the worst I had expected, and this was deeply destabilizing. It was so unsteadying to feel that my mother was baldly attempting to get me to doubt myself, to twist my words, and to shame me for my mistakes, and to sense the smug satisfaction she seemed to get from making childish comments. The worst part was the powerlessness I felt, that no matter how I tried to tell her my intentions were good, she seemed invested in not seeing that.

Thank goodness I had Nicole and David in my life as stable, safe support while all this was going on. I went to work and to the gym and had therapy via phone once a week but otherwise spent time at home. I wanted to experience the pain of this consciously and be as present as possible with what I was feeling. One horrible day, my mother emailed me telling me something was wrong with me and that I was a stranger to her. I came home from work that day weeping. It was astonishing to feel that my mother was refusing to look at herself or take any responsibility and to pathologize me to preserve herself. The focus had irrevocably flipped to what was wrong with me.

After several months of escalating email communication in which I was consistently the target of blame, rage, and shaming and hurtful language, I stopped returning her emails. When my emails stopped, my mother tried to get to me in other ways. Under a veil of concern, she informed me that she had read through all my journals, which were still in storage in her basement. I felt so violated that I immediately drove several hours each way to retrieve the journals. She continued to contact me, despite my requesting space from her, and the longer I didn't respond, the more extreme her communications became, with her even threatening to come to my apartment if I didn't respond to her. She began to see my therapist as the cause of the rift between us and tried to convince me that I was being brainwashed by Nicole. It appeared that my mother began to see me as a helpless victim of a controlling therapist and herself as the concerned mother hellbent on rescuing her child. This unhinged assessment was in stark contrast to the fact that, at that point, my life had never been more successful, stable, or fulfilling. She began threatening to come to my workplace if I didn't respond to her emails.

Looking back, this conflict was a rupture in the mother line, due to how my growth necessitated that I make a break from the toxic dynamics of our relationship. For some, such a rupture may ultimately lead to a healthier level of connection between mother and daughter, but for deeply dysfunctional families, it may mean a permanent break. The family system may not be able to accommodate the empowered version of the daughter, with her capacity to disagree and her sense of worth to speak out, to no longer overfunction, to no longer shrink, to take up space, and to prioritize her own well-being. It was becoming apparent that it was too threatening for my mother to see that my growth was a healthy form of self-actualization based on a decade of my own inner work.

In my family, an adult child's suppression of true feelings seemed to be seen as heroic, an act of love, a form of compassion. My refusal to suppress my pain as my mother had for her own mother was interpreted as the ultimate betrayal, especially as I had a strong relationship with another woman—my therapist— who my mother increasingly saw as her nemesis. She continued, in overt and covert ways, to demonize Nicole's intentionality as one of trying to harm, control, and brainwash me. As extreme and disturbed as this view was, I believe my mother was completely unconscious about her psychological motivations and intentions.

Still, I felt the raw aggression coming at me was a response to me not following the rule of our mother line, which was "Absorb your mother's pain as your own, and someday your daughter will do the same for you." I initiated the rupture by respectfully de- claring my own truth and requesting that we work together to form a new, healthier dynamic. I could not have predicted that I was breaking an unspoken contract that governed our rela- tionship and that of my maternal lineage as a whole. My mother seemed to perceive my continued attempts to be understood as a mean-spirited effort to control her and make her feel bad. The fact that I did not back down and kept affirming my right to my own perceptions seemed to be unbearable to her and eventually ripped off the lid that kept all her own unresolved trauma at bay. I came to see that her extreme behavior came from long unresolved Mother Wound pain in my maternal line. I started looking for clues, and they started to appear all around me. The pieces began coming together as our relationship continued to unravel.

Woman is not born: she is made. In the making, her humanity is destroyed. She becomes a symbol of this, a symbol of that: mother of the earth, slut of the universe; but she never becomes herself because it is forbidden for her to do so.
—*Andrea Dworkin*

A woman becoming healthier and more empowered is often seen as a threat to equilibrium within a toxic family system. The more dysfunctional the family, the less individuality is tolerated, and the more the family will double down on getting the woman to question herself, doubt herself, and feel guilty. All manner of conflict and drama may ensue.

Many mothers may not pass along the same degree of wounding they received from their own mothers. This doesn't translate to an absence of conflict. In fact, daughters healthier than their mothers may feel more comfortable navigating conflict for the sake of growth, something that may be foreign and deeply threatening to their mothers.

One of the hardest experiences a daughter can have in a mother-daughter relationship is seeing that her mother is unconsciously invested in her smallness. For women in this predicament, it's truly painful to see that out of her own wounding, the person who gave birth to you unconsciously sees your empowerment as her own loss.

Ultimately, it's not personal but a very real tragedy of unresolved intergenerational trauma and how our patriarchal culture tells women they are less-than.

We all desire to be real, to be seen accurately, to be recognized, and to be loved for who we really are in our full authenticity. This is a human need. The process of becoming our real selves involves making peace with our capacities to be messy, intense, assertive, and complex—the very things patriarchy portrays as unattractive in women.

Historically, our culture has been hostile to the idea of women as true individuals.

The patriarchy portrays attractive women as people-pleasing, approval-seeking, emotional caretakers, conflict-avoidant, and tolerant of poor treatment. To some degree, mothers pass these messages along to their daughters unconsciously, perpetuating the creation of false selves in their daughters. However, each new generation of women is born with *the hunger to be real*. One could say that with each new generation, the patriarchy weakens and the hunger to be real increases in women; in fact, it's now beginning to take on a certain urgency.

The Longing to Be Real and the Longing for Mother

This presents a dilemma for daughters raised in a patriarchy. The longing to be your real self and the longing to be mothered become competing needs; there's a sense you have to choose between them. This is because your empowerment is limited to the degree that your own mother has internalized patriarchal beliefs and expects you to comply with them as a condition for harmony in the relationship.

The cost of becoming your real self often involves some degree of "rupture" with the maternal line.

On one end of the spectrum, for healthier mother-daughter relationships, while the rupture may cause conflict, it may eventually serve to strengthen the bond and make it more authentic. On the other end of the spectrum, for more unhealthy or abusive mother-daughter relationships, the rupture can trigger unhealed wounds in the mother, causing her to lash out or disown her daughter completely. And in some cases, unfortunately, a daughter will see no other choice than to maintain distance indefinitely to maintain her emotional well-being. Here your mother may see your separation/rupture as a threat, a direct affront to her, a personal attack, and a rejection of who *she* is. In this situation, it can be heart-wrenching to see how your desire for empowerment or personal growth can cause your mother to blindly see you as a mortal enemy. It is a devastating example of the massive cost that patriarchy exacts on mother-daughter relationships.

"I can't be happy if my mother is unhappy." Have you ever felt this?

Usually this belief comes from the pain of seeing your mother suffer from her own inner deprivation and your compassion for her struggle under the weight of patriarchal demands. However, when we sacrifice our own happiness for our mothers, we actually prevent the necessary healing that comes from grieving the wound in our maternal line. This just keeps both mother and daughter stuck. We can't heal our mothers and we can't make them see us accurately, no matter how hard we try. What brings the healing is grieving. We have to grieve for ourselves and for our mother line. This grief brings incredible freedom.

With each wave of grief, we reunite with the parts of ourselves we had to disown in order to be accepted by our families.

Unhealthy systems need to be disrupted in order to find a new, healthier, higher-level equilibrium. It's a paradox that we actually heal our mother line when we *disrupt* the patriarchal patterns in the mother line, not when we remain *complicit* with the patriarchal patterns to maintain surface-level peace. It takes grit and courage to refuse to comply with patriarchal patterns that have strong generational momentum in our families.

We are being called to become true individuals, by decoupling our worth from compliance with patriarchal norms.

Traditionally, women have been taught that it is noble to carry other people's pain, that emotional caretaking is our duty and that we should feel guilty if we deviate from this function. In this context, guilt is not about conscience but about *control*. This guilt keeps us enmeshed with our mothers, depleting ourselves, and ignorant of our power. We must see that there's *no true cause* for guilt. This role of emotional caretaker was never a true role for us; it is simply part of our legacy of oppression. Seen in this way, we can cease allowing guilt to control us.

Refraining from emotional caretaking and letting people have their lessons is a form of respect for self and other.

Our overfunctioning contributes to the imbalance in our society and actively disempowers others by keeping them from their own transformation. We must stop carrying the load for other people. We do this by seeing the sheer futility of it. We must refuse to be the emotional custodian and dumping ground for those who neglect to do the work necessary for their own transformation.

Contrary to what we've been taught, we don't have to heal our entire families. We only have to heal ourselves.

Instead of feeling guilty for not being able to heal your mother and your family members, give yourself permission to be innocent. By doing so, you are taking back your personhood and your power from the Mother Wound. And consequently, you are handing back to your family members their own power to live their own journeys. This is a major energetic shift that comes from owning your worth and is demonstrated by the ways that you remain in your power despite calls to give it away to others.

The cost of becoming real is never as high as the cost of remaining your false self.

It's possible that we may experience backlash from our mothers (and our families) when we become more real. We may experience hostility, withdrawal, sulking, or outright denigration. Shock waves may be felt through the entire family system. And it can be staggering to see how quickly we can be rejected or dropped when we stop overfunctioning and embody our real selves. However, this truth must be seen, and the pain endured, if we are to become truly real. This is why support is essential.

In his article "Healing Your Mother (or Father) Wound," Phillip Moffitt describes the four functions of a mother: nurturer, protector, empowerer, and initiator. Moffitt says the mother's role as initiator "is the most selfless of all the aspects, for she is encouraging a separation that leaves her without." This function is profound even for a mother who has been fully supported and honored in her own life, but almost impossible for mothers who have known great pain and have not sufficiently healed their own wounds.

A patriarchy greatly limits a mother's ability to initiate her daughter into her own personhood, because in a patriarchy, a mother has been deprived of *her own personhood*. This sets up her daughter for self-sabotage, her son for misogyny, and a disrespect for the mother "ground" out of which we all come: the earth itself.

It is precisely this function of mother as "provider of initiation" that launches a daughter into her own unique life, but this role is possible only to the degree that the mother has experienced or found her own initiation. The healthy separation process between mothers and daughters is greatly thwarted in a patriarchal culture.

The problem is that many women live their entire lives waiting for their mothers to initiate them into their own separate lives, when their mothers are simply incapable of performing this function.

It's very common to see the postponement of the grief of the Mother Wound, with women constantly going back to the "dry well" of their mothers, seeking permission and love that their mothers simply don't have the capacity to provide. Instead of grieving this fully, women tend to blame themselves, which keeps them small. We must mourn how our mothers cannot give us the initiation they never received themselves, and consciously embark on our own initiation.

The rupture is actually a sign of an evolutionary impulse to separate from the patriarchal threads of our mother line, to break the unconscious enmeshment with our mothers, fostered by the patriarchy, and become initiated into our own lives.

It's important to see that we are not rejecting our mothers when we reject their patriarchal programming. What we are actually doing is claiming our life force from impersonal, limiting patterns that have kept women hostage for centuries.

Make a Safe Space for the Longing for Mother.

Even though we are adult women, we still long for mother. What can be truly heartbreaking is to feel this longing for mother and know that your own mother cannot fill this longing, even though she has tried her best. It's important to face this fact and grieve. Your longing is holy and must be honored. Allowing space for this grief is an important part of being the good mother to yourself. If we don't mourn our unmet need for mothering directly, it will unconsciously seep into our relationships, causing pain and conflict.

The process of healing the Mother Wound is about finding your own initiation into the power and purpose of your own life.

Of the role "mother as initiator," Moffitt says, "This initiating power is associated with the shaman, the goddess, the magus, and the medicine woman." As more and more women heal the Mother Wound and consequently step firmly into their own power, we finally find the initiation we've been seeking. We become capable of initiating not only our daughters, but also our culture as a whole, which is undergoing a massive transformation. We are being called to find, deep within ourselves, that which we haven't been given. As we claim our own initiation by way of healing the Mother Wound, together as one, we increasingly embody the goddess giving birth to a new world.

At this time in history, women are increasingly feeling the call to step forward to tell the truth and disrupt dysfunctional patterns wherever we see them. This "disruptive truth-telling" is part of our power. The more skilled we are at initiating and navigating difficult conversations, the more we can make profound change in the world wherever we find ourselves. We are surrounded by crumbling systems and ways of being that do not honor life. We have the power to disrupt business as usual, whether in our families, jobs, communities, or nations. The phrase "disruptive truth-telling" does not mean creating chaos or conflict for the sake of it. Rather, it means disrupting dysfunction in order to bring the course of things to a *higher level.*

As little girls, many of us were taught to distrust our observations and intuition. Growing up in our families, telling the truth may have led to punishment, humiliation, withdrawal, or physical violence. Telling the truth may trigger a visceral fear of stepping up and using our voices as a force for change. Our painful histories may have conditioned us to avoid conflict and try to create "peace" at all costs, as a way to keep that fear at bay. It is through addressing those childhood fears that we can dissolve the paralysis we may feel in the face of so many current challenges. I believe that the women who become skilled at initiating difficult conversations will be the most effective and transformative leaders of our time.

Becoming skilled at disruptive truth-telling requires that we practice detachment in two main areas:
1. **Detach from a need for "peace" at all costs.** The more conflict-avoidant we are, the less real we are, and the less authentic we allow others to be. There's a direct connection between our ability

to navigate conflict and our ability to be true. One of the reasons for this is that many of us experienced turbulent, conflict-ridden homes as children and, as a way to stay safe, made a vow to never create or contribute to conflict. That vow may have kept us safe as children, but left unexamined, it can become a barrier to our full power as adult women. Being willing to tolerate the ambiguity inherent in moving things to a higher order requires that we have a deeper source of stability within ourselves that we can find comfort in when the outside world is in flux.

2. **Detach from the need to be liked, understood, and approved of.** It's natural to enjoy being liked and understood. But to "need" it in order to feel OK is a form of giving our power away. As little girls we needed to feel approved of by our mothers and fathers in order to survive childhood emotionally intact. Everything was based on that bond. If that bond was compromised when we were children, as adults we may conflate being liked with being safe, placing our source of emotional safety outside ourselves as we did when we were children. Healing involves cultivating the primary source of our approval within ourselves. This inner source allows us to take risks in being real, telling the truth, and feeling the unsurpassed joy of taking actions in alignment with our truth. There is a delicious kind of freedom in having the capacity to validate your own reality when others around you cannot.

Developing the inner strength to detach from those two "sources of silence" requires that we cultivate a strong relationship with the little girl inside us and address her fears. Your inner child may still believe that truth-telling will lead to some kind of mortal loss, so you may find yourself avoiding her. Often it is the inner child that sabotages our efforts and keeps us silent as a way to keep us safe. The inner child is the gatekeeper of our upper limits. Healing the Mother Wound and becoming a loving "inner mother" to our inner child clears the pathway to voice your truth from a place of inner strength and self-love. Rather than looking to the old, limiting patterns of your childhood as a measure of being safe, the inner child begins to look increasingly to you, your adult self, for reassurance and comfort.

This inner bond between your inner child and your adult self (inner mother) is the firm ground you can stand on for disruptive truth-telling and creating transformation all around you. Here are some brief real-world examples. (Names and details have been changed.)

Maya lived in a home where her parents provided for her physical needs but consistently ignored her emotional needs. Her father was a workaholic and her mother was anxious and so relied on Maya for her emotional support. Feeling her mother's fragility and the emotional tenuousness of the family in general, Maya was chronically hyper-vigilant. She felt she always had to be "at the wheel" to fill the vacuum of emotional safety her parents could not provide. Being silent and vigilant was how Maya kept herself safe.

As a naturally sensitive and perceptive child, she was acutely aware of things unsaid in the home, the moodiness of her parents, and the general tensions in the family and used this awareness as a way to prevent or sidestep any conflict. As an adult, Maya was a respected, high-level executive in a corporation, and because of her childhood history, one of her gifts was being able to discern the unspoken things that needed to shift to bring situations to a greater harmony and move projects closer to the goal. Her biggest challenge at work was feeling safe enough to actually share her observations with the group she was a part of. Her inner child, Little Maya, was terrified that speaking out would cause people to be angry, triggered, or disappointed with her, so for years she kept many of her ideas and observations to herself, constantly questioning and doubting herself.

One of Maya's biggest healing breakthroughs came in the form of connecting with Little Maya and reassuring her before she, Adult Maya, spoke out. Through the deepening of that inner bond and taking increasingly bigger risks in disruptive truth-telling, her inner child began to see that telling the truth was not nearly as unsafe as it was when she was a child. It was actually a form of helping others and being true to herself! She happily discovered that she could survive other people not liking her and that often it was just a temporary disconnection that led to a more genuine relationship overall. The evidence was overwhelming; when Maya began sharing her observations consistently in her job, everything improved. She felt more effective and was more respected and sought after in her company, and the success of her projects improved exponentially. Maya felt increasingly empowered to consciously own her gift of disruptive truth-telling and felt the exhilaration of using each opportunity that presented itself as a way to contribute to the whole from a place of centeredness and self-trust. Prior to this, Maya had tried all kinds of workshops, books, and other methods to dissolve her fear of speaking out. It wasn't until she cultivated an inner bond with her inner child that she was able to move through it.

Sharing our truth serves others, even if their personalities react negatively. Trust that when something is deeply true for you, that truth will serve others as well, even if you don't know how.

Another woman, Liza, learned from an early age that her safety came from suppressing her emotional needs and submitting to her mother's demands. After Liza had a devastating physical accident at four years old, in which her mother patched Liza's physical wounds but coldly ignored her needs for emotional reassurance, she made a vow to suppress her true needs and obey her mother in a desperate bid to get her approval. This pattern continued into adulthood, with her giving her power away to bosses, spiritual teachers, and romantic partners. It wasn't until she developed a chronic illness that she realized she had to speak her truth, no matter the cost. Breaking the pattern involved accessing a healthy outrage on behalf of her inner child, Little Liza, who had been equating obedience and silence with safety. Feeling the healthy outrage on behalf of the child she was and grieving the magnitude of how she had suffered as a child allowed her to increasingly feel her own worthiness and access the strength to speak her truth to her husband, who had been putting his needs above hers for years. By developing a loving relationship with her inner child, Liza began to see the old beliefs operating and how they kept her stuck for years. Liza spoke her truth to her husband and initiated a separation. She has also stood up for herself at her job, where she had been silent as well, tolerating dynamics that were exhausting her for years. With a visceral sense of lightness and a growing bond with her inner child, Liza is stepping into a whole new chapter of her life with greater confidence and more inner strength than ever.

Speaking out in one area can make it easier to do so in other areas.

Michelle is an entrepreneur who is not only savvy in business but also in the visual arts. As a vibrant, talented young girl, she suppressed her craving for artistic endeavors because her mother didn't approve. Every time she expressed her love for painting and desire to be an artist, her mother withdrew or snarled in disapproval. Michelle suppressed this wild, wise, and intuitive part of herself and dove into being a successful businesswoman. This self-suppression bled into other areas, causing her to pick disrespectful partners, overwork at her job, and tolerate inappropriate behavior from her employees. Her healing breakthrough came as she connected with Little Michelle, transforming that sense of shame for being different into a sense of her wild, creative side as being a special, valuable part of her gifts. As she validated the hunger for approval from her inner child and affirmed the goodness and lovability of her wild, creative side, she began to see how often she had tolerated being overlooked and undervalued. This growing awareness and her growing sense of worth supported her in owning her value and asking for more from her employees, her company donors, and her romantic partner. Some people have left her life, but new, more nourishing relationships have emerged. Michelle feels like she is taking a quantum leap. Using her voice has been raising the quality of everything around her, and both her sense of effectiveness as a leader and her inspiration as a painter are soaring.

We can speak the deeper truth wherever we are. Truth spoken somewhere supports truth spoken everywhere.

Times in our everyday lives when we need to speak up and tell our truth may include:

- When people speak over you.
- When you are being misrepresented by others.
- When others are projecting onto you.
- When your boundaries are not being respected.

Becoming skilled in speaking out in our daily lives equips us to be more vocal in larger scale situations when:

- A group is losing sight of its goal.
- Other people or living things are being harmed.
- Rights are being taken away.

The vast majority of the catastrophes we face are sourced from the deliberate, continued silencing of women and people of color and devaluing of the earth itself. Any way that we can speak out, we must. And any way that we can support other women and people of color in speaking their authentic truth, we must do so. Women of color experience even more risk for their silence than white women. For those of us who are privileged in any way, we must hold space, remain silent, listen to the voices of other groups, and amplify their voices whenever we can.

Each of us has the opportunity in these times to own our voice and contribute to positive change. Let's look to each other for support and solidarity as we take bigger risks in being true.

We can find the fuel to speak out within ourselves through *reclaiming* our observations and intuitions as sources of truth and no longer suppressing them as a means to be safe or accepted. *And it's also found through sisterhood.* May each of us be a woman that other women can look to for inspiration and encouragement in being true to themselves, voicing their truth, and putting that truth into action.

Questions for Reflection

1. How was conflict handled in my family?
2. What typically stops me from initiating difficult conversations?
3. What do I need to believe in order to get better at disruptive truth-telling? What beliefs do I need to let go?

Chapter 8

BOUNDARIES

AT THE CENTER OF the fallout with my mother was, in my view, the issue of boundaries. To have boundaries means to have a separate self. In my family, a daughter setting a boundary with her mother seemed to be considered a betrayal, a sign of ungratefulness and immaturity. My rupture in the mother line revealed what I saw as an unspoken contract in our family that a daughter should always agree with her mother, be relentlessly cheerful, absorb her mother's negative emotions silently, soothe her mother's fears, and always prioritize her mother over herself.

To my family, a child creating boundaries seemed to convey disrespect, a lack of love, and an attempt to control. I had always sensed this very acutely, but it had never actually been articulated. This open conflict with my mother made it glaringly clear that my perceptions had been more painfully correct than I could have imagined.

My mother continued to contradict my lived experience, choosing to blame me, call me a bad daughter, and communicate to me and the rest of my family that something was wrong with me. She seemed unable to take responsibility for pain she may have caused me and invested considerable effort in trying to convince me how wrong I was. She went so far as to blame my therapist, Nicole, and even tried to get a meeting with her under a false *name. Nicole had security cameras installed on her property and spoke to a Connecticut state trooper, who I understand called my mother directly and told her that if she did not cease and desist her harassment of Nicole, the state of Connecticut would press charges against her. My mother continued to threaten to come to my apartment and workplace unannounced if I didn't agree to meet with her. It eventually got to the point where I felt so unsafe that I felt I had no choice but to request a restraining order against her to make this behavior stop. (My request was denied because my mother had not threatened me with physical harm.) This felt so tragic and surreal.*

I had believed firmly that if a family loves each other, they'll do what it takes to work things out. What was being slowly revealed, however, was that my family's definition of "love" was not the same as my own. To them, love seemed to mean enduring abuse silently, pushing things under the rug, forgetting your own pain, and putting on a happy face. Love meant denial. Love meant silence. Love meant keeping secrets. And ultimately, love meant abandonment of oneself. This form of silencing and self-suppression in my family felt like an echo of the wider patriarchal demand that women accept their role as lesser, inferior, and undeserving of owning themselves.

Setting boundaries like pursuing a restraining order and standing up to my father when he insisted that I continue to be my mother's "therapist" was both terribly frightening and empowering. So much weight I had carried my entire life was lifting off me, including the roles I had played in buffering my father from my mother, and my brother from my father—absorbing the shock waves of their pain and unconscious emotions like a sponge so they wouldn't have to. I also realized just how truly powerless my parents felt in the face of interpersonal conflict and how bereft they were, because of their own upbringings, of skills, tools, or models to work through it. How deeply resistant they seemed to be, despite their visible suffering, to grow and change.

The more I healed, the less I was able to tolerate and go along with the long-held dynamics I had maintained in keeping the peace in my family. This new capacity to set boundaries was such a freeing experience for me. I'll never forget one day after I set a boundary with my mother by email, my physical vision seemed to become sharper and the colors around me more vivid. It was like I had been sitting in a haze that was now dissolving. I was shocked that my physical sense of sight was immediately made sharper by setting a boundary. It was as though my life force was returning to me with every interaction in which I held my ground.

Deep down, I had always known that setting a boundary for myself would result in a chaotic rift in my family. But with my eyes newly open, I could finally see that breaking the cycle meant breaking through to my own life, a life that would become truly mine.

I will choose what enters me, what becomes
flesh of my flesh. Without choice, no politics,
no ethics lives. I am not your cornfield,
not your uranium mine, not your calf
for fattening, not your cow for milking.
You may not use me as your factory.
Priests and legislators do not hold
shares in my womb or my mind.
This is my body. If I give it to you
I want it back. My life
is a non-negotiable demand.
—*Marge Piercy, from "Right to Life"*

There is so much to say about boundaries and how foundational they are for our sense of self. Without firm boundaries, we can easily become enmeshed with others, causing us to emotionally caretake, be overly responsible, or neglect our own needs. When boundaries are too rigid, we isolate ourselves and push others away.

Healthy boundaries are "selectively permeable." They are not too rigid or too loose. Rather, they are flexible and can be opened or firm when needed, much like a healthy cell.

Boundaries are related to our early attachment needs as children. They pose the question: "Where do I end, and where do you begin?" All of us started out in life as a "we," as infants bonded with our mothers. Being securely attached to our mothers helped us internalize this sense of security and became the foundation for our own sense of self. If we were not securely attached to our mothers, we may have developed a background sense of inner insecurity, and on a subconscious level, we may still be looking for this security as adults.

This can cause some of us to have very weak boundaries, letting in anyone who remotely relates to us with care and affection, being too trusting, or having a very high tolerance for poor treatment from others. Weak boundaries can leave us open to being taken advantage of by others and can cause us to be on an emotional roller coaster, because our sense of security is not yet fully anchored within ourselves.

Confidence and Feeling Safe in Your Own Skin

An important step in developing healthy boundaries is learning that no outer person can provide the inner safety that you need; the time for that is only in early childhood, and that time is over. However, as adults we can mourn that lost opportunity and develop inner safety.

Knowing ourselves as individuals is essential for true intimacy and connection with others. As we fine-tune our self-awareness, we can know more fully our own needs, desires, and preferences. Taking the time and space for our inner work is an important form of self-care, and it reinforces a deep sense of integrity. The more centered and grounded we are in our own inner sense of self, the better partners and friends we are able to become.

The Old Paradigm: Compliance with Others = Acceptance from Others

You are the expert on you. It's OK to be yourself, to have needs and preferences different from those of the people around you. This may seem obvious, but we're surrounded by images of desirable females being the most yielding and most willing to be dominated. These messages will remain in our subconscious until we actively dismantle them.

What you say no to determines the success of what you say yes to.

Our boundaries determine what we say yes and no to. Learning how to say no is a skill and an art. Before asserting a boundary, it's important to take the time we need to process emotions that may be initially present, like rage and fear, so that we come from our highest integrity in the exchange. Anytime we can communicate a clear and clean "no," devoid of bitterness or negativity, we are demonstrating a high level of self-worth.

Sometimes loving someone involves affirming your separateness, not your sameness.

We give our power away when we accept the shame that others project onto us because of their own unprocessed pain. We support others not by accepting their pain as our own, but by highlighting their ability to make new choices. Don't feel obligated to absorb pain that isn't yours.

Healthy Boundaries: Sovereignty of Self

Shame is a toxic emotion instilled in us from childhood that causes us to soften our will, to feel less sure of ourselves and less powerful and, thus, more compliant to the wishes of others. When we set firm, healthy boundaries, we are reclaiming ourselves from the toxic shame we may have experienced in childhood and asserting our sovereignty as individuals with the power and right to define who we are and what we will or will not allow into the sacred space of ourselves.

Having Compassion *and* Strong Boundaries

As an extension of the cultural ideal of the "ALL Good Mother," who self-sacrifices and puts the needs of others before her own, many of us grew up with the unconscious belief that we are "good women" when we tolerate poor treatment by giving others the benefit of the doubt or "taking the high road." But the problem is that, too often, we allow our compassion for wounded people to soften boundaries that should be quite firm, unwittingly opening us up to harm. In other words, there's a common belief that if we are to have compassion for people who harm us, it's wrong to hold them accountable for their actions because they didn't intend to do harm.

The truth is that you can have BOTH. You can have compassion *and* strong boundaries. They must go hand in hand. Don't feel guilty for holding people accountable. Our compassion need not disable our instincts to protect ourselves. Our compassion need not open us up to harm. I like to use the metaphor of a rabid dog. If a dog that was clearly sick with rabies approached you, you would understand that you need to keep a distance from the animal in order to stay safe, yet that distance wouldn't stop you from *also* feeling compassion for the sick animal. You would likely feel both simultaneously: an obvious need to keep your distance and a heartfelt empathy for the dog's condition, which it incurred through no fault of its own.

A clear balance of compassion and containment is something we must feel entitled to in our relationships. Having strong boundaries and limiting interactions with unconscious people is a form of mothering ourselves. Tolerating toxic behavior can come under the guise of "taking the high road," or "being the bigger person," particularly for those of us who as children had to survive by coddling our abusive parents or watching our mothers coddle our fathers (or vice versa). Know that as an empowered adult woman, you don't have to be around people who don't honor you. You don't have to be the dumping ground for someone else's unconscious behavior or the unhealed wounds of others. Sometimes when we set boundaries, people become angry because those boundaries leave them to manage their own emotions instead of you carrying their emotional burden. Don't take responsibility for their pain; it doesn't serve them or you in the end.

You are the authority of your own energy, of what you allow or don't allow into your space. And you don't owe people an apology or explanation for doing what's right for you. This is a form of claiming your personal power, a form of self-love. I invite you to contemplate these questions: What are you tolerating in your relationships? Where do you need to have stronger boundaries? How has tolerating this put a drain on your energy? How would setting a firmer boundary free up your energy and vitality?

For others, being in your life is a privilege . . . not a right.

As we continue to realize our true worth, we are less willing to tolerate the people, circumstances, and situations in our lives that do not reflect our worth and self-respect. No one has a right to be in your world, nor is anyone entitled to your time. If people want to have the privilege of being in your life, that privilege must be earned by treating you with consideration and respect. As you emerge into greater self-worth and set new boundaries, the people who in the past have felt entitled to a place in your life may protest or object, unconsciously seeking to instill a sense of guilt or obligation in you, perhaps calling you ungrateful or selfish for holding your boundaries firm.

Know that you are always at choice. You don't have to acquiesce to the demands of others and give your power away. Communicating your boundaries and holding firm even in the face of outer disapproval is a powerful expression of your self-worth.

Healing the "Good Girl" Syndrome

As little girls, we were rewarded for being relational, compliant, quiet, and invisible. The covert message is that you don't deserve to have ownership of yourself. Messages about the primacy of appearance and sex appeal also communicate that "your body is not your own. It exists for the pleasure of others." These early cultural and familial messages may have also contributed to the development of a false self.

Maturity involves shedding the false self and discovering our authentic self—separating out our true needs and wants from the fake ones we took on in order to survive.

In the process of discovering our true, authentic needs and desires, things may change in our lives. This can be very challenging, but ultimately the changes will bring new forms of relationships, situations, and dynamics in our lives that reflect who we really are. People who have been used to us being compliant, submissive, or docile may feel surprised, enraged, or inconvenienced when we assert our boundaries. Their feelings are their own responsibility.

Are you willing to give other people permission to not like your boundaries?

We can expect to feel uncomfortable as we venture into new territory, places our friends or family may have never gone before. Much of our ability to succeed and to create the world we want directly hinges upon our ability to endure the discomfort of being misperceived and disliked as we evolve and grow on our own path. Boundaries are an expression of unapologetic self-ownership.

Setting Boundaries While Financially Dependent

Setting boundaries may present certain challenges for women who are still dependent on their mothers financially. For some of us, while our mothers could not offer us emotional availability or support, financial support is one thing that they can offer, and there need not be any guilt in receiving that. For other women, the mother's behavior may be so problematic that it's not safe to receive financial support from her because she may use it as a tool for control or manipulation. You are the expert on your own situation: trust yourself, get support, and take action that prioritizes your own physical and emotional safety.

This situation of financial dependence on one's mother offers particular opportunities as one heals the Mother Wound. It's a powerful context to begin establishing yourself as your primary inner source of support and developing a sense of separate self while receiving financial support in the relationship. For example, even though you may receive financial support, it's powerful to assert *to yourself* that you are not owned by your mother and do not owe her a certain mask, story, or role in compensation for that support. How you show up in that relationship, while receiving support, can shift in healthy ways, and starting small is the best way to go. How your mother responds to that will provide you with more information about the relationship and your next steps as an individual within that relationship. Getting support from a therapist or counselor can be extremely helpful as well.

When I had to rely on my mother for housing while getting my master's degree, I had a conversation with her shortly after moving in when we both were in a positive mood. I explained that while I appreciated her offer of housing, my boundaries were different now as an adult. I said in order for this to work smoothly, I ask that you not speak to me about personal issues you have with my father or other members of the family. She seemed to hear me and did not push back. From then on, I made sure to keep things light between us, not share any personal information with her beyond the bare minimum, and to remove myself or change the subject if she started disrespecting my boundaries. This is an example of how to filter yourself around your parents as a way of protecting yourself, staying centered around their dysfunction all while staying in your integrity.

You are your own treasure. You belong to you.

Having healthy boundaries involves being connected to your worth, being anchored to your own center of truth, and being willing to communicate respectfully and authentically with those around you. It's a skill that is learned, practiced, and refined over time. When you're starting out, it may seem scary, but each time it gets easier and more empowering. Over time, we start attracting more and more people who are willing to respect our new, healthy boundaries. The people who are unwilling to do so will pass out of your life.

When we have healthy boundaries, we feel increasingly safe and supported within ourselves, and we also become more effective at everything we do.

Facing the pain of what you went through births a fierce, protective love that takes no shit.

Our "no" moments can define who we are, what we value, and what we envision for ourselves. One of the most profound things a woman can do is to learn to say NO in an empowered way.

Your "no" is a sword that cuts away the nonessential so that you can live the fullest life.

A powerful point on our journey is when we feel fed up, when we feel as if we've had enough. This is a potent place for change. It can happen for a number of reasons, usually in response to something we've been tolerating that we simply can't tolerate any longer. It could be an emotional NO, or a simple mandate from the body that something cannot continue.

We live at a time where we are straddling two paradigms: an old paradigm of struggle and competition and a new paradigm of abundance and cooperation. All our small, daily actions have powerful ripple effects in the culture.

The word "no" is an expression of individuality and separateness, which is very threatening to any system of patriarchal domination, whether it's a family system, a corporation, or a political body. And that is precisely why "no" is our greatest ally in upending oppression in all its forms. Many little girls missed the chance to say "no" without experiencing loss, punishment, or rejection as a consequence. As adults, learning to set healthy, strong boundaries is part of stepping into our full individuation. "No" is a muscle that must be strengthened through the practice of actively expressing our truth and refraining from resolving tension for others.

New empowering beliefs may include:

- "I can be my own separate self and be lovable."
- "I can tolerate people not understanding me."
- "I am safe even when people don't like me."

Healthy female assertiveness is a by-product of inner work.

True female assertiveness becomes accessible as a result of feeling anger on behalf of the child we once were, the little girl who was exploited to whatever degree. Finding the healthy impulse to protect the child we were is the raw material for not tolerating any form of exploitation as adult women. If the inner child still believes that compliance and silence will bring her some form of "mommy," then the woman will continue to give her power away. We stop fearing our anger as we decouple it from the echoes of abandonment we experienced in our childhoods. The answer is to mourn the powerlessness we experienced in the past and to call up healthy adult outrage about what happened. As long as we postpone doing this inner work, we'll keep creating experiences of feeling powerless as adults.

This inner work is a form of rinsing our "no" of the residue of the past, working through the defensiveness or the fear it may be laced with so that when expressed, it can be "clean," ringing with the power, clarity, and radiance of the true self. This creates incredible momentum in one's life as each situation becomes an opportunity to live into your truth. Each "no" is a doorway into your greater "yes."

Lindsay C. Gibson explains, "Research suggests that what has happened to people matters less than whether they've processed what happened to them." Getting support with this is crucial. Working through what happened and placing our anger in its correct context liberates it to transform into self-knowledge and self-worth. The world needs more adult women who have reckoned with the truth about their childhoods. Only then can we really face reality *as it is now* and take action that will change the perilous course we are on.

Women of color have always been pressured to resolve tension for white women, due to the power differential inherent in a white-supremacist patriarchal society. That's why it's essential for Black and indigenous women and other women of color to refuse this pressure to resolve interpersonal tension for white women and to support one another in doing so. It's time for women of color to rise and own their power like never before. It's also time for white women to become educated about racism and unconscious bias, as they are part of the cultural and familial inheritance passed through generations, to some degree. This knowledge is crucial in disrupting that unconscious impulse in ourselves to look to others to resolve our tension. White women can support one another in taking more responsibility in this way as an even deeper commitment to our integrity during these transformational times.

The truth is that owning your value is not frivolous. It's fact.

Author and psychologist Mario Martinez says that to go beyond what the culture has permitted us, we need to create a "subculture of well-being" that validates and celebrates the new paradigm. We need each other, and we need to work together in this if we are to transition to a new culture that values the feminine and life itself in every way: in ourselves, in men, children, animals, and the planet itself.

Being loyal to your essence, to your soul, to your authentic self ALWAYS serves the whole better than any compliant, attenuated, small version of you could.

It's going to feel uncomfortable in some moments, that's for sure. But it's totally worth it. We can support each other in those uncomfortable moments.

Embodying the new narrative comes from highlighting the evidence of your worth.

To endure the tension that comes with being a leader and a pioneer, find evidence of the value that you hold within you, the wisdom, the experience, the commitment, and the love that make up who you are. Find the facts, and remind yourself of them day after day.

The truth is that owning your value feels like betrayal in many ways because that's what it is. We are betraying the old paradigm by creating the new one. It's a necessary betrayal, as the tectonic plates of our lives and the world shift to create something new.

One could even say that intergenerational betrayal is necessary for evolution.

As Dr. Mario Martinez says, how would we evolve if no one was willing to risk being shamed for going into new territory?

YOU are worth every bit of discomfort it takes to embody and express more of who you truly are in this world. It's worth it for you in terms of how it creates a powerful inner environment of self-love and because what you offer the world as you radiate from that place of realness is pure gold.

It's the epitome of a win-win, and it's the foundation of the coming world.

The Ultimate Boundary: Navigating No-Contact

For some of us, healing the Mother Wound while staying connected to our mothers is possible. In this scenario, the healing eventually creates a new, deeper connection between mother and daughter, which is a beautiful thing to witness. I've seen it happen, and it's truly inspiring. But for some of us, it gradually becomes clear that the severity of the dynamics in play make it impossible to heal ourselves and remain connected with our mothers.

It's still considered taboo to be estranged from one's family; especially to be estranged from one's mother. For some, the distance can be brief and short term. For others, the estrangement can be permanent. It takes enormous strength and fortitude to follow through and do what's best for you.

What Can Lead to Estrangement?

There are many reasons why people make this choice. A core theme leading to estrangement is realizing that your mother's dysfunctional behavior has demanded an enormous cost to your mental/emotional well-being, and you're simply no longer willing, or able, to pay that cost.

I believe that this isn't something chosen in a flippant, cavalier way, but rather it is often a choice made after years of trying every other possible avenue to preserve the connection and see it evolve to a higher level. At a certain point, you may reach a crossroads where the cost is too much, and you have to make a choice.

It may be the hardest thing you ever do in your entire life. And it may be the single most empowering thing as well.

Families are complicated systems. When one person stops playing their usual role in the family, the system will usually experience some degree of disequilibrium or chaos. Conflict can serve to transform the system to a higher level, if the family members are willing and open to grow and learn. Unfortunately, sometimes, in an attempt to resist change, the family attacks the person who wants to grow. That person has the choice to stay and suffer the toxicity or leave the unhealthy system and heal. The choice to terminate contact is often made when it's clear that it's impossible to heal while remaining in that family system.

Daughters often play the roles of family mediator, scapegoat, keeper of secrets, emotional caretaker. If a daughter on a path of growth wishes to evolve beyond her role in the family (perhaps by being more empowered, having firmer boundaries, speaking her truth, being less tolerant of disrespect), the degree of chaos that ensues is indicative of how dysfunctional the family system is as a whole.

If the family members are each relatively healthy, stable, and open, the family may be able to find a new equilibrium without much chaos. However, if the family members are deeply wounded or traumatized themselves, a daughter's evolution can be perceived as deeply threatening to the family system. This chaos can be deeply unsettling and extremely hard to navigate. Support is essential.

In an unconscious attempt to maintain equilibrium and resist change, family members may launch attacks against the daughter. A common and virulent form of backlash is "pathologizing" the daughter: seeing the conflict as a result of some form of defect or pathology in the daughter herself. The message is, "Your unwillingness to continue in the family system in your established role indicates that there is something deeply wrong with you." This shame-based narrative abdicates the mother and other family members from having to honestly examine their own behavior and take responsibility. The daughter's level of mental stability, her sexual activity, her past mistakes, everything about her may be openly questioned, that is, *except the role of the mother in the conflict.*

We can't save our mothers. We can't save our families. We can only save ourselves.

It's amazing how vehemently people resist looking at their stuff and the lengths to which they will go to remain in denial of it, including ostracizing their own child. This is actually an unconscious attempt to resist change by projecting all the conflict or "badness" onto the person initiating the transformation of the family system. Ultimately, this is not personal at all. This is what happens when people who have not been dealing with their inner life are confronted with their disowned pain through a catalyzing event, like a woman in the family growing beyond the predominant dynamics that have kept the family in a stable state for generations.

You don't need your mother (or other family members) to understand you in order to fully heal.

It's heartbreaking to realize that your mother or family is simply unable or unwilling to understand you. No matter how much you explain or how many attempts you make to convince them where you're coming from, you get nowhere. They may be unconsciously invested in *not* understanding you, because it poses too much of a threat to their deeply held beliefs and values. Understanding you may cause a seismic shift to the very foundation upon which they've built their identities and worldview. It's a painful thing to realize, and yet it helps to create a singularity of spirit within yourself. It becomes clear that your own understanding of yourself must be enough. Your validation of yourself becomes primary. You begin to realize you can be OK even if others do not understand you.

See their negative opinions about you as comfortable illusions that protect them from truths they're unwilling to face about their own lives. Truly, it has nothing to do with you.

After you go no-contact, your life may begin to improve in many areas. I've seen chronic illnesses clear up, neurotic fears vanish, and lifelong patterns dissolve. In fact, sometimes the challenge then becomes enduring the pleasure of your own life. With each new level of increased prosperity, increased intimacy, joy, and freedom, you are reminded that your family is not there to share it with you, or reminded of the punishment that would follow expressing independence or experiencing pleasure. It's particularly at these horizons that we may experience the turbulence of grief. There's nothing to do but feel the grief as it comes and allow yourself to move forward.

The grief doesn't mean you've made the wrong choice. It's actually a sign of health and healing.

Keep yourself grounded in the new paradigm that gave you the strength to leave the toxic connection. If you don't, you could get pulled back through guilt or shame. It's so important to get lots of support and give yourself time and space to process all the emotions that come with this choice. Ground yourself in exactly why you're doing this, and use it as an opportunity to birth you into a new paradigm in your life.

Estrangement as a Launch Pad to Empowerment

You may discover something deeply profound that many people never do: you can survive your mother's rejection. This can birth a level of freedom and determination within you that may initiate quantum leaps in your life. It can spur a fierce commitment to truth and carve out a radical integrity that extends to other areas of your life. It stokes a fire of truth within you that has always been there, but can only now blaze fully. You feel your own source energy within.

Grief, grief, and more grief gives way to . . . FREEDOM.

Grief may arise every time you go to a new, higher level to which your mother or family has never been. It may feel like a bone-deep ancestral grief, of having to go forward in life on your own. But it gets easier and easier with time. I find the more we lovingly allow ourselves to grieve, the more space is created in our lives for magic, beauty, and joy. There is something deeply sacred about the grief that comes from making this choice. It can serve as an opportunity to deeply connect to your truth and to embodying it at the deepest level. We must find meaning in this loss and use it to enhance our lives in new ways. That's the key to long-term healing. Your integrity becomes the solid foundation for the rest of your life.

It's OK to walk away from the toxic people in your life, including toxic people in your family.

Healing intergenerational wounds can be a lonely path at times. But with the space created, soulful connections will come into your life. Our attachment needs are the most powerful needs we have as humans. To face this level of estrangement is to confront the depth of your pain, of your humanity, and to claim the full value of your own life. Our greatest fear is that we will be alone. But the aloneness we fear already happened long ago in the trauma of our families. I'm here to tell you that in time, you will find your soul family, the people who are capable of seeing and valuing you for who you are.

Estranged Daughters Are Spiritual Warriors

In a world where women are predominantly expected to stay silent and cater to the needs of others, and where the shadow side of mothers is not acknowledged, the experience of estrangement can be an initiation into a new level of awareness that many people never get the opportunity to experience. A space is cleared that allows your light to shine at full radiance. What will you do with this light blazing within you?

Estranged daughters are finding each other, creating a new mother line; a connection of authenticity, realness, and truth in each other that supports the arising consciousness in all. I've seen instant camaraderie between women who have walked this path. There's more of us out there than many people realize. You're not alone!

You have to do what is right for you. Trust yourself.

Estrangement doesn't necessarily mean you don't love your family. It doesn't mean you're not grateful for the good things they gave you. It simply means you need the space to live your own life the way you want to live it. Women who feel no choice but to go no-contact with their dysfunctional mothers create the break because it's the only way to send the powerful message that "Mother, your life is your own responsibility as my life is mine. I refuse to be sacrificed on the altar of your pain. I refuse to be a casualty of your war. Even though you are incapable of understanding me, I must go my own way. I must choose to truly live."

Questions for Reflection

1. Growing up, girls often receive messages that it's not attractive or polite to say "no." As you grew up, how did your mother and other adults around you respond to your "no"?

2. Did you internalize any beliefs that create guilt for setting boundaries? What are some of those beliefs? (For example: Saying no is a form of rejecting or abandoning others. Boundaries mean you don't love the other person. Having limits means putting the relationship in jeopardy.)

3. What new beliefs might support you in setting boundaries more confidently now? (For example: Boundaries are a normal, essential part of human relationships. Boundaries are a form of self-respect. I am a singular and separate being. My boundaries enhance, not detract from, my relationships.)

Chapter 9

THE TABOO OF QUESTIONING MOTHER

OVER THE NEXT FEW *years, I began to learn how the complex and disturbing dynamics I was experiencing with my mother had their roots in deeper generational wounding in my mother line.*

My refusal to meet with my mother seemed to ignite a deeply seated rage within her, and what appeared to be her obsessive behavior began to correlate with other events in my family's history that I had heard about. I was beginning to see that I was not the true cause of my mother's reaction and toxic behavior—that it likely took root in her relationship with her own mother, long before I was born.

Years prior to this, I had heard from other family members about some sad and alarming events that had trickled down to my mother, which my mother herself had never talked to me about: how her own mother had been an alcoholic, how as a young child she'd had to take care of her five siblings on her own when her mother was incapacitated from drinking, and how her own paternal grandparents had stalked her mother routinely when she got married. This history of pain, jealousy, alcoholism, aggres-

sive behavior, and relationship triangulation had run through my maternal line unhindered, unquestioned, and unruptured— until me.

I also began to understand much of this behavior through a mental health lens. Several members of my family had died too young—some from alcoholism or illness, and I had to imagine as a result of the challenging dynamics and legacy of traumatic experiences they endured as children under the veneer of "everything's fine."

Why was it so hard for my mother to look at her own childhood pain, and to see how she was inadvertently passing on these patterns to me? What was this rage being directed at me all about? Why was this behavior not being questioned, generation after generation?

My parents married very young to get out of their own families and never went to therapy. It was my turn to follow suit in my lineage, to "suppress and move on." I recall reflecting on this and feeling such a deep ache inside me, a longing for the freedom of self-actualization, to be a separate, independent, individuated being, to own myself, to belong to myself, and how deeply I craved the blessing and support of the women in my family; but in my mind's eye, I saw all the women in my lineage with their backs to me, withholding, cold, jealous, deprived, full of rage, and impervious to my pain. The shadows I had sensed underneath the warm surface now had a cold, visceral reality to them. I knew that to be my full self, I would have to trust this process of rupture and endure the cost of becoming real. I had come too far now, and there was no going back.

The Death Mother
and the Apocalyptic Mother

For some women, approaching the taboo of questioning mother can feel like life or death. Many of us sense some deeper pain within our mothers that may be unleashed if we question what may feel like the fragile stability of that relationship. But that questioning and possible rupture must occur for a woman to have her own life, her own individuation.

When considering this intergenerational initiation, I think of the "Death Mother," an archetype first introduced by author and Jungian analyst Marion Woodman and further explored by Bud and Massimilla Harris in their book *Into the Heart of the Feminine: Facing the Death Mother Archetype to Reclaim Love, Strength, and Vitality.*

Using the myth of Medusa as a guide, they explore the denial and devaluation of the feminine in our culture and how it manifests as a particular negative energy present within our own psyches. They write: "When the feminine principle is repressed into our unconscious, it becomes part of our collective shadow, and this shadow projects itself as a longing, or even a demand, for power."

In a powerful conversation between Marion Woodman and Daniela Sieff in an article called "Confronting Death Mother," Sieff sums it up by saying:

> . . . when we are wounded during childhood, we become
> vulnerable to the Death Mother, whereupon our lives become
> ruled by shame and its concurrent fear of exposure. We fear
> being exposed as inadequate for who we are. We fear being
> exposed as inadequate for what we have done and what we
> have not done. We fear that our supposed inadequacies,

if exposed, will lead to our abandonment and annihilation. Once we are ensconced in this toxic and shame-fueled world, we act out the Death Mother we have internalized. We develop an embodied, yet unconscious, longing for death and at the same time we attack or abandon anyone who might expose what we work so hard to keep buried. We also try to compensate for our terror of abandonment through the unconscious and insatiable drive for power.

The drive for power and the taboo of questioning mother can keep female pain disowned for countless generations, cloistering it deep in the unconscious, but inevitably it seeks expression in some form, often against other people and ourselves, as in the many manifestations of the Mother Wound. One can see how the Death Mother archetype becomes particularly damaging in mothers and daughters in a patriarchy, as it keeps our power captive in an unwinnable struggle within ourselves and with each other.

However, there is another archetype that we can call on for support, the "Apocalyptic Mother," which may seem similar in name but is wildly different in character. Unlike the Death Mother archetype, she isn't Death in Resistance to Life, but rather Death *in Service to Life.* The word "apocalypse" derives from the Greek word meaning "revelation of that which was previously hidden." Daniela Sieff coins this term to mean "death of the obsolete and birth of the new." The Death Mother perpetuates the Mother Wound through enforcing the taboo of questioning mother. The Apocalyptic Mother archetype is an energy that clears the way for a woman to be initiated into her own life, even in the face of a rupture of the mother line. With support, strength, and compassion, a woman can turn a confrontation with the inner Death Mother into a confrontation with the inner Apocalyptic Mother. Apocalyptic Mother is represented in the Hindu tradition as Kali, the goddess who is the natural cycle of birth and death, or as Baba Yaga in the Russian tradition. Marion Woodman explains, "A life that is truly being lived is constantly burning away the veils of illusion, gradually revealing the essence of who we are. Apocalyptic Mother burns us in her hottest flames to purify us of all that is not authentic. Her energy is impersonal. She doesn't care how painful or terrifying the process is. Her only purpose is to serve life."

Woodman goes on to say: "How we respond to the Apocalyptic Mother determines whether we experience her as friend or foe. Early on in our journey, when Death Mother's strangle hold is particularly ferocious, and when consciousness is afraid to open itself to the otherness of the unconscious, we experience ourselves as victims of the apocalypse; in time, we bring the Death Mother to consciousness and begin to experience life beyond her clutches, we may gradually come to see ourselves as partners in the apocalyptic process."

The Death Mother archetype could be seen as the gatekeeper of our true power that lies beyond the taboo of confronting mother, keeping us trapped in shame, guilt, or fear. The fear of being seen as a "bad daughter" in pursuit of our own healing can be one of our greatest obstacles at the gate of our power, preventing us from accessing the many gifts and powerful transformation that lie within the pain of the Mother Wound.

There are many variations of the taboo that says, "Don't look at your relationship with your mother." Most of these beliefs equate the desire for healing from painful feelings in relation to your mother with "mother-blame." This is a false equivalence that instills guilt and shame. This can greatly thwart a woman's process and keep her stuck in adolescence. When we believe these thoughts, we are being controlled by the Death Mother. With support we can develop the power to override the voices of guilt, shame, and doubt and transform the Death Mother, who keeps us stuck, into the Apocalyptic Mother, who assists us in transforming our pain into consciousness, our shame into liberation.

We may be pressured to ignore our feelings and blame ourselves, by people who are in denial of their own Mother Wound.

Others may say to us:

- "She didn't have it easy. Don't put more of a burden on her."
- "Your mother tried her best. You know she loves you."
- "Focus on the good in the relationship. You only have one mother."

These things may well be true: your mother may love you; she may have tried her best; you only have one mother; she didn't have it easy. *However*, these things, even if true, shouldn't be cause for you to swallow your pain, stop seeking healing, and silence yourself. This silencing is in accordance with the silencing of women as a whole.

This pressure can even come from our own mothers; no matter how diplomatic, empathic, and compassionate we may be, we may face backlash for speaking our truth. Depending on how much your mother has avoided her own Mother Wound, she may respond with outrage, martyr-like sulking, cutting sarcasm, or the cold shoulder. She may manipulate or try to shame, guilt, or blame you for bringing this to her attention. Especially if she was raised to never question her parents or voice her own difficult feelings. If your mother has been able to achieve some measure of personal growth in terms of handling difficult emotions, there could be a chance of growing together through it.

There are also a number of stereotypes that instill shame and may prevent us from breaking this taboo and differentiating from our mothers. These stereotypes reinforce shame and cause us to blame ourselves because we don't measure up. They include:

- The mother and daughter who are best friends and share everything.
- The myth of the perfect family.

- The ungrateful daughter and her self-sacrificing mother who is never appreciated.
- Mothers are always right, so if you're having issues with your mother, it's *your* fault.

Our culture instills shame for our authentic feelings about our mothers, which always include some not-so-positive feelings. Refuse to feel guilty about this.

The guilt that we feel is *not* because we are not good people. We've been taught that feeling guilt is a sign that our value as a person is in question. The fear of "being a bad daughter/person" keeps so many women silent about the truth of their feelings, truth that if spoken could set them free in many ways. In actuality, this guilt is an *artifact of control*, the larger patriarchal control of women's voices and feelings. The guilt we feel is caused when we transgress the age-old mandate that we stay silent about our pain to maintain our relationships. To speak out is to refuse to be controlled, and this is a *good* thing. Similar to dealing with fear, I tell women to "feel the guilt and do it anyway," meaning don't see the guilt as a true barrier but as an old feeling that must be ignored when it comes to speaking our truth and doing what we know is right.

The pressure that precedes breaking the taboo of questioning mother is the pressure of women's evolution.

This taboo must be broken if women as a whole are to heal. This is utter blasphemy to older generations, who were taught from every angle in society to "honor thy father and thy mother." From a religious standpoint, if you broke this commandment, you could burn in hell for eternity. Parents could not support their children's growth because it questioned their own power and defied all the other acts of suppression and denial they themselves had endured to get through life; this could unlock all kinds of feelings that they were taught not to feel. But that way of living is no longer an option. The more we deny, suppress, and avoid the truth of our experience, the more we whittle our lives down to narrow confines, and the less resilient we become over time.

So many taboos must be broken:

- The taboo against listening to yourself as your own highest authority.
- The taboo of honestly feeling your feelings even if they offend others.
- The taboo of feeling fully deserving and worthy of big things.
- The taboo of loving yourself and owning your worth.
- The taboo of process, patience, and things taking time.
- The taboo of imperfection and making mistakes or changing your mind.
- The taboo of acknowledging the truth of our childhood histories.
- The taboo of vulnerability.
- The taboo of focusing on self-exploration (labeled "selfish," especially for women).

Healing the Mother Wound is a form of honoring your entire female line: the generations of women who came before you and the generations of women to come.

Due to the cultural atmosphere of female oppression, women have historically felt caught in a bind: honoring your mother may seem to necessitate disempowering yourself, and likewise, empowering yourself may feel like not fully honoring your mother. This either/or bind has been a problem in women's empowerment. This is because of the power dynamic that has been passed down through generations of women living in patriarchy, which creates a sense of scarcity that makes it seem challenging for mothers and daughters to both be empowered individuals at once.

Honoring your mother should be seen as in full alignment with honoring yourself.

As more generations of women become individualized and live their authentic truth, it will no longer be taboo for daughters to reflect on the Mother Wound and seek healing. It will be known that healing the Mother Wound is essential to taking responsibility for oneself and to living life consciously and with integrity. And it will be seen as a critical step in fully owning one's brilliance and power.

We must resist the cultural pressure to avoid questioning our mothers by denying painful emotions or unhealthy patterns in that relationship. This task of resistance is essential to our realizing our wholeness.

If we ignore the pain of the Mother Wound, we risk living our lives indefinitely with persistent feelings of deep shame, self-sabotage, competition, comparison, self-doubt, and attenuation. We also risk passing it along to our daughters and sons. The template that we inherited from our mothers (with its patriarchal distortions) will remain intact until we consciously act to transform it so that we can live in alignment with our deepest truth and thus experience deep fulfillment.

In the healing process, there may be moments of experiencing challenging emotions toward our mothers, like sadness, rage, and disappointment. They are temporary phases on the cycle of healing. If we stick with the healing process, those feelings eventually transform into greater peace and acceptance.

We have to believe that we are worth it and have what it takes to come out on the other side of this wound.

Healing the Mother Wound is a personal journey and does not require that your mother heal herself alongside you. It does require you to question the things you think you know about your relationship with your mother. This line of inquiry will focus on YOU and your own healing and transformation. However, it is very possible that your own healing process may trigger your mother in some way. The trigger can be viewed as a valuable opportunity for mother and daughter to potentially come to a deeper understanding. It could also be an opportunity for the mother to reflect and have insight on herself and her own life, if she is willing.

Healing the Mother Wound is characterized by:

- Examining the mother-daughter relationship with the intention to gain clarity and insight in order to create positive change in one's life.
- Transforming limiting beliefs you've inherited with the intention of adopting new beliefs that fully support you in flourishing as your authentic self.
- Taking responsibility for your own path by becoming conscious of previously unconscious patterns and making new choices that reflect your true desires.

Healing the Mother Wound is not a rejection of mother, it's a powerful form of claiming oneself as whole.

Because our relationships with our mothers served as the foundation for our relationships with ourselves, the healing process offers massive potential for growth and transformation. That is the point of questioning to heal the Mother Wound: not to blame, not to judge or reject one's mother, but to experience the peace and freedom of self-actualization, which is the birthright of every woman.

If our mothers try to shame us or guilt us for doing the work of our own healing and breaking this taboo, we must stay strong. You have a right to differentiation and a separate selfhood.

We truly honor our parents and our children when we take responsibility and do the work of healing our own wounds.

If enough of us do this inner work, rejecting the shaming voices of the culture and the voice of the Death Mother archetype within us that would keep us silent, fearful, and compliant, we can transform the collective Death Mother into the collective Apocalyptic Mother, ushering in that new earth in which we no longer fear change due to toxic shame stored in our inner basements, but rather, all change can be seen through the life-giving lens of "death in service to life."

Questions for Reflection

1. What myths, stereotypes, or cultural messages have caused you to feel any form of guilt or shame for your true feelings toward or experiences with your mother?
2. What taboos do you experience in your daily life that prevent you from being more authentic? What experiences early in your life reinforced those taboos?
3. What do you think could be possible for you if you ceased obeying these taboos and moved forward with what you truly desire? How would your life be different?

Chapter 10

GIVING UP THE IMPOSSIBLE DREAM

WHAT FOLLOWED AFTER THE court hearing to request a re-straining order against my mother was a brutal turbulence of emotions. Now that I had stepped further outside the family system and its chaos, I had to face the chaos within myself. This felt like the ground beneath me was constantly shifting as I attempted to walk in a straight line. Part of me was thrilled and proud of myself for standing up to my mother and setting strong boundaries with my family members. This sense of empowerment emerged in fits and starts, punctuating longer periods of intense grief, nostalgia, anxiety, and longing. I'd wake up in a start, feeling like I should reach out and connect with my mother in that familiar old hope of "What if I just explain it better this time? I think she may finally understand where I'm coming from." Thankfully, each time, I managed to remind myself that I had already tried to explain it over and over again, and it had never worked.

Months would go by with no word from anyone in my family. I noticed in moments an old narrative emerging, that old refrain that used to give me a sense of control: "If I just change myself to meet them where they're at, they'll finally 'see' me and things will improve." I began to understand that this had been the guiding force, a North Star, for me as a child. And I began to see that there was never going to be a payoff for my bottomless support and gratitude for crumbs of respect. I knew that this yearning represented the "impossible dream" of my childhood, and could recognize it operating in full force.

I had learned through working with my therapist, Nicole, and immersing myself with her in deep Internal Family Systems/inner parts therapy work, that the impossible dream is a common survival strategy for survivors of childhood trauma; it had protected me from the unbearable truth of how emotionally unavailable my parents had been. Adult survivors of abuse, neglect, or familial trauma often translate this early childhood dream into striving to be perfect, good enough, and liked by everyone; people-pleasing; and caretaking in an unconscious bid to be loved in a way they never were as children. It takes an incredibly long time to undo this personality accommodation to traumatic pain.

I remember lying in the grass in the park near the West Side Highway in New York City on a Sunday afternoon. I was telling my inner child, "Little Bethany, Mom is never going to become the mother that we need. It's time for us to give up on this now. She's not capable of giving you what you need. I'm here for you now to take care of you and love you." I was shocked when I felt my inner child respond to me with "That's OK, I'll wait forever for Mommy. I want her to see me more than anything in the whole wide world. I'll happily wait until the day I die. Her love is all I want in this world, and I don't care what it takes to get it. I need it. I need her love in order to be OK." Right then, I realized just how deeply entrenched this impossible dream really was for me and that it was going to take time to help my inner child let go. I also began to recognize how that same energy of one-sided attachment had borne out in other areas of my life: relationships, jobs, and friendships that were all "dry wells" with nothing to offer me but to *which I clung with a false hope that kept me deeply stuck, waiting. I could now feel how my inner child was driving that stuckness in a false attempt to get my mother's love and how this had been projected onto other people and things for most of my life.*

Over time, my impossible dream with my mother began to steadily dissolve, layer by layer, as did the impossible dreams in other parts of my life. It was as though the impossible dream with my mother had been fueling the other impossible dreams as well. As the fog lifted around that primary relationship, I could see all my other relationships more clearly, including those with David, my father, and my brother. I began to direct more of my attention to personal pursuits, like community activism and my writing aspirations. The more I healed, the more I felt excited about things like world travel and simply having time and space to write and rest.

As the impossible dream was evaporating, I felt waves of grief and yet moments of solid ground appearing beneath me. My therapy focused on helping me integrate all these changes. I couldn't help but feel like I was going through some kind of initiation; my senses felt incredibly heightened and attuned. I felt as though, in my willingness to consciously feel the immense pain of having to break away from my family, I was breaking open somehow, as though part of me was dying and a new part of me was being born.

To cope with emotional pain and confusion in our families, many of us squeeze our life force into a secret dream that continues to unconsciously constrain us into adulthood. Left unrecognized, this dream gets projected onto other people, situations, and things, asking them to provide what they cannot, keeping us in a perpetual state of dissatisfaction and self-loathing.

The impossible dream is a coping mechanism in which a child hopes that one day, when she becomes "good enough," her mother will finally recognize her and give her the love that she has always longed for. At its most basic level, it's some form of "When I _____, Mother will finally see me and love me for the real me." This impossible dream gives a child in a dysfunctional family a powerful form of hope that will sustain her amid the confusion or pain she is experiencing in the family. It also gives the child a sense of control over her environment, allaying her fears and protecting her from the painful truth that she is actually powerless to change the dynamics in her family.

The impossible dream protects us against the painful realities that we didn't have the cognitive capacity to cope with as children.

In many ways, the impossible dream is a brilliant survival strategy for getting through some form of trauma. Like a safe haven, it takes the focus off the mother (who feels unsafe or inaccessible to the child to some degree) and instead puts the child's focus on herself, giving her a sense of control and a focus on a future time when all will be well, helping her to endure the daily pain and confusion she may be experiencing.

Unconsciously, the child believes, "There must be something wrong with me. My control lies in *changing myself* into what she wants me to be."

It's a false hope because the truth is that no matter how "good" you were, it wouldn't have changed anything in your family. Even if it were possible to be the perfect child who pleased your mother in every way, it wouldn't have changed the painful, dysfunctional dynamics of your childhood. Here's why: The truth is that pain you experienced in your family had nothing to do with you. It was entirely related to your parents handling their own challenges, personally and as a couple. Your mother having a child may have been a catalyst for pain that was arising within her, but you as a child *did not cause* her pain.

Giving up the impossible dream is accepting the fact that your mother's pain had nothing to do with you. You did not cause it. And it was never your responsibility to help her heal it.

In adult life, the impossible dream becomes a defense against the pain of the present moment. It's a barrier between you and what's actually happening. It gives a false sense of control and a false sense of hope that often gets projected onto other areas of your adult life.

As women, our impossible dream can manifest in many different ways, including:

- **Constant Self-Improvement:** A background sense that "there's something wrong with me" and a perpetual pressure to work hard to become worthy.
- **"Will You Be My Mother?":** Projecting an unconscious need to be mothered onto other people such as spouses, partners, and children. This can manifest as an attachment to being liked, idealization of others, or a feeling of being owed.
- **Safety in the Future:** Projecting hope that future external circumstances will bring some final sense of calm, acceptance, and "arrival." A sense of always looking for the "next thing."
- **Self-Sabotage:** Often an unconscious sense of hesitation of "not without my mother."
- *Over*active mind: Constant thinking, strategizing, and planning to buffer against painful feelings arising in the present moment.

Effort, Exertion, Struggle, and Striving: The Pain of Keeping the Impossible Dream Alive

It actually takes an enormous amount of energy to keep the impossible dream alive, but since we have been doing it for so long, this effort is invisible to us. It's only when it stops, like when a motor that's been running in the background suddenly stops, that we realize how loud it has actually been.

"I'm the one I've been waiting for."

I'll never forget one woman who attended a workshop I taught in Colorado. She said to me, "I remember thinking to myself when I was a little girl that 'this woman can't be my real mother because my real mother would never treat me this way. Someday my real mother will come and get me.'" Through tears she said to me and to the group, "I realize now that I am the good mother that my inner child has been waiting for. I'm here for her now. I'm the one that's able to give her what she needs. This is the moment my inner child has been waiting for."

When you release your attachment to the hope that your mother will change, you release your attachment to the hope that other people in your life will change as well. Because the relationship with our mothers is the blueprint for our other relationships, changes there automatically get reflected in our other relationships, sometimes immediately and sometimes over time.

Giving up the impossible dream is getting back in touch with reality as it is.

Intellectually, you may be very aware that your mother "is who she is" and will never change. However, below your conscious awareness, there may be a little girl within you who's still waiting and hoping for her mother to give her what she needed.

The impossible dream can show up in many different ways:

- Do you find yourself experiencing frustration after spending time with your mother?
- Do you find yourself feeling hopeful about your visits with your mother, only to experience a kind of predictable disappointment and self-doubt for hours or days afterward?

- Do you find yourself idealizing people in your life, only to be repeatedly disappointed?
- Do you feel as if you're perpetually on hold in some way? Perhaps waiting for some external permission to act on what it is you really desire?
- Is self-sabotage an issue for you? Do you get very close to a breakthrough, only to find yourself collapsing at the last minute?
- Do you fall in love with a person's potential instead of the person they actually are?

The impossible dream keeps us in perpetual childhood.

A major shift can happen when we see that it's safe to let go of loyalty to the patterns that we thought would grant us the mothering we needed, patterns such as:

- Staying small.
- Feeling guilt and shame.
- Being fearful and hypervigilant.
- Believing in scarcity.
- Depriving ourselves in some way.
- Playing the victim.
- Solving other people's problems.
- Suppressing our true feelings and responses.

These patterns may have been taught to you by your mother overtly and/or through simple observation of her behavior. They were likely passed down to her by her own mother and/or her own cultural conditioning. Because we live in a patriarchy that tells us women are less-than, we all have these beliefs to some degree. (These beliefs can be even more damaging if our mother was unhealthy or mentally unstable.) They may be very hard to let go of because on some level, letting go of them feels like letting go of "Mother"—and for our unconscious and inner child, this can feel like death. For example, if your mother was very fearful, you may have unconsciously taken on her fearful beliefs as a way to feel close to her. Letting go of a fearful approach to life may feel as scary as if you were letting go of your mother herself. Another example is letting go of self-blame. If you were taught to blame yourself and were rewarded for that, letting go of self-blame may feel like you are betraying your mother.

Because these patterns were associated with being mothered, the patterns themselves begin to unconsciously represent a mothering presence. These patterns may have afforded us temporary approval, validation, or acceptance in childhood. But now, as adult women, they only serve to keep us down. Because they were formed so early in our development, these beliefs and patterns tend to be quite unconscious and can endure for years before we see their origin. These patterns may have even served you in some ways. For example, being a striver to get your mother's love may have helped you to achieve a lot in the world. Being an emotional caretaker may have helped you be skilled at tuning into people's feelings. Being controlling or rigid may have helped you be exceptionally productive. However, the most important thing is to see how these strategies or patterns of behavior did *not* bring us what we wanted most: for our mother to show up for us in the ways we needed her to. As we mourn that loss, we can free ourselves to live and act in new ways.

Accepting how powerless you were as a child is a major step toward owning your true power as an adult. Your parents' inability to give you what you needed had nothing to do with you. Fully letting this realization in requires grieving and getting support. The real letting-go is in the grieving, which makes space for new ways of being in the world that truly nurture and fulfill you.

It's important to identify new, positive beliefs or patterns to replace the old negative ones. Then commit to taking action on those new beliefs.

Examples:

- It's safe to step through fear and believe in myself. (Action step: Soothing yourself through fears as you take a new risk and start a project that requires you to be visible to others.)
- I give myself permission to honor my needs and speak my truth. (Action step: Speaking out on your own behalf in a situation in which your boundaries are not being respected.)
- I honor my truth even when those around me disagree. (Action step: Doing something that you know is true for you even when others reject you for it.)

The action step gives you a new experience that sends your subconscious a powerful message: it *IS* safe to act counter to what you learned as a child. In other words, not acting in accordance with the patterns will not cause rejection, humiliation, or abandonment the way they could in childhood. In a way, it's as though you're bringing your inner child into the present moment, where she *can* experience being supported for who she is, because *you* as your adult self are there for her in the ways your mother could not be. This creates deeper integration within yourself and more detachment and distance from damaging patterns that were unconsciously adopted in childhood. The key here is consistency. Small, consistent steps lead to bigger transformations over time.

It's important to acknowledge how childhood strategies did not work.

Examples:

- Being really quiet did not cause people to approve of me.
- Solving my family's problems did not create lasting peace or protect me from rejection.

- Agreeing with her did not lead her to see me for who I was as a separate person.
- Absorbing my mother's fearful beliefs did not cause me to feel safe.
- Staying small and silent did not lead to my mother's approval or validation of me.
- Focusing on my mother and her problems did not cause her to listen to or support me.

When we see how these strategies did not work, we can more easily let go of the unconscious hold they have on us.

When we admit that "the good mother is not coming," we can grieve this and give ourselves permission to choose new ways of being and acting in the world that actually bring us fulfillment and joy. Our lives begin to automatically shift around this realization. Rejection of these negative patterns is *not* a personal rejection of your mother. Moving beyond these early patterns is about *you* choosing to heal and create new, healthier ways of living and being in the world. Your mother may view the shift in you as a personal betrayal, to the degree that she is closely identified with these patterns in *herself.* Her response to your divergence from these patterns is a statement of where she is at within herself; it's not about you. You may see how futile and unhealthy these patterns are in your own life, but your mother may not; she may still see them as valid ways of acting in the world. Her opinions do not have to dictate your reality. Let her have her own experience without rushing in to explain or emotionally take care of her; this is a form of respect for her and for yourself.

For generations, wounded mothers have been unconsciously asking their daughters to compensate them for what patriarchy and their families would not give them: a sense of purpose, control, and personal validation. Daughters cannot provide this. It cannot be given; it can only be found within the mother by the mother herself, by committing to her own healing and transformation. This toxic cycle is broken by refusing to comply with the unspoken message from a wounded mother: "Do not abandon me by becoming fully yourself." Woman, you have a right to your own life. Letting your mother have her own experience and healing process is not cruel (as patriarchy would tell us); it is healthy and necessary. A major shift happens when your integrity becomes more important than your mother's opinion of you: you show up powerfully and model a new way of being for others.

There is only one thing that will bring you the satisfaction you're seeking: the truth at the center of your being, and living from that place of deep authenticity, no matter the cost.

Because this taboo against exploring our inner truth has been operating with momentum for countless generations, we are each presented with a dilemma: Do we continue with business as usual, with the persistent background pain, but with an illusion of peace and security? Or do we directly face the pain for the sake of moving through it to arrive at a place of genuine truth and clarity and the deep fulfillment it brings?

In the new paradigm into which we are moving, family honor will *not* be equated with silence but rather with honesty, integrity, and authenticity, even if that involves confronting painful, uncomfortable feelings. The uncomfortable feelings that come up in the process of healing from emotional wounds will not be avoided due to fear, but seen realistically as an integral part of a healthy process that ultimately delivers you to clarity, deep wisdom, and compassion.

Our hunger for truth is starting to exceed our hunger for cultural and familial approval.

The fact that our culture has equated honest examination of our histories with treason or blasphemy illustrates how perfunctory honor is a form of exerting control, not about genuine love. Love that is commanded is not love. Examining our histories, if we stay with the process, may ultimately bring us to genuinely honor and love our parents. No commandment needed.

It's an act of love to continue to bring this painful truth to the inner child: Mommy isn't coming. And you're safe.

Putting the emotional pain in its true, proper context releases a person to more fully embody their individuality with confidence. The inner child stops blaming herself. This is the process of clearing the projection of the abandoning or invading mother away from current situations so that you are living more in the now, no longer seeing your current life through the distorted lens of the past. This process is very slow and can take many years, but with each layer you remove, more of your true self becomes accessible and your life becomes more completely your own. Your inner child feels supported in being "her own girl," and as a result, you know in your bones that you are a woman who belongs to herself. Being separate and being lovable are no longer competing needs but rather interwoven cornerstones of oneself. Paradoxically, this inner singularity births an ever-deepening experience of interconnectedness with all.

Questions for Reflection

1. In what ways did you see the impossible dream showing up in your childhood and now in your life as an adult woman?

2. What were some unconscious strategies you used in childhood to feel more safe, secure, and approved of?

3. What are some new beliefs that you can adopt to help you replace negative beliefs from your childhood that, if embodied and acted upon, would create some tangible change in your life, moving you beyond the legacy of your family in some way?

Chapter 11

ACCOUNTABILITY

THE FALLOUT WITH MY mother, *while devastating and shocking, had served to sharpen my understanding, and had validated my earliest perceptions and observations about what had caused me to disown myself as a child to survive my family. I felt like I was putting together a puzzle; I had been whole when I was born, but through the necessity of having to adapt to the dysfunctional dynamics of my family and the wider patriarchal culture, I had become fragmented and dismembered, split off from myself. Now I was in the process of putting myself back together through the act of naming the experience I had gone through as a child. I was discovering a deeper wholeness that had always been within me but that I had never recognized before. Only through surrendering to the emotions in the wake of those realizations was it possible for me to really understand this on a visceral level. It felt like a second birth, stepping truly into myself, being more self-possessed, speaking out, saying no, and discovering my integrity to be by far the most nourishing force in my own life.*

As I reflected on my parents' apparent inability to have empathy for my pain or take any responsibility for their part in our dynamic, I came to the conclusion that it likely stemmed from their belief that in their own eyes, they had been better parents than their own parents. My dad didn't beat me to a pulp the way his dad beat him (he did beat my brother, though not to such an extent). My mother didn't pass out drunk for days and leave me to take care of the entire household the way her mother had, but she did emotionally burden me with way more than any little girl should ever be burdened with. I understood how, in their eyes, they had improved on where they had come from. But the fact that they hadn't done any inner work around their own childhoods made them aggressively resistant to any evidence I presented that showed I had still experienced harm at their hands.

I felt that my request for accountability was perceived as an attack. The way I saw it, their denial had permitted me to be abused; unfortunately, I believe they saw this denial as love for or loyalty to their own parents. Unearthing the truth wasn't seen as healing but rather as a blasphemous betrayal of the family. My view was that the effort required to get out of denial was the most powerful expression of loving oneself and one's children. Being accountable is necessary to create change. When each generation serves the denial of their parents over the well-being of their children, we end up with a traumatized society.

At this point, I had over a decade of therapy under my belt, having built a long-term therapeutic relationship that provided the things I missed in my childhood. As a result, I could see these patterns and felt empowered in expressing my desire to change them. But I firmly believe that because my parents hadn't done similar inner work, they couldn't be proud of this, only threatened by it. The outcome was that the family system could not accommodate me in my empowered state, and I was ousted from it. All families seek equilibrium and homeostasis, and for some families, the most empowered person must be exiled; otherwise, there's too much turbulence for the system to remain stable.

Learning that I could survive my mother's rejection of me gave me an increasing ability to recognize and speak out against toxicity whenever I saw it. And with each layer of taking in the accountability, more layers of anger and grief emerged. I noticed I felt immense traction and inner momentum when I was able to process my grief and rage about the true magnitude of what actually happened to me as a child, and not put the primary focus on the secondary situation that may have triggered those feelings to come up. Often after processing my feelings about the original cause, a calm clarity emerged about next steps to take in the current situation.

My growing accountability of my history and the increasing dissolution of my "impossible dream" was increasingly positioning me to be a truth-teller and whistleblower in my personal life and in the communities I was part of. I could more easily recognize toxicity and dysfunction in everyday interactions and was using those experiences as opportunities to step more into my fierce integrity. My mother was out of my life, but the Mother Wound was still showing up. I approached each new manifestation as an opportunity to be true to myself in ways that I never could in relation to my own mother, practicing being authentic, continuing to own my part, respectfully setting firm boundaries, and staying transparent to the projections of others, all while maintaining my center and caring for my inner child. I could feel an almost visceral shift every time I did so, as though my cells were reorganizing in a new way.

Patriarchy's chief institution is the family.
—*Kate Millett*

Nothing is more important for the future of our culture than
the way children develop.
—*Gabor Maté*

When it comes to childhood wounds, the sobering truth is that love
is not enough. Love for children is not enough to prevent parents from
unconsciously wounding them. And love for our parents is not enough
to make our childhood wounds go away. This is true among friends,
partners, and colleagues, too. Even if we have the very best of intentions, our unresolved Mother Wound will determine the ceiling of our
positive impact on others. It will show us how limited our capacity is
in any given moment. Trauma will trump love.

It's not that love or good intentions don't matter. It's that loving
someone and your intention to *not* hurt them are secondary to whether
you have taken accountability for your own history. Our unconscious
will override our conscious intentions unless we have attended to it.
Whatever we refuse to see or prefer to ignore about the pain we experienced as children *will* show up in our adult relationships and be the
biggest determining factor in the level of pain and dysfunction present
in those relationships. Without insight into our histories, our relationship problems will feel like unsolvable mysteries, we'll feel ourselves to
be victims of repeating patterns, and we'll look outward, blame others,
and always feel some level of shame.

Protecting our parents from accountability is not love. Preferring
to remain blind to how they've harmed us is equivalent to permitting
harm to the next generation.

Our definition of love must expand to include accountability.

Accountability is insight and clarity about how we were harmed as
children, the myriad ways that harm impacts us now as adults, and
the steps we can take now in order to heal ourselves and care for the

child within us. In older generations, the definition of "love" included silence about our pain. But now we must expand our definition to include accountability. An alternative definition of love could be, "Being cognizant of how my childhood pain is linked to my current behavior, I commit to taking regular steps to heal and grow so that I don't unconsciously project that pain onto you."

"My mother tried her best." I hear this from many women suffering from the Mother Wound who would prefer to not look at the relationship. The reason their pain persists is because this is only *half* the picture.

The full picture is "My mother tried her best AND I suffered as a child." I see some women unconsciously trying to bypass this second part. But it is precisely this second half that allows us to mourn, heal, and ultimately move on and thrive as the women we are meant to be.

It's nearly impossible to be fully emotionally present to our children if we have not sufficiently healed our own inner child. In other words, we can be attuned and empathic to our own children to the degree that we have empathized with what we went through as children ourselves. The better we can care for our *inner* child, the better we can care for our *outer* child.

There is no blame. Ultimately, both parents and children are victims in a patriarchal culture. Both are victims of the mandate of silence; silence about our feelings and about our true experiences. However, it is only accountability that will bring greater awareness to the plight of children in our society and thus effects change for future generations. The deeper accountability that is needed is that adults heal their inner children. Otherwise, we'll continue to look at the problems of the world without truly seeing them for what they are: symptoms of the unhealed, disowned collective pain that lives within all of us.

All children are innocent. The child within us is innocent and our children are innocent. It can be heart-wrenching to see how we've harmed our children and how we've been harmed as children. But this willingness to SEE the painful truth of how we have been harmed is the only way to keep from passing it on. This willingness to be aware, the willingness to endure the pain of this awareness, is *key*. When we come to a place of accountability, our healing takes on a powerful momentum.

Accountability involves several steps:

- Account for the truth of exactly what you went through as a child and empathize with your inner child. Be sad and angry on her behalf. (In this way, you become the compassionate witness that she needed in the past.)
- See how those painful experiences impacted your life as a child and how you've had to compensate for them now as an adult.
- Take into account that as a child, you had no power over the situation. The responsible people at the time were the adults.
- Finally, become skilled at grieving the layers as they arise, and feel the reality of your own incorruptible goodness as you step into personal power.

The most powerful form of accountability is within yourself to yourself, about the facts of what you went through. Whatever happened to you as a child was not your fault. This is the liberating insight that allows you to shed the shame and redeem the child within you. But it has to be a felt insight, not just an intellectual one. You must feel it in your body. This is precisely what reconnects you to the REAL within you: your real instincts, your real feelings, your real observations.

Whether you confront your mother and/or father or not isn't primary.

It's a personal choice to hold your parents accountable by actually speaking to them directly. It can be very healing, yet timing and delivery is critical and to be considered carefully. In some situations, it's a wise choice to *not* confront directly. What is primary is that you, in your heart, have put down the burden of blaming yourself for the pain you experienced as a child. The ability of your mother/parents to see or understand you is secondary and not necessary to you moving forward. You don't have to have a harmonious relationship with them to heal yourself.

It was not your fault. This simple and profound insight takes our power back from the Mother Wound and puts our center of gravity back into ourselves. It is the antidote to the unconscious belief that the acceptance of one's family is contingent upon our willingness to accept their pain and shame as our own.

To a child, painful feelings seem to have the power to kill. They have such a threatening power that they must be suppressed. As children, we have to split in two in order *not* to feel so that we can survive. As adults, we can heal the split by giving ourselves the experience of feeling our emotions fully and realizing that these painful emotions do NOT have the power to kill us. We can discover that we are more powerful and spacious than any painful emotion. We can discover that a painful feeling does not mean we are "bad." In fact, we can learn that accessing and processing the truth of our pain is part of our goodness, our realness, and our truth.

We cannot heal from the wounds we refuse to acknowledge.

There is a high cost to not accounting for childhood wounds. Due to his/her developmental cognitive limitations, an abused child cannot help but see itself as the cause of its own wounding. This lack of awareness and lack of accountability prevents the necessary grieving that is only possible after honest adult reflection on the sobering facts of childhood experiences that caused pain. Without this grieving, the unhealed child will continue to live in the adult body, projecting its pain on others and reenacting the painful situations over and over while blaming itself.

Why do we fear accountability?

Many fear examining what they've been through because they see it as equivalent to blaming our parents; they see them as one and the same. This erroneous conflation is a symptom of the dysfunctional enmeshment that patriarchy has fostered. We must uncouple the two. This belief permits abuse to run rampant through generations. The more adults who grieve their childhood wounds fully, the more our society will no longer see accountability as a threat to the power status of the parent. Instead, parents (who have done the necessary grieving for their own childhood wounding) will see their accountability as a source of honor and pride.

Accountability brings the greater awareness necessary for meaningful change to occur.

We have the potential to really see and mourn the tragedy of how our unconscious, unhealed pain can cause us to blindly harm others without knowing it. We must have the courage to see clearly how we have been harmed *by* the unhealed pain of others and how our unhealed pain has caused *us* to harm others. Seen together, this recognition is the birth of compassion, forgiveness, and meaningful change. This recognition is the product of grieving our own pain sufficiently to the point where we understand that the behavior of others really has nothing much to do with us. How others treat us is the culmination of their own inner state. This creates a psychic space in which we no longer feel compelled to respond with reactivity or hostility to others who act out of pain. However, until we grieve our own childhood wounds, we will take the behavior of others personally, because this is the limited perspective of an unhealed child who cannot help but see itself as the cause of events. Until we grieve sufficiently, we will be compelled to repeat the pain. Mourning childhood wounds fully is a powerful act of maturity that opens the way for a new world.

Some acknowledge that while childhood wounds may be painful, they feel the angst or pain helps them be creative, eccentric, and passionate. Some fear that if they heal, they may be less quirky or lose a drive that keeps them motivated and successful as an adult. The truth is that as we heal these wounds, we don't lose what makes us unique; instead, our true creative energy is unleashed in ways that help us become truly innovative and original, allowing us to have the psychological spaciousness to see beyond the confines of family culture and into new possibilities that are beyond our perception limited by childhood wounding.

One of my challenges on my healing journey has been to trust that rest and relaxation don't leave me open to negative outcomes. This is based on the erroneous belief I developed as a child that being safe requires being always mentally hypervigilant and always striving toward the next goal. It felt very unsafe for me to relax as a child. As an adult, I've had to develop a different relationship with rest and see it as a partner in my creativity and productivity, not an obstacle to it. I remember one day I was exhausted and felt I should push myself to work toward a deadline. Instead, I took a radical step and gave myself the entire day off. I didn't do a single productive thing the entire day. I didn't zone out to Netflix or social media. I made a point to rest consciously and deeply. For a while I stared out the window watching squirrels play in the trees next to my house. For a while, I just watched the minutes go by on the digital clock. Then some grief came up, and I cried for a while. I followed my own rhythm moment to moment. All this felt incredibly soothing and comforting. I allowed myself to just BE. I was amazed that after that day of total rest, I was incredibly productive and organized in the days following, and none of the tasks felt like a burden or a slog. In fact, I felt so rested that completing mundane tasks felt fun and energizing.

Based on what I learned through reworking that pattern, I now make sure to take one full day completely off each week, and this has helped my creativity and productivity enormously. This is an example of how accounting for my childhood hypervigilance helped me break the loop of burnout. Unless we have the courage to look at these things, they can keep us trapped indefinitely in patterns that don't work.

Why Is Accountability Necessary?

Grieving is impossible without accounting for the truth of what we've been through. And grieving is precisely what reconnects us to our deeper selves and widens that space between stimulus and response, so that more possibilities and choices can be accessed.

Healing the Inner Split

When we do this work, we validate the inner child who was forced to suppress her feelings, see herself with suspicion, deny her instincts, and reject her core. This splitting is what helped her survive the unbearable truth. When we do this accounting, we become "real" again. The truth was unbearable, and we had to suppress it as children. But we must reconnect with that truth as adults in order to truly live.

The answer to personal and societal change lies in empathizing with the abused child within each of us.

In order for women to stand fully revealed in their power, we need to create a world where a child does not have to choose between her personal power and the love of her mother.

The highest act of accountability is mothering ourselves. In doing so, we cease asking others to mother us. We stop asking our children, partners, and friends to give us what they cannot. The compulsion to unconsciously reenact the pain gradually dissolves. There's no way to effectively mother ourselves without first empathizing with the truth of what we've been through. In order to do this, we have to connect with our inner child, listen to her, validate her, and allow her to grieve. This opens the way for her joy and indestructible goodness to flow into everything we do.

Questions for Reflection

1. Are there any memories or experiences from your childhood that you know would benefit from deeper exploration and healing? What about your childhood have you not yet accounted for within yourself, that if embraced and acknowledged could provide some deep relief and momentum in your current life?
2. What are some parts or aspects of yourself you had to cut yourself off from or downplay in order to be more approved of in your family?
3. What are some nourishing ways you can embrace or bring these buried traits to life in yourself now? What are some action steps you can take to begin welcoming these qualities back into your life?

GRIEVING

AS I PROCESSED THE dissolution of my family and what was starting to seem like the possible dissolution of my marriage, there were moments when I felt like I was being ground to dust. While I functioned in my day-to-day life, my inner structures felt like they were evaporating quickly, like sand slipping out of my hands. All the strategies and coping mechanisms that I had always relied on seemed useless now. The very tools I had used to make sense of myself and the world were either too painful to employ or had become obsolete. The "good girl" role felt hollow. My concern about being liked and approved of had been replaced with a raw hunger for truth. The motivation to be an overachiever "in pursuit of excellence" was gone. It felt like there was nothing to strive for anymore. And in the wake of those rotting masks and strategies, layer upon layer of anger and grief came to the surface from my earliest moments of feeling unlovable, bad, and never good enough. It began to feel like I was living life moment to moment, breath to breath.

Therapy was particularly intense at this time. In therapy with Nicole, I began working with what I called the "black hole": the raw, searing center of the Mother Wound. It felt like total internal disorganization and despair. It was always preceded by what felt like a familiar melody of doom that had played faintly in the background for my entire life, composed of confusion, self-doubt, and exhaustion. In my daily life, I usually avoided this feeling or numbed out. But recently it had begun to assert itself in my everyday existence. I was confused by this progression: I had had moments of intense clarity and freedom, but now I was being plunged into deep despair.

Nicole explained to me that the more healed you become, the more trauma you become capable of processing. It's a different form of progress than we typically imagine. We assume we will go in a straight line toward "better," but in healing trauma, it's more like a spiral or a wave. This spiral involves frequent regressions during which one repeatedly confronts echoes of traumatic material while very gradually developing the capacity to digest, integrate, and evolve beyond old traumatic narratives, beliefs, emotions, behaviors, and ways of being and relating.

During one therapy session, I told Nicole, "I can feel the black hole approaching. This sense of being stalked by a malicious force."

She said, "Well, let's bring it out into the open, let's get a good look at it. I'm right here with you. You're safe. Let's look at this together."

I asked, "Are you sure? This feels like if I look at it, it will kill me. If I open to this, it will surely destroy me."

She replied, "Yes, I'm sure. I've got you. You're safe."

OK, here goes, I thought.

I allowed the feelings to wash over me. It felt like falling into an abyss. Nicole asked me what I was experiencing as I wept. I spoke from this place and said, "I'm so bad. I want to die. I'm the most awful, bad, horrendous, horrible being. I'm hideous." And then it moved to a deeper place, as if I was actually speaking to my mother. "I can't make my needs go away. Please don't leave me. I've tried, but I can't stop needing. I want to kill me so you'll love me. I'm so bad. I hate me." I was witnessing the self-abandonment and suppressing of my soul that I had to go through to maintain the bond with my mother.

The traumatic aloneness, the terror, the helplessness, the sense of never-ending doom, the sense of self-hatred, the longing for my mother. While I was speaking and weeping, I felt the most intense powerlessness and loss of hope, as if every cell of my being had been permeated by despair. Somehow the feeling of another person being there with me helped me to stay present with it. Nicole reassured me multiple times that I was safe, that she was with me. "You're not alone. You're safe." My legs were shaking the entire time. I just allowed the feelings, the words, to come out as they wanted to and my body to shake as much as it needed to. It seemed to come in waves. There would be an intense movement of weeping, words, and shaking, and then a deep stillness for a minute or two, and then it would start again. There were no pictures; it felt preverbal, or from a time in the first few years of my life, like a shadow that had been stored in the deep recesses of my being ever since.

During one of the brief periods of stillness, I was taking a deep breath when I became aware of a palpable benevolent presence around the pain; a pure, clear, loving awareness that was witnessing the pain and yet was undisturbed and unfettered by it. I then saw that this benevolence was my own essence, my very existence, and included both the excruciating pain and the vast, loving, tender awareness that surrounded it. This visceral recognition felt so liberating.

This emotion of complete despair did not kill me as I feared it might. I was standing on the ground of my deepest pain . . . and I was alive! This moment was a powerful turning point in my journey.

> Pain is important: how we evade it, how we succumb to it, how
> we deal with it, how we transcend it.
> —*Audre Lorde*

Sitting with our pain is such a simple act, and yet it can be one of the hardest things to do.

Feeling our pain and not rushing in to fix it, numb it, avoid it, or cover it up takes enormous courage. This is where surrender comes in. We reach a point in our healing where we've read all the books, consulted all the gurus, or tried all the fancy techniques, and all that is left is the last thing we want to do: feel our painful feelings. Ironically, sitting with our pain is precisely what will eventually bring us all the things we were looking for through avoiding it.

A major key to healing emotional wounding is the willingness to endure discomfort for the sake of transformation. This willingness is essential to truly coming out on the other side of childhood wounds.

Discomfort can come in many forms:

- Being misunderstood by family members.
- Sitting with your own pain and just feeling it and allowing it to be there.
- Going through periods of anger and outrage as you wake up to the reality of how you suffered as a child.
- Letting grief come up and not knowing when it will pass.
- Having low energy or a feeling of being lost and unsure.
- Allowing yourself to be vulnerable and receive support from others.
- Alienation from people with whom you used to be close.

Our culture promotes the idea of immediate gratification and instant results. It takes enormous courage and strength to stick with the unglamorous process of healing that has a timeline of its own. In addition to the cultural component, there are also the survival instincts within us that tell us to fight or take flight when we feel threatened. That is why having support in the healing process is essential.

To an unhealed inner child, the only way it knows how to soothe itself is to act in accordance with the patterns that were imprinted by the family of origin—usually the precise patterns that are causing the pain. This keeps us trapped in a loop. The answer is to cultivate the skill of inner mothering and soothing our inner child while we make new choices that better reflect our true desires and needs. This inner bond is what helps us to effectively separate from family and cultural patterns that cause suffering.

For many of us, growing up involved a series of self-betrayals in which we had no choice but to create an inner split in order to survive. The split usually involved some form of numbing our feelings and rejecting ourselves in order to be accepted by our families. Healing involves the recovery of our ability to fully feel our feelings and thus to feel and express the truth of who we are without shame.

Eventually the longing and hunger for living your truth overshadows all other desires, including the desire to be free of pain.

This hunger for truth is trustworthy and will lead you to what you need in each moment. And sometimes what you need is to embrace yet another level of inner pain. The moments of relief and bliss that open up through having embraced your pain make it all worth it. Over and over we learn that the act of embracing and being present with our pain is what connects us with the larger truth of who we are.

A new inner space will be created where you have permission to live from the REAL.

As we do the inner work, eventually a conviction arises: a quickening, a hunger, and a fierce commitment to living one's truth. As we increasingly face the truth of what we experienced as children and how it's impacted our lives, a desire develops to live each moment from within the fire of your original self. Each moment begins to represent a new, fresh opportunity to live from simple, open awareness of what is.

We see that awareness itself is an embrace.

We start on the painful periphery. As we become increasingly skilled in enduring discomfort and uncertainty, we discover the potential to merge with the holy presence that lives at the center of our pain, and realize that is the truth of who we are.

Many of us have a feeling of homesickness deep within, a nameless longing and aching grief. Many of us experienced this feeling of being groundless and adrift as children in relation to our mothers. Embracing the homesick feeling within the Mother Wound leads us to eventually come to a place where we realize that we can never be truly abandoned. This becomes possible when we become a loving inner mother to our inner child as we embrace her deepest despair.

In that despair is a door; a door to our source, the unified consciousness in which we are one with all.

In this way, our pain is a messenger telling us it's time to come home to the primordial home within, which is the realization of our true identity as consciousness, the knowing that we are spirit and can never be truly harmed or abandoned because we are one with all.

Feeling our pain is what allows us to become liberated from it.

By sitting with our pain and bringing tenderness and acceptance to it, we begin to recognize that the pain we have felt is not the truth of who we really are. We begin to see that the open, loving presence we embody as we embrace our own pain is who we are, our true identity underneath all our other identities. The culmination of living as a "self" is to live as the "no-self": the vast, generous space that lovingly witnesses our pain and embraces it completely.

Through that primary, holy wound, we are called to become that loving mother to ourselves . . . and to all life.

As we embody the unconditional love of the inner mother, we become reconnected to life itself. We become reconnected to the birthless and deathless center that is constantly being born and dying in countless forms. This is the evolutionary step that lies within the pain of the Mother Wound.

As women, we grow up believing that a holy power lies *outside* of ourselves, and in the healing process, we start to realize that what we most desire, that which is most holy, eternal, and pure, is *inside* of us and has always been there. In fact, it *is* us. Not just in one or some of us, but living equally in all of us, in all life.

Because we are all connected, each time we lovingly embrace our own pain, we activate the power of oneness in all.

Grieving is how we emotionally process our experiences and move beyond them. To our culture, which is obsessed with productivity and perfection, the experience of grief, its sadness, anger, and feelings of loss, can feel like taking steps backward or being in a stuck place. But that is an illusion. Grief is the great accelerator.

According to physician and author Gabor Maté, as humans, we have two primary needs: the need for attachment and the need for authenticity. In dysfunctional families, a child will typically suppress his or her authenticity needs to preserve the attachment with the primary caregiver, typically the mother.

The primary human need is attachment. Left unaddressed, our attachment wounds will persist into our adult lives and may cause us to unconsciously arrange our lives around not triggering the emotional memory of traumatic aloneness. This is what can keep us stuck in relationships, jobs, or situations that we need to move on from.

The need to suppress authenticity to preserve attachment creates an "either/or" mind-set that can stay with us and get projected onto other parts of our lives. The healing comes from mending this split so that both authenticity needs *and* attachment needs can be abundantly met within ourselves, and subsequently in our relationships.

This reunion in the self opens us up to the possibility of perceiving an even larger "and," the larger bond of love and belonging that pervades all life.

Authenticity needs: The experience of having our real selves being seen, accepted, and validated, including our:

- Flaws and limitations.
- Failures and mistakes.
- Quirks and idiosyncrasies.
- Gifts and talents.
- Greatness and uniqueness.

Attachment needs: The needs for love, safety, and belonging, including:

- Being seen and responded to with kindness.
- Being emotionally held.
- Feeling a sense of belonging to a dyad and larger groups.
- Physical touch and affection.
- Being supported and understood.
- Feeling emotionally safe.

We don't have many models for what it looks like to persevere on this healing journey, and many stop prematurely. A crucial piece is the willingness to be present with our own pain. As humans it's natural to want to avoid pain, but usually the avoidance of pain is more painful than the actual pain. That's why support is so crucial. The wound begins in relationship, and the ultimate healing occurs in relationship as well.

Without accompanying resistance from a mental storyline, emotional pain can be deeply cleansing, clarifying, and liberating.

When the pain of that original aloneness of childhood is contacted and felt, there arises a powerful sense of *ground*. When we can stand conscious and face our own emotional pain, we are standing on the bedrock of self. There is immense relief in realizing that you are feeling the deep pain of the core wound and that you are alive. The emotional pain that you feared might destroy you has only birthed you into the realization of your vastness, into seeing that you are larger than any painful emotion.

There's a difference between despair and grief. Despair is when we are reliving the pain of our past as though it is happening in the present. It's the projection of our pain of the past onto a current situation. It's the pain of the inner child without a loving adult witness. You can tell when this is happening by looking at your mental narrative alongside the emotional pain you're experiencing. In despair, the narrative is usually negative, focused on how bad things are and how there's no hope. This is the narrative of a child experiencing pain alone without support. When we are in despair, the inner child is abandoned again and again as we replicate this childhood pattern within ourselves.

Grief is different. Grief transpires when a loving adult consciousness is present alongside the pain, a narrative of loving presence, a feeling of "I'm with you in this pain. You're not alone. This is the pain of the past. It's safe to feel it now. I've got you. I'm sorry you suffered so much and were so alone. It's safe to feel this and let go of this pain." Through this act of empathizing with our own pain, the presence of this inner consciousness allows us to digest the pain, to move through it into a place of increasing lightness and freedom.

Do you remember your little child self? The one who conversed with bees, flowers, and butterflies? By facing the pain within you, you reclaim the little child waiting for you within. Your presence in the pain opens a door, for her innocence, vitality, playfulness, creativity, laughter, and wisdom to flow into your life again.

In that moment of staying conscious in the face of your own pain, it's possible to glimpse a larger you, the you that is part of all things. And to sense her mind-shattering compassion that has always already loved you in every nook and cranny of your life. You can see that nothing has ever been separate from her love.

The Mother Wound can be a portal to realizing a deeper, indestructible "attachment" bond that interconnects all life.

By being willing to stay conscious in the pain of it, a veil is lifted.

Every bit of emotional pain that you courageously face births you into a more robust expression of the *real*.

Over time, we realize that the ultimate security does not come from what the mind tells us, but from living from that raw, open, real core of presence within us; that core "ground" that is revealed in the center of our own pain. Over time, perhaps over a lifetime, we become increasingly accepting that safety does not come from struggle or mental activity, but from a raw, open not-knowing that can only guide us from moment to moment. Through this we are able to access both childlike wonder and the depth and wisdom that has been carved out by the radical integrity of facing our own pain.

This radical integrity is the foundation upon which we build our lives of authenticity and service to the whole.

It's a paradox that by entering our deepest aloneness, the traumatic aloneness of childhood, we have the chance to see that we've never been separated from the divine. The whole world then becomes our secure base for exploration. This safety is so vast, this embrace is eternal. You can begin to identify with this aspect of your being and practice embracing whatever arises inside with a gentle, loving curiosity.

Life becomes a series of infinite sheddings down to the real.

Metabolizing your own pain makes you capable of embodying a more potent level of truth. As you embody this, you are serving those around you in a profound way.

Your deep authenticity, your originality, your eccentricity, is the most potent and exhilarating expression of the divine. Ironically, the very things that we had to suppress as children often become the vehicles through which the divine seeks to express itself through us.

The truth is that your own presence is one with the presence of the divine.

You don't have to do or be anything in particular for this to be true. You already are and always have been infinitely accepted and thoroughly loved by the divine. This becomes viscerally self-evident in your direct experience over time. At first, it's in glimpses, but those glimpses begin to expand until it gradually, over time, becomes your primary mode of being.

Feeling Safe in Your Originality and Owning Your Sovereignty

The painful emotions of the Mother Wound serve to help you shed the layers of dysfunctional adaptations from your childhood and to reach the living core of fire within you . . . and to increasingly walk in the world as the light that frees.

In this way, the Mother Wound is a teacher. As we heal, it transforms from a source of pain into a source of wisdom. Facing the pain doesn't annihilate us as the ego would purport, but instead births us into a new relationship with life, from separation to oneness. That presence within us, the "inner beloved," is inviting us in each moment into deeper communion with it, to hand over our masks, our falseness, our reliance on the mind, and our defenses and live life from an undefended intimacy.

When a new level of pain presents itself to be processed, we can increasingly see it as the inner beloved beckoning to us to merge with it in the fire of truth, to shed down yet another layer into oneness with the all, to realize the vast embrace where absolutely nothing is left out.

On a deeper level, the Mother Wound is a wound with life itself. And as we heal it on the personal level, we step into something universal. As we detox from the cultural and familial messages, our life force gets rinsed of painful defenses and a new space is created within us to radiate powerful energies that benefit all life.

How Do We Live This Every Day?

The truth is shattering to the ego. It is counter to everything that our culture has taught us. In fact, our culture is designed to distract us from the very investigations that are necessary to realize this in our direct experience. It takes courage and radical integrity to really *live* this. But there is nothing more nourishing or exhilarating.

From the real, our most powerful place is one of the unglamorous facing of our feelings in each moment.

- Facing our pain, taking the time to process, investigate, and gain insight.
- Seeing our adaptive defenses and choosing to remain open.
- Embracing our places of shame and actively practicing self-love.
- In terms of productivity, acting only when inspired; otherwise, rest.
- Scrutinizing our moments of falseness and choosing to be real.
- Working in each moment to not flee into the concepts of "final, done, destination."

Healing the Mother Wound takes time. It's common for people to reach places of intense discomfort and think, *What am I doing wrong? I thought I was healing, but I feel miserable! When is the pain going to end?!* It's at this point that people can get down on themselves, get distracted, or doubt their ability to heal. Yet it's also at this place that it's important not to give up, to hang on and get the necessary support to keep going.

A common misconception is that people who are "evolved" never feel challenging emotions like rage, anger, grief, or jealousy. I'd say quite the opposite. Being awake, aware, and centered means embodying the benevolent space for the full spectrum of emotions to emerge and be seen without judgment. Emotional intelligence comes from the ability to feel all kinds of emotions without getting stuck or identified with any of them. One could say we have the ability to become emotionally "fluent."

As children, we needed outer approval to survive, but as adults, the approval we must find is our own.

My sense is that the true gift of the pain of being unseen is having no choice but to find and claim one's worth within oneself first, without getting the approval or validation of others. In doing so, a singularity of spirit emerges. This strength can only emerge after a sufficient amount of grieving has been done; feeling healthy outrage on behalf of the child you were, grieving for what you legitimately needed that you did not receive, accepting that it was not your fault, seeing that the unconscious wounds of your parent/caretaker were the cause and were always completely out of your control. When we follow our grief where it takes us, our hearts break open to a compassion for all people, for all life. Grief doesn't weaken or deplete us, it restores, fortifies, and renews us.

Grieving Is an Expression of Self-Ownership

Have you ever felt the joy and relief that comes from feeling a difficult emotion all the way through? That sense of clearing, of a weight lifted, a sense of freshness and newness? Every difficult emotion offers us this transformation. Many of us did not grow up learning that all emotions eventually run their course and come to completion. Because the adults around us were often afraid of emotions, we may have been cajoled, distracted, or shamed out of them. The truth is that all emotions are temporary. When embraced and allowed, they always pass.

We must realize that it's necessary for a deconstruction to take place within us. By virtue of living in a patriarchal culture, we've had to internalize structures and beliefs that are actually *built to prevent* our empowerment and self-realization as women. So, without this necessary deconstruction and the discomfort it brings, no authentic transformation can take place. That's why I'm so passionate about being brutally honest about the fact that this work takes a long time *and* emphasizing that each woman is worth the time and effort it takes to do this work.

If we continue on the path of healing the Mother Wound, something truly miraculous and profound may begin to awaken within us. We may become aware of our own presence in a palpable way, perhaps a presence that feels familiar. It may feel like a divine longing, a bliss, a source within us that is always there, and always has been there from the beginning. We may begin to realize its power as an overflowing emanation from within, the core true self, the source of all. What results in this stage is knowing. Knowing your divine nature gradually dawns in your being, and with it a sense that you have within you a source of love that is always there, always available.

In order to fully let go, we first need to feel fully supported. We have to first make sure we have a safe environment in our lives to support this work. In my opinion, the most ideal environment for the support of this work has three elements simultaneously; however, while ideal, this is not necessary for everyone. Each of these elements are wonderful on their own, but together they form a powerful base of support that can move you through the Mother Wound to the other side. You may experience one or more at different times of your journey.

1. **Long-term individual psychotherapy** with a relationally based therapist who deeply resonates with you and has years of experience in attachment wounds and complex developmental trauma. This allows you to go deep into the emotional processing that needs to happen to create meaningful change in early patterns and beliefs. It can take a while to find the right therapist so patience is important. (And we need more therapists to do this deeper work themselves so that they can help others go to this level of depth of healing and transformation.)

2. **Coaching with a competent, compassionate mentor/coach** who has already been through many years of healing herself and continues on her own path to the present day. This person supports you to take action on the shifts and insights that happen as you process and heal the Mother Wound. This is the service I provide through my private mentoring.

3. **A supportive, stable community** that fosters safety, authenticity, and transparency. This could be an informal group of friends or a formal community that meets regularly with the intention of supporting each other's unfoldment. The important thing is that the group is long-standing, reliable, trauma-informed, and consistently available.

The courageous, lifelong commitment to healing is not a reason to judge yourself; it's a cause for deep self-respect. This healing process is done over time, step-by-step, tenderly, gently, and with compassion.

Modern society tends to judge those who do long-term therapy or coaching as being somehow flawed and maladjusted. I encourage you to refuse to buy into this. The truth is that it usually *does* take many years of inner work to heal intergenerational wounding, most especially if we're on the more acute end of the spectrum of childhood trauma. I've seen myself and others try to do it alone, and frankly, that is just postponement of doing what is really required.

Longing for relief from pain is natural. It is human. But if we are to truly mature as a species and truly heal, we must change our focus from *seeking relief away from our wounds* and instead seek relief through *the transformation of ourselves through them.*

We don't grow and evolve through hating our wounds or judging our pain. We grow through the embrace of our pain and by realizing that no painful emotion can harm us. That deep seeing is only possible through letting go of attachment to being "done," surrendering to the process, and getting professional support. This powerful shift in mind-set toward one's own healing journey is crucial to really harvesting the gifts of a life consciously lived.

Your desire for ongoing healing isn't pathological; it is a deeply healthy and life-giving impulse. The tendency to judge ourselves for our wounds is deeply embedded in the culture and our families. We may feel like an outsider or as though there's something wrong with us. But the truth is that the people seeking healing and growth are often the healthiest people in a dysfunctional family system.

Specialized support is required to keep the necessary mind-set toward our process to truly come out the other side and abundantly harvest the gifts of our ongoing growth.

Stop making relief from the pain your main goal. Stop pushing yourself to be "done." Start seeing the wound as a portal to your power.

The more you heal the Mother Wound, the more you can consciously embody your own divine nature.

It's as though the healing process clears out all the limiting debris we've accumulated in our families and in the culture. And as we clear out, there is more space for us to hold the energy of our true essence, and to embody our identities as divine beings, capable of bringing forward new ideas and solutions to the world that is in a time of great transition.

While this work of healing generational wounds is challenging, overwhelming, and lonely at times, it is a privilege to be conscious enough to do this work. So many of our ancestors pushed their pain down, and it crippled them in many ways. Now we are blessed with the consciousness and the tools to heal our wounds.

Questions for Reflection

1. What feelings do you tend to avoid or downplay in yourself, which, if embraced and felt, would greatly lighten your emotional load?

2. If you feel inspired, the next time this challenging emotion arises, visualize yourself calmly embracing that emotion with sincerity and affection. Are there any supports you can put in place to support that experience?

3. What were your authenticity needs as a child? What were your attachment needs? In what ways did you have to suppress your authenticity needs to secure your attachment with your mother/caretakers? What are some ways you can give those suppressed authenticity needs some expression and support now?

Chapter 13

DISCOVERING THE INNER MOTHER

DAVID AND I HAD *grown apart over the years and decided to end our marriage, but agreed to remain friends. I was relieved that the divorce process was going relatively smoothly. During this time my therapy continued to deepen and focused on grieving my illusions, my losses, and the old narrative of my childhood history. I was also getting more skilled in working with my younger traumatized parts, soothing and regulating them, and taking more responsibility for my internal self-system. I was proud of how my then seventeen years of therapy had helped me love myself enough to make choices that, while unpopular and unconventional, reflected my true self and my true desires. With my marriage officially over, the possibilities for my life felt wide open.*

At this time, there was no communication coming from my mother, father, brother, or anyone else in my family. My writing was getting more exposure on global platforms, on podcasts, and in magazines. I became trained as a coach and developed my own seven-step process to support other women in healing the Mother Wound. While not traveling I was spending time at home, running my business and being with friends. I started hosting women's "new moon circle" potlucks at my house to connect with other women, which was vital nourishment for me.

I had been on the path of learning to be my own inner mother, and this newfound inner safety and growing inner resilience created the possibility for me to find the kind of romantic relationship I had always wanted and deserved. After about a year of being single after the divorce, I found myself with the desire to be in a relationship with another powerful woman and a sense that it would open my life up to all kinds of possibilities. It felt like the natural next step on my journey.

I met one of my best friends, J., through doing environmental activism locally, and had been friends for over four years at this point. J. was an out lesbian and old soul who seemed, to all who knew her, wise beyond her years. She came to my potlucks, and we enjoyed swimming, going out to dinner, and dancing together. She had been single for a couple of years and, like me, was determined not to settle for anything but "the real thing."

I realized I had been falling in love with J. for some time but feared losing our close, long-standing friendship. One night, after we went swimming at a nearby lake, I revealed my feelings for her. While she was also scared to jeopardize our friendship, we agreed to take the risk together, and committed to stepping into a romantic relationship with clear and open communication.

Part of healing the Mother Wound and healing from patriarchy is that we begin to feel safe enough to disregard the patriarchal norms we were raised with and to be more authentic, and our relationships can reflect a new level of safety, love, and openness that we've created within ourselves. For me, the journey toward my authentic self meant saying no to the old ways of my family system and finding new strength and fortitude to say yes to a new way of being. With J., in our first embrace as a couple, I viscerally felt a door open within myself and to a whole new world that my former self would never have considered possible.

During the first year J. and I were together, I wept often. So many things were coming together for me. New insights, realizations, and deeper truths, about myself, my Mother Wound, and the influence of patriarchal culture on women, were constantly emerging.

Through being in a healthy, supportive, romantic relationship with a woman, and the particular woman that J. is, I was discovering my erotic power, not as something purely sexual, but as an essential part of my power as a female human being. This included intellectual, spiritual, visceral felt experience, humor, playfulness, and undefended transparency. It felt as though my being had expanded into more of my true self, beyond my family, and beyond patriarchal norms. I felt like I was experiencing what it would be like to live in a nonpatriarchal world. Through the safe container of our trust, I saw my understanding and experience of myself blossom in ways that had never been possible before. With heteronormative roles removed, I felt more free to be more fully myself, with a fluency of masculine and feminine energies, moment to moment, without the same level of expectations, stereotypes, and obligations that many heterosexual relationships engender.

I had the space to reflect on how patriarchy and relationships with men had affected me and my sense of self throughout my life. Things that I had considered to be "the way things are" were revealed to be old relics purely rooted in the norms of heteronormative patriarchy, not relationships in general. One of my biggest epiphanies was that my role as "dismantler of walls" wasn't just endemic to being in a romantic relationship; it was part and parcel to being in a relationship with men, at least the wide range of men I had been with. That role was not needed at all in my relationship with J., and this was stunning to me. The duty of deciphering how to emotionally connect with someone, to find a way to bring them out of their shell, and to coax them into connection, which I considered an inevitable part of partnership—had evaporated, leaving an enormous spaciousness. The level of reciprocity, clear communication, and depth of emotional connection with J. was beyond what I imagined to be possible in a relationship. I wept because of how much I blamed myself in the past for "not getting it right," for exhausting myself by taking the high road, for convincing myself that I was fulfilled in relationships when I hadn't been.

I had entered a world of women, from my partner, to my colleagues to friends, to the authors of books I read, to the musicians I listened to. As I entered that world of women more intentionally, the distance from men gave me the space to admit to myself how exhausted I was from years of propping them up, fighting for crumbs of respect, and the constant gymnastics of pleasing, enticing, decoding, bearing the burdens, shrinking, and contorting myself to create a modicum of connection—and, most painful of all, believing that that was my role, my place, the best I could hope for. I hadn't been conscious of just how taxing and fatiguing it was to maintain relationships with the men in my life. Finally I was strong enough psychologically to admit to myself just how bad it really had been and to grieve.

All romantic relationships have honeymoon periods followed by a stage of differentiation, a time of defining one's individuality within the relationship. The bliss and expansion of the honeymoon stage with J. began to give way to an uncomfortable time of increasing tension between us. This time of differentiation presented very unique challenges for me due to my template for attachment that had originated through the dynamics with my mother.

Because J. and I had such a strong emotional connection, it offered me an opportunity to heal more of my Mother Wound, in particular a specific aspect of it that had so far remained untouched. Up to this point I had done an incredible amount of healing around the abandonment side of my Mother Wound through developing a loving, supportive inner mother to soothe and reassure my inner child from that original devastating abandonment of my childhood and the triggers that ensued from emotionally unavailable partners who, up to that point, had all been men. However, I hadn't yet addressed the invasion side of my Mother Wound, largely because I did not feel like my previous partners were emotionally engaged with me enough for that aspect of the wound to even be triggered.

J. and I embarked on a journey of loving one another and seeing our relationship as a sanctuary for more of our own healing and transformation. Because I had never been able to emotionally differentiate from my primary attachment figure, my mother, it was very challenging for me to navigate the differentiation stage with J., my female primary attachment figure as an adult.

I had learned from a young age, through my relationship with my mother, what I call a "template of emotional servitude" for relationships. To preserve a primary connection, I would "submerge and merge," meaning submerge my own feelings and merge with the other person, prioritizing their needs and desires over my own. I had learned that my sense of separateness, autonomy, and boundaries was shameful and cause for rejection, humiliation, and withdrawal. Over time, I began to see how automatic and almost invisible this dynamic was in my relationship with J. Because I didn't feel entitled to set boundaries early and often, I would "submerge and merge" with her and then resentment would build, causing me to feel invaded and burdened, and I'd collapse into exhaustion. Through lots of inner work and couples therapy, I discovered that my anger wasn't really at J., but at both my mother and the patriarchy as a whole, which taught me the illusion that I must suppress my need for boundaries and abandon myself to preserve my connection with my primary female attachment figure.

Continuing to heal my own inner parentified child meant embracing my anger as legitimate AND setting firm boundaries early and often, things my mother would never tolerate from me. J.'s loving encouragement of my boundaries was incredibly healing. Over time I have increasingly embodied an inner "non-patriarchal" mother who not only comforts and soothes my inner child, but who also protects and expands the freedom of my inner child as well.

One of the most empowering things I've realized is the difference between what true empathy is and what it isn't. I discovered this through witnessing myself getting defensive and impatient when J. would be in deep emotional pain. One time J. was expressing how she longed for more quality time with me and how she felt distant from me. As she was vulnerably explaining this through her tears, I noticed that I was feeling increasingly angry and ashamed. I realized I was interpreting her sadness and need for empathy as a demand on me to be inferior to her, and my anger was acting as a form of self-protection. As she and I worked through this, I began to realize that this response was linked to how, as a child, I equated empathy for my mother with "emotional annihilation" of myself.

As a child, my mother's emotional demands felt linked to a shameful shortcoming in myself as I could never solve things for her, and thus, never get any empathy for myself. It was a powerless situation for any child to be in. I remember one particular time I visited home from college, during a period I was really struggling with depression. Almost immediately after I walked through the door, my mother began talking about herself, what things she was stressed about at work and how she was considering divorcing my father. I remember sitting there listening to her, aware of my own inner suffering being unimportant to her, and realizing that I was being used. I saw how I was being related to as an object she was using for her own relief, how unaware she was of this, and how alone I had always been in the relationship. I felt a despair, exhaustion, and hopelessness wash over me. Her demand for my empathy felt like quicksand suffocating me, with no end, no relief, and no reciprocity in sight.

Through mothering my inner child and grieving how deeply I had to abandon myself in the face of my mother's emotional demands, I've discovered that true empathy is not a place of subordination or servitude as I once experienced. Empathy does not include fixing problems, carrying the pain of another as our own, accommodating their illusions or silencing oneself. True empathy comes from a place of calm inner power, from a place of separateness, inner sovereignty, and safety within oneself. As I began to feel more deeply established in my own inner separateness within my relationship with J., I've been able to be much more empathic, to really see her and hold her in her pain with love, affirmation, and acceptance. And because I'm no longer equating empathy for her with a loss for myself, I'm able to be present to her without agendas of self-protection or self-preservation. It's been amazing to realize that empathy does not perpetuate dependency in another, but creates a space for the other person to feel their own inner power and strength, which actually clears obstacles to connection. In this way both people get to feel separate AND seen, singular AND connected.

In the container of my relationship with J., I'm so grateful for how I've been able to identify and transform so many painful traumatic scripts from childhood and for us to continue to heal and grow together as a couple. Relationships are truly the ground on which we create these new lived experiences, going beyond the "maternal horizon," and into our own individuated, liberated adult landscape.

And the Great Mother said:
Come my child and give me all that you are.
I am not afraid of your strength and darkness, of your fear and
    pain.
Give me your tears. They will be my rushing rivers and roaring
    oceans.
Give me your rage.
It will erupt into my molten volcanoes and rolling thunder.
Give me your tired spirit. I will lay it to rest in my soft meadows.
Give me your hopes and dreams. I will plant a field of sunflowers
    and arch rainbows in the sky. You are not too much for me.
My arms and heart welcome your true fullness.
There is room in my world for all of you, all that you are.
I will cradle you in the boughs of my ancient redwoods and the
    valleys of my gentle rolling hills. My soft winds will sing you
    lullabies and soothe your burdened heart.
Release your deep pain.
You are not alone and you have never been alone.
—Linda Reuther, from "Homecoming," a poem featured in Her Words,
    edited by Burleigh Mutén

The mother-daughter relationship lives within us as adults. Our mother's voice can be the voice of support and encouragement, and it can also be the voice of the critic in our head—keeping us feeling stuck, discouraged, and doubtful. Our task as we heal the Mother Wound is to transform our inner mother from a duplicate of our human mother—with her limitations—into the mother we always wanted: an inner mother who can accurately and abundantly meet our needs, and who can support us as we flourish and love ourselves for who we truly are. We create this unconditionally loving mother on the inside through consistent dialogue with our inner child while actively increasing our ability to care, nurture, and comfort our child selves. Over time, inner mother and inner child form a safe inner bond, which fills the gap of mothering that we did not receive from our own mothers. In this way, the primary attachment bond is no longer with our "outer mother" but with our inner mother, bringing enormous freedom and vitality. We cease searching for this foundational love on the outside because we are finding it within. This takes the pressure off the other people in our life to fill a hole in us that is impossible for them to fill, allowing us to be more present and less defensive in our relationships. It also creates enough inner security for us to be more fully expressive, inventive, bravely original, boldly true, and honest with ourselves and other people.

Many people don't realize that what we ultimately want is our *own* love, which is truly infinite and without limit. The reason it seems that, as adults, we still want our mother's love is because a mother's love is what gives a child *permission to love herself.* When we mourn the loss of the chance to get that permission from our mothers (because we can't go back to childhood), it gives us our power back. We see that it is not our inner child's fault that her mother couldn't give her what she needed. Believing it was your fault was a way of hanging on to the false hope that your mother would one day change into the mother you needed. Understanding the truth—that your mother will not change, and that her wounds are not your fault—shifts the primary mother from outer to inner and gives us a second chance to get the mothering we missed.

Inner mothering is a skill that can be learned and, with practice, can create a whole new relationship within. Through inner mothering, we experience firsthand that our childhood is not our destiny, but merely the soil we were born into, which can be transformed. Inner mothering enables us to form a deep well of inner safety that allows us to reach into our greater potential.

We mother our inner child by consciously making new choices that we couldn't make in the past, and in doing so receive emotional nutrients that replace earlier deficits. For example, someone who was shamed for speaking her mind as a child can shift this pattern by taking the risk to speak her mind as an adult, even if it feels uncomfortable, in order to experience a different outcome. When we act counter to the original pattern and have a different experience than we did as a child (perhaps by being supported rather than shamed for speaking our minds), our inner child gets the message that things are different now.

If others respond similarly to how our parents once did, with perhaps some level of rejection or withdrawal, the inner mother aspect of you can always show up differently, with more support and affirmation. This makes every experience an opportunity to rewrite the past and, in doing so, open up new possibilities for the future. This new outcome demonstrates that you are not frozen in the past, stuck in that pattern, but that you, as an adult, are capable of new experiences of yourself and life.

Creating an inner bond starts with the willingness to dialogue with your inner child on a regular basis. Depending on the level of trauma you experienced when you were a child, your inner child may be reluctant to trust you at first, and it may take time for her to open up to you. Even just a little dialogue every day over time reaps massive returns in the form of physical energy, positive emotions, and general well-being. Over time, your inner child will begin to trust you more and more. Be persistent, and you will be amazed at the results.

The Role of Triggers and Self-Honesty as True Safety

Emotional triggers indicate that we have projected old fears or patterns onto others around us. They signify an emotional flashback coming up for the inner child, a pocket of trauma that is ready to be processed, digested, and healed. Triggers offer the opportunity to inquire into what unhealed pattern from the past has been activated so that it can be healed and released. Many of us fear that if we become the powerful women we're meant to be, then we will be a threat to those around us. We may hide our light so as not to offend others or trigger their insecurities. The child in us fears that claiming our full individuality will cause us to be left alone. Understandably, this aloneness was very threatening to us as children. But there is a different kind of aloneness that we may find in adulthood, an aloneness that is a kind of nourishment.

To some degree, we're always operating in the tension between evolution and safety or individuality and belonging. Attachment theorist John Bowlby introduced the concept of how children use their mothers as a secure base for exploration. If the mother conveys sufficient safety to the child through her attunement to the child, the child feels safe enough to venture out and explore the environment. We must transfer our source of safety from the outside to the inside.

The Miraculous Power of "Presence Alongside the Pain"

As inner mothers, we're not trying to make our pain go away. We're not rushing the inner child out of her feelings, as our mothers or other adults may have done. We embody a loving presence alongside the pain, and we allow the feelings to be there as long as they need to be. The old neurocircuitry must be activated in order to be reworked.

We can't do this all in our heads; we have to feel it to heal it. Only in that original emotional activation is it possible to heal and rework that traumatic response. In the moment, the inner mother can provide a loving, benevolent presence that says, "I see you. I'm with you in this pain. You're safe, even though you're feeling this emotional pain. Let's allow this pain to be here. And let's do something soothing. How about we take a walk or put some lotion on our hands or look out the window at the trees?" Doing something physical and simple *with* the pain there helps the inner child to experience, in a visceral way, that she is safe in the present.

Below are what I consider the main pillars of inner mothering. With consistency over time, they begin to fill the mother gap and build trust between the inner mother and inner child. At different times some of these pillars may be more needed than others as you heal through different layers of your Mother Wound.

Pillars of Inner Mothering

Acceptance of Emotions: Accepting feelings that arise and embracing them with empathy and a loving curiosity.

Comfort: Consistently comforting the child, doing things that help the child feel nurtured, comforted, and safe. This means physical comfort as well as emotional comfort.

Freedom: Giving the child time and space to feel her own energy, to receive things she wants, to follow her own rhythms, like when to start things and when to stop doing things.

Play: Giving the child time to use her imagination, feel unencumbered, laugh, delight, and enjoy life.

Structure: Providing the child with the sense that you are a safe, reliable, and consistent container of support. Having predictable routine to some degree.

Consistent Communication: Regularly checking in on her and reassuring her, letting her know she matters, and listening to her, asking her questions, and having your actions be consistent with your words. Gaps in communication are opportunities to repair past ruptures from our childhoods.

Listening: Listening to the fears or worries that she may have and quickly responding with reassurance, empathy, and evidence that she's safe. Example: "Tell me everything you're angry about. I want to hear all about it. I'm here for you."

Discipline: Proactively doing things on a regular basis that benefit the inner child as well as your adult self. This can mean things like making doctor's appointments, and getting enough sleep.

Some examples of affirming things you can say to your inner child are:

- "I'm so glad you were born!"
- "You are thoroughly good and wonderful."
- "You are lovable and special."
- "You are safe."
- "I respect you."
- "I am so proud of you."
- "I'm so happy you are here!"
- "You can do it!"
- "I'm right here for you whenever you need me."
- "It's OK to have needs. I love filling your needs!"
- "I love taking care of you."

- "It's OK to make mistakes."
- "All your feelings are OK with me."
- "You can rest in me."
- "There's nothing you could say or do that would make me not love you."
- "You don't have to work or manage anything. You get to be a kid and learn, play, explore, and grow. It's safe for you to relax and rely on me to take care of things."
- "You don't have to take care of me. I'm an adult, and I have all the support I need. You get to be a child and receive support from me. You don't have to reciprocate."
- "I love you as you are, no matter what."

Some examples of questions to ask your inner child are:

- "How are you feeling today?"
- "What do you need from me in this moment?"
- "What can I do for you right now?"
- "I sense that you are feeling _____. Would you like to talk about it?"
- "What would you like to do right now?"

Your Inner Mother

Your inner mother is your adult self, with all your knowledge and power, supported by higher forces such as the universe, God/Goddess, and your higher self.

As the inner mother, you help your inner child see that the past is truly in the past. You do this by being conscious of your inner child's emotional state and making new choices that demonstrate the fact that the dangers she faced in early childhood are no longer present.

You, as the inner mother, have the ability to care for your inner child and provide things that your mother may not have been able to. Some examples:

- Soothing her when she is scared.
- Comforting her when you are moving in a new direction that seems risky to her.
- Supporting her by affirming her worth, value, and deservingness.
- Protecting her boundaries.
- Supporting her in her desires to play, learn, explore, and grow.
- Affirming her goodness and that it is indestructible, no matter what happens in life.

The Inner Bond That Will Change Your Life in Profound Ways

You move back and forth between being the inner mother and the inner child. In this way, you receive the nurturing you need, and you provide the safe container that you needed as a child. One could say that through this relationship, you create a center of wholeness and safety within that allows you to truly thrive and flourish in the world. This relationship continues to deepen over time and brings a great richness to life. For women who were parentified daughters, this must also involve reminding the inner child that she doesn't have to work or manage anything as she did when she was little; now she can rest, play, and be a child, as she now has a capable adult who can protect and care for her.

When your inner child really understands, with your help, the truth that her pain was never her fault, a major shift happens:

- The primary attachment bond begins to shift from the limited outer mother to the unconditionally loving inner mother.

- You become increasingly able to feel the reality of your own lovableness and rejoice in your own goodness and value, no matter the outer circumstances.
- You are better able to receive love from others because a part of you is less invested in seeing yourself as "less-than" as a form of being loyal to your mother (waiting indefinitely for your mother to show up in the ways that you needed her to).
- You are able to see yourself more accurately. You can see your own faults, flaws, and mistakes while remaining firmly rooted in your basic sense of goodness and value. External approval may come, but you no longer need it to feel OK.

Ways to Cultivate the "Good Enough" Inner Mother

By cultivating the "good enough" inner mother, you are developing a new relationship within yourself. You don't have to be perfect; you will make mistakes. The important thing is that you are willing to keep going. And every little bit goes a very long way.

What were some of the things you wanted when you were little that you never got? As a little girl, did you wish your mother would:

- Lovingly brush your hair?
- Lay out your school clothes the night before?
- Read you a bedtime story every night?
- Deeply listen to what you had to say and respond empathically?
- Console you and help you brainstorm solutions when you were upset?
- Support your interest in music, art, or dancing?

- Give you lots of hugs and be physically affectionate toward you?
- Support your independence, allowing you to play for hours, immersed in your own imagination?
- Be overjoyed at your successes and breakthroughs, enthusiastically celebrating you at every opportunity?

There is something so pristine at our core . . .

The child that we were is not just a snapshot of our history; she is a vital energy that lives within us right now. Our inner child is part of our authentic self, the self we were before we had to wear masks and take on a false self, to some degree, in order to survive in our families and in our cultures. When we care for our inner child, we begin to recover our authentic, natural self. We begin to restore a sense of goodness and worthiness to those things we may have had to put into shadow.

Welcoming back the parts of ourselves we had to reject is incredibly liberating!

We can welcome our rejected parts back into the embrace of ourselves and act in new ways that demonstrate to our inner child that the past is over and that it is safe to be her full self.

Some examples of taking actions that heal and liberate are:

- Setting boundaries when it was previously forbidden.
- Using your voice to speak your truth when it caused you to be rejected in the past.
- Giving yourself time to play or do nothing when you were taught that your value only comes from effort.

We have to be rebels to heal. Healing requires that we have the courage to undo the dysfunctional patterns that were laid early in our lives. It is a long journey and can be so challenging, but it is so worth it. Ultimately, it expands our capacity for radical new levels of joy, pleasure, creativity, and connection.

We can find a love within that has no limits.

In our culture, it seems that children are rewarded more for *growing out* of childhood as soon as possible, and not so easily loved for whatever stage they are in as children. Because of this, many of us grew up feeling punished or abandoned for the simple fact that we had needs: the need to eat, the need to be held, the need to be seen, the need to be listened to, the need to rest, the need to be understood, etc. Many of us learned to hate our needs and to hate ourselves for having needs. We may be carrying this self-derision within, and it can keep us stuck.

As we work with the inner child, our vitality and inner safety is restored.

We all need to feel adored, cherished, comforted, nurtured, and honored for the unique person we are. When we help our inner child feel these feelings, new energy and vitality comes into every area of our lives because we are releasing shame and anointing ourselves in goodness and blessedness. This gives us new confidence, lightheartedness, and joy.

Creating a Safe Inner Environment for Your Inner Child to Thrive

Listen to what your inner child has to tell you and feel the energy shift in your body and in your emotions. Paint, draw, journal, write letters, dialogue with an empty chair, pull out your favorite old toys. Have fun with the process. You are creating a sanctuary within where everything is OK—no matter what. A sanctuary where it is safe to be a child, where it is safe to have feelings, where it is safe to be messy and ungroomed, where it is safe to cry, where it is safe to play and have fun!

Discovering and Embodying Your Indestructible Goodness

I had a photo of a fox on my desk, and I recall one day when every time I looked at it, I felt the urge to weep. Sensing something potent under the surface, I sat down with the photo and allowed myself to feel what was coming up. As I stared into the eyes of the fox, I sensed its innocent and pure presence. I began to weep and realized I was weeping for the innocent and pure presence of my own inner child. And as I wept, I had a major realization. I realized that the innocence and purity had not been destroyed by early trauma as I had feared, but was actually present with me in that moment. In fact, it could never fully be destroyed, nor could I ever be fully separated from it, because this innocence and purity were the very essence of my being and part of my connection to life itself.

Loving our inner child gives us access to our essence, our truth, and our vitality in a way that nothing else can.

The indestructible bond that we create between our adult self and our inner child replaces the deficits of our early childhood with the emotional nourishment that create the strength needed to live as our full, brilliant, authentic self. It is a process of building a new foundation to support the vastness of who we really are.

One of my favorite sayings is "We Mother Ourselves into Mastery." With each new level of empowerment, the inner child needs reassurance that it's safe to go into new territory beyond where our families or friends have gone, reassurance that she will not be alone, which is at the heart of so many of the fears we carry.

Every time we go to new levels in our lives, the little girl inside us will need extra reassurance and support.

The profound healing energies of inner mothering include:

- Bringing softness and gentleness to our fears and anxieties.
- Allowing ourselves more space to be with our emotions.
- Making time to differentiate the pain of the past from the safety of the present.
- Giving evidence of all the good, beautiful things in our lives each day.

- Allowing ourselves to move more slowly through the day, hour by hour.
- Creating new nonnegotiables that protect our boundaries.
- Taking calm, clear action as an adult while internally soothing the fears of the inner child.
- Celebrating our wins and owning our magnificence regardless of external approval.
- Having the courage to end relationships that deplete or disrespect us without guilt.
- Creating new consistent habits of self-care and nurturing in our schedules.

With Each Level, Getting More Skilled at Inner Mothering Brings Amazing Shifts into a Woman's Life, Such as:

- An expanded sense of possibilities and excitement about the future.
- A fierce self-love in the face of anything that would diminish her.
- A clear sense that she is capable of creating anything she wants.
- A feeling that she is worthy of infinite support and connection with others.
- A sense of abundance and space for all beings to get what they desire.
- A sense of her special place in the world that can never be taken away.
- A joyous generosity and desire to support other women in their dreams.
- A willingness to step into the discomfort of the unknown for the sake of what is true and real.

Inner mothering isn't a walk in the park. Yes, it includes a lot of softness and gentleness. But it also includes being willing to be uncomfortable, firm, and patient, as well as:

- A willingness to feel the uncomfortable, often painful emotions that were suppressed when you were a little girl.
- A commitment to consistent contact and dialogue with the inner child.
- The courage to get support and not do it alone.
- A willingness to try new things that may feel awkward and take time.
- A willingness to let go of instant gratification and look from a long-term perspective.
- A willingness to make your inner life a top priority and listen to your body and your emotions, acting on what you know from within.

Clues that you would benefit greatly from inner mothering include:

- You find yourself regressing into feeling like a little girl in situations that cause stress.
- You feel helpless and powerless in moments more than usual.
- You push yourself to exhaustion and burnout with work.
- You numb out to cope.
- You find repeating patterns from your childhood coming up in relationships.
- You struggle with fears of being alone through rejection or abandonment.
- You feel paralyzed in moments to make changes in your life due to guilt, shame, or obligation.

Here's a powerful truth . . .

There's a paradox that as we slow down to nurture the small child inside us, we accelerate our forward momentum in our lives as women.

Questions for Reflection

1. Do any of the above clues resonate with you? If so, which ones?
2. Find a picture of yourself as a little girl and look at it closely. Notice the details and delight in the innocence and how unique you were. As your adult self, send that little girl some loving energy of kindness and acceptance. "I love you and I'm here for you now." Put the photo where you can see it every day.
3. What is one activity or thing you could do to nurture your inner child today? What would help you feel most nurtured, loved, supported? Think of it and then actually do it. Notice how you feel afterward.

Exercise: 6 Steps to Dialoguing with Your Inner Child

1. **Connect:** Speak to your inner child inwardly, out loud, or in writing; greet her with words like "Hello! I'm here with you." Communicate that you are present and available to her. (If you're just starting out with this, simply doing step 1 throughout the day can be hugely comforting.)
2. **Inquire:** Ask your inner child questions such as "What's happening for you right now? How are you feeling? What do you need right now? Would you like to talk about what's upsetting you?"
3. **Listen:** Actually make space to listen and observe closely what is coming up. Pay attention to the words, images, and sensations that arise from your inner child.
4. **Empathize:** Validate your inner child's emotional experience by repeating back to her, in a gentle tone, what you heard her say, and respond with empathy: "I see. Yes, that makes total sense to me,

of course you would feel that way. It's normal and natural that you would feel like that, given what you've been through."

5. **Internal Holding:** Envision yourself holding and soothing her physically, gently and respectfully holding her hand, making eye contact, carrying her, stroking her brow in a nurturing, motherly way, etc.

6. **Positive Reframe:** Create an empowering narrative to help her make sense of what has happened in the past and what is happening now. Gently explain that the past is over and she is safe now. This positive narrative must be honest, encouraging, and heartfelt. Show concrete evidence to validate the new narrative that affirms your inner child's worth and safety in the present moment.

Chapter 14

LIFE BEYOND THE MOTHER WOUND

J. HAD MOVED INTO my house in the woods, and it was so fun to finally live together, making meals, sitting by our woodstove, and hiking on the trails behind the house. We also spent time envisioning the kind of house we wanted to buy together, one in which we could garden on the land, host friends and loved ones, and provide space for large gatherings, community building, and connection among women. We envisioned this house as a space where people could come together to find their truth.

Within just a few months, we had miraculously found the perfect home—and had connected with a group of women we started hosting who quickly became our dear friends and "chosen family." Moving into our new house, we joked that we were transforming the Victorian-era home, constructed in a time of female repression, into a house of female freedom of expression. J. and I got to blend our respective libraries. We read aloud to each other from books by Audre Lorde, Adrienne Rich, Alice Walker, Judy Grahn, Mary Daly, Andrea Dworkin, Denise Levertov, Muriel Rukeyser, Leslie Feinberg, and more. I had moments in which I looked back at my former self and realized how ignorant I had been, how blind to the depth and power and resilience of my feminist foremothers. I felt incredible humility, grief, and gratitude for all that I was learning and living. I felt proud to find myself among other revolutionary women.

Loving a woman felt like the most natural, holy, and liberating thing I had ever experienced. Unlike many, I didn't have the experience of "coming out" to my family, as I had had no contact with them in about four years at that point. I realized that I had been ostracized and excommunicated not because I came out as a lesbian, but because I had come out as an individual; and that act of patriarchal disobedience and self-reclamation was a precursor to discovering my sexuality as a lesbian, an important step in my evolution.

Over time I began to accept that while my family believed they loved me, they didn't have the capacity to love me as the empowered woman I was becoming. I kept bringing myself back to that truth over and over again: that it was really over, and I would never see them again. That no matter how much I loved them, no matter how my intentions were good, they were not capable of seeing this. Bringing myself back to this inner refrain was painful yet important, especially to prevent the impossible dream from forming again. The more I grieved and accepted that reality, the more my new life with my partner and our new house and community felt like my own. I began to feel enormous pride that while it was painful to have so much loss in my life, everything now felt authentic and nourishing and real. Even though I continue to process the trauma of what I went through, my life feels truly mine, and I feel so alive and grateful. What was once a void for me is now a new local community of friends, a healthy relationship with J., a soul family, and a global network of collaborators. Out of that pain has emerged more love and abundance than I could have ever imagined.

Life is more like a devotional practice with more layers appear-

ing for healing, but with each layer, more clarity and freedom are realized. With each layer, it's about embracing whatever triggers come up, mothering the child within me, differentiating the past from the present, and meeting life more fully, trusting that whatever comes up is for the best, even if my mind doesn't know how or why yet. My overactive mind is no longer functioning as "mother," but rather a calm substrate of being is increasingly the foundation of my life. With each layer, I've become both more tender and more fierce. I feel more integrated, like a blend of an innocent child and a wise crone, and this energy expresses as the adult woman I am.

Over time, I've come to a place of what I call "benevolent defeat," an acceptance that all the strategies that helped me survive my family of origin have ceased to serve me. As a child, I thought I had to dominate life with my mind in order to survive. I needed to figure out the rules of life and master them through striving, struggling, strategizing, being the good girl, being hypervigilant, and overfunctioning. I believed that these mental strategies would create desirable circumstances and THEN I'd be able to rest. But all that striving and mental effort failed me because they didn't get me to my primary goal: for my mother and family to love me and see me as I painfully longed for.

Grieving has pulled me to a place of sobering depth and clarity. At the bottom of it all, what my inner child has always wanted is to rest and just BE. And for a long time, I believed that I needed my family's love to allow myself to do that. Relief has come from surrendering to ever deeper levels, to accepting that I cannot control life or circumstances, no matter how hard I try. The nourishment that comes from Being cannot be achieved through work; it can only be felt and experienced in the now. And in the now is where all true creativity and knowledge reside.

My desire for truth and living from integrity constantly brings

232 | BETHANY WEBSTER

me back to the fact that nothing in this world, no matter how beautiful, validating, expansive, or ecstatic, can ever erase the trauma I endured and my responsibility to tend to the pain within me. The nourishment for me now comes NOT from finding comfort in mental strategies that promise some future rescue or payoff, or in the hope of being able to dominate circumstances, but in the power of being in the present moment, where there's a love that doesn't need mental strategies. It's as though the inner mother is saying in each moment, "Accept the benevolent defeat and stay here with me. You don't need to run or protect yourself or seek for anything. I'm always here now; holding you, holding everything."

Everything in this world will change or disappear. Mental striving pulls us away from what we want, not toward it. By courageously facing our pain through embodying the inner mother, in being present with our own brokenness, we may find the nourishment we've been looking for. This sets us up to be in full contact with life, without the insulation of avoidance or denial. This full contact with life, with truth, is what I believe we are really seeking.

Through healing the Mother Wound, we can discover what true power is and begin to embody it. This is not the power of patriarchy as in "power over," but the power of Being, as in "being with." Here we are no longer relying on or complying with an external authority, but tuning into inner authority based on our truth, finding that flow, and living moment to moment from there.

Healing the Mother Wound is not about seeing transformation as a way to get rid of the pain of your past, but as a way of embracing life now. There is not an easy path. It takes courage, grit, and resilience, but it's worth it. This process has its own organic timing for everyone. There is no end to the journey, only more opportunities for evolution, shedding more of our illusions, and manifesting our true self as increased aliveness, freedom, and joy.

You thought that union was a way you could decide to go. But
the soul follows things rejected and almost forgotten. Your true
guide drinks from an undammed stream.

—Rumi

As the Mother Wound is increasingly healed, you realize that there's
never been anything wrong with you. Incredible energy is returned to
you. Slowly, over time, it becomes clear on a direct, visceral level that
you are divine and connected to all life. The medicine is in the wound.
As we heal, the Mother Wound doesn't just disappear. It transforms
from a source of pain into a source of wisdom that goes on to nourish
every part of your life. The wound itself, when tended for healing,
reveals in perfect timing all the breakthroughs, shifts, and insights
necessary to seed a new life and a new world.

As you move through the wound and make your way to the other
side, you will transform, and so will your vision of yourself and your
life, often in unexpected and magical ways—because your connection
to life is gradually being restored. You begin to realize that you really
belong. There becomes more space for more play, pleasure, creativity. You will continue to experience pockets of grief and residues of
trauma, but with each layer, more of you is liberated to explore more of
your purpose and potential.

Surfing the Waves of Healing

The best metaphor I've found for life beyond the Mother Wound is
surfing. I first started surfing with a group of friends when I was seventeen. I spent the entire summer without even standing up on the
board, but instead learning to read the waves, developing my upper

body strength, learning the timing of how to identify which waves to catch and which waves to let pass me by. In the beginning, the waves pummeled me and took me down, sometimes scraping my face against the bottom of the sea; sometimes the board would pop up and hit me in the head. But I kept going. Over time, I learned how to anticipate the waves, harness the forward movement, leap up at the right moment, and surf upon them with exhilaration instead of being overpowered and threatened by them. This is the process of healing the Mother Wound: to learn to ride the waves of healing, to harness them, to allow them to move you forward, to learn how to steer their power, to welcome them.

Over time we come to a real place of gratitude and genuine compassion for our mothers and their journeys. We may feel gratitude for whatever our mother could give and compassion for what she could not give us. It's incremental. It's an evolution. We heal on a spiral. There is no final "done" moment, and as time goes on, it becomes less of a focus or destination. Rather, the focus becomes the empowerment and freedom we experience as we move through each layer. Surfing the waves of healing becomes less like a chore and more like an adventure, constantly moving you into the unknown, finding support along the way, and treasures as well.

Permission to Be Real

The permission to be real is something that happens in the intimate space between you and yourself. As you heal the Mother Wound, you increasingly become the secure base for exploration for *yourself*. As the inner mother to your inner child, you become the profound space for everything to be OK. There is a powerful circle of love that flows around and through this inner bond, allowing you to increasingly let go of limiting patterns from your family of origin and the larger patriarchal culture. Exploration, experimentation, and mistakes are all welcome. Here there is no such thing as failure, only learning. As we become safer within, we become free to take risks, to chart new territory, to really explore the inner landscape without the usual fear of "What will they think of me?" This fear may still come up, but its power to stop you diminishes.

Patriarchy has demanded that women be small and give away our power in exchange for external approval. As we become awakened women, we become small, not in yielding to any outer authority, but in yielding to the truth at the center of our being, the divine, the source within. This becomes what guides our lives. Our lives then become lived in devotion to *that*. The process of becoming small in this context is the ultimate exaltation, because we become an instrument of a higher power. From here, everything we do can be lived as an expression of this truth. Our true authority is inner. This is so healing, because patriarchy tells us that we must split and betray ourselves in order to be accepted. Here our authority is squarely placed in the center of ourselves. Here we realize our innate wholeness. In her book *Radical Acceptance*, Tara Brach encourages us to let our suffering be the gateway to the awakened heart. Seen in this way, our suffering is not something to get rid of, but a doorway to deeper truths. Brach talks about seeing our pain as something that is entrusted to us. To cultivate inner safety, we mother our own inner child in the ways our outer mother could not. We replace those original deficits by first feeling them fully. We have to feel the feelings that were off-limits when we were young. This is the first step in becoming really authentic.

As we increasingly live as our original self, we are periodically asked to depart from the known and to find rest in the unknown. It asks us to befriend our ultimate aloneness and to find safety in our own presence. In that stark simplicity, there is a profound fullness that is not of this world. The ego quiets down and becomes in service to the organic mystery of your own evolution. There is a connection between the longing for mother and the longing for the inner beloved. One could say that this longing flows through the same channel, the child's longing for her mother and the adult's longing for the ultimate truth in the form of God/Goddess/all that is. That is why when we heal the Mother Wound, the way becomes clear for us to embody the spiritual power that wants to be expressed through us.

When we go deep enough into our own pain and existential aloneness, we discover that we've actually never been alone. There in our own pain and messy feelings is a loving presence alongside everything we've ever experienced. As we increasingly feel safe within, our loyalty shifts from the beliefs we inherited from our families and culture to our own inner truth and integrity. Over time, our ability to be honest with ourselves about what we're feeling becomes our true source of safety. This innate safety begins to outshine the illusions of safety we thought we'd attain through the old defenses we adopted in childhood.

The integration of the increasingly healed inner child and the conscious, wise adult self culminates as a new way of being, a bridge of spirit and matter, the new earth itself. We embody the Goddess when we mother the traumatized child within ourselves. As we mother ourselves, a greater sense of peace and freedom pervades, and we increasingly release the need for others to change in order for us to feel OK. We can let others be who they are and release attachment to being seen accurately by them. This becomes possible when we've reached the point where we can accurately see and appreciate *ourselves* enough to let go. We do this by mothering our traumatized inner children into the safety of the present moment. We mother ourselves in real time by feeling the pain of the past trauma *and* any pain of a current situation, by mothering ourselves on both levels simultaneously. It is a point of great power to live with awareness of many levels at the same time; to be aware as the adult in present time and as the inner child, and also as the formless divine presence that we are at the deepest level.

The best use of a traumatic childhood is to use your family's short-comings to birth your greatness. Your greatness is simply being more of who you are at your core. This is the deeper gift available in the pain of our abuse. This is the true resurrection. When we discover the light in our deepest pain, we become capable of seeing it everywhere and in everything. Unity consciousness and existential belonging become a felt reality. Being the sovereign feminine is being both tender *and* fierce. Allow yourself to be large. Allow yourself to take up space. Over time, we reach a point where our inner child feels safe enough to start to let go of the early beliefs that tell us we must be small in order to be loved. And in doing so, we are increasingly able to experience vitality, wonder, creativity, joy, bliss, excitement, comfort, and receptivity. The inner bond allows us to emotionally separate from the toxic messages of "less-than" and "shrink to be accepted" that women receive from the wider culture.

Many of us are craving the ability to be fully authentic, to be real, to be seen and loved as who we truly are. We are collectively longing to have a visceral experience of our true creativity, power, and beauty, undiluted and unmitigated by the limiting structures of the wider culture. Each of us holds the potential to bring our original selves forth in a way that transforms our world. The time is ripe for whatever you want to bring forward.

Will You Come Forward?

Whatever external permission you are waiting for is not coming. The only permission that can liberate you is your own.

Potency is embodying your indisputable value and giftedness.

We are out of integrity when we discount and devalue ourselves. It's time to finally dump the idea that self-diminishment is noble. The biggest gift we can give others is the example of our own lives working, stepping forward in our power and being who we truly are without apology, without shame, but with a sense of inner blessedness and celebration.

Potency is the flower of legitimacy. Claim your legitimacy and right to take up space.

We can't embody our potency if we don't first feel truly legitimate. No one and nothing from the outside can confer the feeling of legitimacy that we crave, yet this is the foundation for everything else. Legitimacy is the sense of basic worthiness and goodness. The time for developing that was when we were small children and our mother conferred to us a sense of legitimacy through her own felt sense of belonging in the world. If she did not feel *she* belonged, our basic sense of legitimacy and value was compromised. We cannot go back in time and get this sense of legitimacy; we can only mourn that lost opportunity and create for ourselves the inner legitimacy we crave.

Because our mothers grew up in patriarchal cultures, we each have a sense of being lost to some degree. Once the Mother Wound is embraced, it actually transforms into a gift—leading us to the feeling of legitimacy that we long for. Legitimacy is the right to be, the right to flourish and act as an entity with agency and power. Despite cultural messages that tell us otherwise, we are each legitimate by the fact that we exist, that we *are*. Life itself has given us legitimacy by the fact that we were born. We feel this more and more as we remove the layers of limiting beliefs and traumatic residues that cover our essence.

Dare to own your potency.

Our essence, our spirit self, is that spark of potency. The more we trust it, the brighter it shines through our human form, the clearer its guidance becomes, and the greater the transformation we offer to those around us by virtue of vibrating with our potency.

The solidity of the felt sense of legitimacy forms a kind of container to hold that spark of potency within. The container of legitimacy supports our potency and allows it to flourish. One could even say that your basic sense of legitimacy is the human container for the potency of your God/Goddess self.

Owning your potency is the undefended courage to live and embody the undiluted truth of your being, no matter the cost.

Owning your potency is living as essence, beyond the personal ego. It is surrendering to your deepest truth and trusting wherever it leads you, even if your mind thinks it should look different. It takes guts and fortitude to do this.

Ultimately, it's about dismantling the inner walls of the individual ego self that feels it has to defend itself against life. When these walls come down, your personal will merges with the divine will like a stream meeting the ocean. Suddenly, there is a power living within you that provides incredible energy, support, and inspiration. You are no longer a single stream—you are the ocean itself. Daily life becomes about finding that flow and allowing it to carry you to all that you need, all that you're meant to know, and all that it wants to express through you.

What is standing in the way of you living in alignment with what you know is true for you? What is that costing you?

We have to look at how we've been brainwashed into self-flagellation and reclaim our life force by choosing new thoughts and beliefs that accurately reflect and articulate what we know is true. Many women hit a ceiling right before a major breakthrough. We tend to first *look for external permission* to thrive, to succeed, to excel. Patriarchy has gaslighted women into believing in our lack of value or power. The legacy is long, and the beliefs deeply entrenched. Our mothers and grandmothers had no choice but to believe and pass those beliefs down to us. We have to legitimize ourselves in ways our mothers could not. There's no other way. As the saying goes, we are the ones we've been waiting for.

There is no excuse not to follow your dreams. Now is the time. Don't underestimate the effects of simply making a powerful decision to do so. Trust that whatever follows this decision will be exactly what is needed to bring it about. It's not easy, but it's worth it. Nothing compares to the bliss of living from the depths of your being.

Attenuation is the impulse to diminish oneself, to be small, to disappear, to be invisible. Attenuation seems to be one of the central wounds we incur as females in this world. From early on we are taught that there are things about us that are shameful, so we learn to hide, contort, and manipulate ourselves to be acceptable to the world. We had to believe in our own defect in order to survive. We had to be compliant with our own oppression.

We can transform the shame into a fierce love.

The fact that we were not accepted—by our families and by society—does not mean that we are not legitimate. It does not mean that there was something wrong with us. It means that there was something deeply wounded in our society and in our families. To admit this is not to cast blame, but to come into truth so that healing can occur.

The end of attenuation comes when we are willing to be misperceived, when we are willing to risk offending others for the sake of what is real and true in ourselves and in the world. We must be willing to be uncomfortable and to be seen as inconvenient.

One must contact a certain rawness within, a fierceness, a "won't stop until I fully own myself" determination.

In our culture we tend to rush into forgiveness, compassion, and solutions. And as women we have learned so well to sugarcoat the things that make us and others uncomfortable and slip them under the rug. This includes accepting less than what we deserve for the sake of "peace."

The time of compliance is over. We must be determined to own ourselves, to know in our bones that we belong to ourselves.

As female children we had to say yes to a world and to families that had wounds, wounds that have cost us years of our lives. As the current carriers of generational and collective pain we have the ability to consciously transform that pain into consciousness. As children we had no choice but to give away our power. It's now time to rectify that "yes" with a powerful "no" to the things that continue to oppress us—starting with the ways that we oppress ourselves.

To liberate ourselves, we first have to locate the ways we are divided within ourselves. The ways we are divided within must be identified and acknowledged. Otherwise, they will continue to control us and limit us. Compliance is very costly.

How are you compliant? In what ways do you attenuate yourself?

The path to owning oneself can be long and treacherous because it involves facing all the grief, pain, and rage that blocks our true self. These frightening feelings must be faced. The love that we are is not afraid of the places of fragmentation we have accumulated. That is why it calls forth in us the courage to face our pain and move through it.

The love that we are metabolizes the pain and turns it into itself . . . love.

We've learned to turn away from the things that scare us and make us uncomfortable. This is a form of giving away our power. As we embody greater awareness, we realize that we must shift and turn *toward* those things that make us uncomfortable and bring the light of awareness to them—for the sake of our own transformation.

Healing the Mother Wound is impossible without the container of a therapeutic relationship with a therapist who is skilled in attachment and trauma, especially for those of us who experienced severe abuse and trauma. The wound happened in relationship and the healing ultimately happens in relationship. Part of mothering ourselves is getting the quality support we need. See the appendix on page 257 for some recommendations on what to look for.

Our safety lies in this willingness to turn toward the places of fragmentation.

The love that we truly are is not afraid of brokenness. When our brokenness is embraced, it transforms into an unbreakable wholeness that we realize was there all along—an eternal, timeless wholeness that is who we really are. It's called forth by our willingness to be uncomfortable and to look into the shadows within ourselves. It is fed by our loyalty to what is real and true, no matter the cost.

Walking the Razor's Edge of Fierceness and Tenderness

As we process the places of fragmentation within us, we literally dissolve the layers that have obscured our light. As the layers dissolve, a deeper aspect of our true identity emerges—a consciousness of pure love that has been pristine and untouched throughout all the pain. We discover this as we confront all the beliefs that tell us we are not good enough or powerful in our own lives. This message is not that of a quick and easy fix, but it is the undiluted truth. You are worth every ounce of discomfort and inconvenience it takes to own yourself, to love yourself.

The most powerful intimacy is when no emotion or experience can separate you from yourself. That is true safety and true freedom. This is the gift awaiting us in the Mother Wound.

Questions for Reflection

1. As female children, many of us were forced to say yes to things we wanted to say no to. We may have had to endure experiences that felt unbearable or challenging without being able to express our suffering. What were some of your experiences like this?
2. Imagine connecting with your inner child. Express empathy for how difficult it was to feel alone, powerless, or without a voice in those

moments. Imagine telling her that now you are there as her adult self to protect her right to say no and have her needs and boundaries respected.

3. What are some ways you can support your right to say no in your daily life that would affirm your sovereignty now as an adult woman and would also nourish your inner child's sense of being protected and heard?

CONCLUSION

Emergent Woman: Releasing the "Pleaser" and Making Peace with Our Power

> . . . the connections between and among women are the most feared, the most problematic, and the most potentially transforming force on the planet.
> —*Adrienne Rich*

The Mother Wound has been a blind spot of women's empowerment up to this point. Even the most evolved among us have avoided looking at this issue. Healing the Mother Wound is the next frontier of feminism, as it functions as the linchpin of our most insidious forms of self-limitation, the very subtle and invisible ways we hold ourselves back in order to secure love, safety, and belonging. These insidious self-limiting patterns have been passed down from mother to daughter for centuries. The time to stop the cycle is NOW.

Historically, male children were dependent on their fathers only until they became the heads of their own households, but the dependence of female children, mothers, and wives on their fathers/husbands was lifelong. There's an old English saying: "A man is a son until he takes a wife, a daughter is a daughter for life." The familial arrangement throughout history of women being powerful *only through male protectors* has limited the development of a consolidated female solidarity and group cohesiveness over time, as has the illusion that class and race privileges could protect white women from misogyny.

For many women throughout history, throughout different life stages, safety was found through some form of male "protection," preventing women from outgrowing a childlike state of being under continual male subordination throughout the course of their lives. In this way, the family dictated the obligations and roles an adult daughter would follow throughout her life, from father to husband to son, with her mother and/or mother-in-law often there to help enforce this indoctrination to some degree. This, combined with the lack of a tradition that affirmed the autonomy and independence of women, leading to the invisibility of women of significance, has long prevented women from ever imagining anything beyond this arrangement, in which life was lived from birth to death in subordination to the dominance of the family.

Once a woman became a mother herself, for many women, the home became her domain; her prison as a daughter became her place of power as a mother to enact dominance in her own way. For much of the history of Western civilization, with few opportunities for women outside the home, this has been the way of things. If a woman rebelled against the family or societal norms, she could be cast out, left to fend for herself, or experience slander, torture, or death. For some, her mother or mother-in-law might have been the one to cast the first stone or drive the woman out of the home. In some places, these incidents are still a daily occurrence.

We stand at a particular place in time, in 2021, in which many of those patriarchal arrangements have shifted across recent decades: women now make up most of those awarded college degrees; are opting to have fewer children, if they elect to have children at all; and hold more political posts than ever. And yet women's reproductive rights are being continuously threatened, Black women are still dying in childbirth in record numbers, indigenous women are still going missing, and the majority of the poor are nonwhite women.

In the digital age of feminism, more information is available to us than ever before, and women are finding one another, opening up the potential for large groups of women to liberate ourselves from patriarchal subordination. But in order for this to happen in a large-scale, sustainable way, we must do the inner work of healing the Mother Wound, addressing how the toxic cultural atmosphere of patriarchy has caused our human needs for love, safety, and belonging to be fused with beliefs about being "less-than," resulting in the insidious ways we oppress ourselves and each other. For white women in particular, we must not collapse into shame or guilt for the legacy of white supremacy we inherited, but instead fall back into a vast humility that understands that our stepping back to listen and learn from Black women and other women of color is an essential act of reclaiming our humanity from white supremacy and patriarchy.

Healing the Mother Wound helps us become conscious of our history, both personally and culturally, so that we can formulate a truly feminist, postpatriarchal future for all. This work is long term and will take generations. It also helps us cultivate a healthy mothering consciousness within ourselves, a transpersonal inner mother, a benevolent intelligence within to which we can turn at any moment for strength, comfort, and guidance.

We stand at a point in time in which many women are healing themselves and becoming intolerant to toxic systems and choosing to leave them behind, whether they are walking away from families of origin, organizations, companies, churches, or communities. As we heal the Mother Wound, we become more fearless, disrupting the status quo, having difficult conversations, knowing when to walk away, refusing to prop up dysfunction, and creating our own systems of support that prioritize ourselves and other women. Facing the pain within us, and living transformation as a way of life, we begin to stop projecting our unmet attachment needs onto situations or people. We become more sovereign, separate, singular. We become more reality-based, more connected to ourselves and the higher flow within us. There's less striving, pushing, or forcing and more of a deep "tuning in" to our own truth, discerning the higher wisdom within ourselves and no longer mistaking it for the patriarchal garbage we've been taught about ourselves.

Gerda Lerner, in the conclusion of her book *The Creation of Patriarchy*, recommends two things for women to end patriarchy: (1) that we at least for a time become woman-centered, and (2) that we step outside of patriarchal thought. She explains that centering women means that we trust our own female experience, that we no longer believe the lie of inferiority that we are surrounded by in the culture. It means we learn to identify and ignore the male commentary in our heads and look to ourselves, other women, and our feminist foremothers for validation instead.

Stepping outside of patriarchal thought means we must be skeptical of every known value system of thought, as our erasure is baked into every one. She advises that we also be critical of our own mental narratives, which have been trained in a patriarchal context. And finally she explains that ending patriarchy requires us to have great courage: the courage to question ourselves, the courage to stand alone, the courage to accept ourselves, and the courage to name our experiences as inherently valid. She says perhaps the biggest challenge of all is to go beyond the illusion of safety rooted in external approval into the audacity to assert ourselves as rightly entitled to transforming the world by unapologetically defining and centering ourselves within it.

As I continue to guide women to heal the Mother Wound through my courses, mentoring program, and retreats, I have witnessed a groundswell of exactly these two developments. As women heal the Mother Wound, we automatically begin to center ourselves and other women, and we become increasingly conscious of ourselves as a collective throughout time. Individually we dismantle the baggage of our foremothers in the patterns of self-suppression, and in so doing, we discover our true energy, our life force, and it begins to become a North Star, guiding our lives and seeking its own expansion and expression. This process naturally involves connecting with and up-lifting other women, who we increasingly see as sisters in upending the very same oppressions that we and our foremothers experienced. We also become more conscious of the necessity of reclaiming our humanity from patriarchy through the dismantling of social ills in-cluding white supremacy, homophobia, classism, and more. Central to this is a growing resilience, cultivated to make space for the pain and suffering of other women. Pain is no longer seen as a dead end, a weakness or a threat to our own power, but as a doorway to self-knowledge and liberation.

On Lerner's second point, I've also seen healing the Mother Wound cause women to question patriarchal thought, to see it not as some-thing that is universal and to be respected because we were taught so, but rather seeing it accurately as an obsolete historical relic of the control of women with no possible payoff for women in the equation. No longer is deference to family or male institutions and way of think-ing mistaken as a passage to safety. Women begin to find their safety, worthiness, and visions within their *own* authority, within themselves and in collaboration with other women. Through healing the Mother Wound, we set ourselves free of outside patriarchal distortions we in-ternalized and declare ourselves no longer beholden to patriarchal systems that have been imposed upon us since birth.

Some relationships won't survive the real you.

On a personal level, as women, many of us are in the process of emerging from the core patriarchal mandates that tell women to be small and to be quiet, to accept our role as the dominated, inferior sex. One of the central ways this shows up in our everyday lives is so commonplace and familiar that we take it for granted, and yet within it lies an untapped power to upend patriarchy. It's *how we show up in relationships.*

Personal relationships are the ground on which the revolution really takes place.

As women, we are conditioned to believe that our value lies in making relationships work; that the emotional realm is our domain, and if relationships fail, it's always our fault. Even when we know it is best to let go of a relationship, there may remain a subtle residue of self-blame that continues to plague us under the surface, long after the relationship dissolves. Cultural messages about gender reward us for being the "emotional" sex and valorize those among us who attempt to rehabilitate immature men and tolerate unending disrespect from friends, family, and colleagues. We can see this in the subtext of countless sitcoms and romantic narratives.

"Authenticity" has become a cliché buzzword in the wider "female empowerment industrial complex" that is present-day coaching and personal growth. But the authenticity that we are craving is much more radical and subversive to the status quo than we realize. It requires an unwavering fidelity to that core of inner truth that is covered up through our experiences of growing up female, and a commitment to reclaiming and embodying our truths even when we're met with external disapproval and rejection.

One of the things I hear most often from women is a fear that their true authenticity will cause injury to their relationships; this includes relationships with romantic partners, friends, coworkers, and family members.

Women ask themselves:

- "Can my marriage survive my real self?"
- "Will my honesty crush my partner?"
- "If I become who I want to be, will I lose my close friends?"
- "If I come out as my real self, will my family disown me?"
- "Will I be able to remain in my job if I can no longer tolerate certain things?"

The fear of loss of relationships is a key way in which patriarchy holds us back. We keep our voices down, we exaggerate the truth, we manipulate to get our way, we dilute the truth, we stagnate our growth as a form of loyalty. These patterns are not a cause for self-judgment or self-blame. These are intergenerationally transmitted survival mechanisms for enduring misogyny, and a cause for self-compassion. And it's urgent now that we mature out of them and into a new relationship with our truth and power.

Women's undiluted honesty is a huge threat to patriarchy.

We break down the patriarchy in the small, private, unglamorous moments that the external world will likely never see:

- When we listen to the small voice that tells us something is off about a situation or person.
- When we choose to make space for our grief rather than force ourselves to put on a happy face.
- When we acknowledge how furious we are and refuse to ignore it.
- When we are brave enough to acknowledge our racism, ableism, homophobia, etc.
- When we choose to stand up for others who are disenfranchised.
- When we let ourselves be inconvenient and displeasing to others for the sake of our own well-being.
- When we slow down the frenetic pace of our day and honor our need for space, silence, or rest.
- When we feel the clarity of an uncomfortable truth and resolve to voice it even though it may disappoint the other person.

Every time you unapologetically and respectfully honor your own truth and express it without diluting it to protect the feelings of others, you give a gift to others. When you are firm, clear, and respectful, you empower others, even if they are triggered by it. Triggers are actually ruptures in the status quo; turbulent openings that release to a new way of being if we're brave enough to do the inner work they require.

We have to be willing to risk loss in relationships in order to:

- Not pass along the trauma we've experienced personally and collectively.
- Be truly creative, original, and innovative.
- Change oppressive, intergenerational patterns for the children of the future.
- Stop white supremacy, anti-blackness, racism, and homophobia in our organizations and communities.
- Save life on this planet.
- Engage with people who have different experiences than us (this is especially true for white, privileged women, those who are straight, able-bodied, wealthy, etc.).

Some relationships that may not survive include:

- Relationships with family members who relied on you to play a certain role that protected their own insecurities and denials.
- Relationships with family members who have more limited worldviews and values.
- Relationships with friends who may feel threatened by your growth.
- Romantic relationships in which your partner is not committed or willing to also take responsibility for his/her/their growth.
- Relationships with colleagues who may feel threatened by your courage to speak out and would prefer that you not rock the boat.

Making peace with our power involves accepting the fact that our authenticity will inevitably trigger painful feelings in others, and knowing that we can survive it.

When we stop overfunctioning in our relationships, it releases enormous energy back to us to use for our own evolution. And it gives others their power back to process and use their own emotions for their own transformation. Triggers are keys to healing that belong to the person who is triggered—keys to a door that lies inside them. It's their journey to use the trigger to unlock greater freedom in themselves. It's their opportunity to take, or not.

There's a delicious kind of freedom in making mistakes, in being misperceived, and in being disliked.

It's delicious when you know that those things no longer have the power to diminish your self-love. When they happen, they may feel uncomfortable in moments, but they no longer take you out of your center. In fact, they begin to serve as opportunities to more effectively mother yourself and anchor even deeper into your truth.

This delicious freedom is *not* the same as being rebellious or oppositional simply for the sake of it. It is delicious because it is part of the freedom to be a full individual. An individual means the right to have all kinds of emotions and feelings that deserve respect, even if others don't agree. Being a true individual was a freedom that was not afforded to most of our grandmothers and great-grandmothers. Claiming the right to be an individual could have meant injury, death, or banishment. And for some women today, especially Black and brown women, this remains the case. Staying small has indeed been a way to be safe and out of harm's way.

Making peace with our power also means reckoning with our power to oppress, especially for those of us who are white women, as we are closest to white men in the hierarchy of who benefits from patriarchy.

Culturally, we need to grieve. Personally, we need to grieve. And the situations in the outer world reflect this mounting inner imperative to look at our own pain. There is an exciting evolutionary step within the Mother Wound—that is, *if* we listen to the call to go within, face our situation, and grieve. However, if we choose to continue to be in avoidance and postpone the grief, we'll continue to act it out and harm the earth. The more individuals do this work, the more the culture will transform.

As women, we feel guilt based on the false assumption that it is our job to make people feel good all the time. If they don't feel good all the time, we think it represents a failure on our part. Give yourself permission to put down this ancient guilt. It was never a true obligation.

We have to let go of this "pleaser" role in order to step into our full power.

The truth is that we cannot protect people from their own painful feelings. Distracting others from their pain doesn't serve them. It only prolongs their suffering and postpones their healing.

There will be discomfort when we cease to derive our sense of value from pleasing others.

We'll be uncomfortable because we're releasing an ancient pattern that feels so familiar. And others will be uncomfortable because the buffer between them and their "stuff" will be gone. They will be forced to be in contact with their own pain. Your ability to endure the discomfort of this change is critical. Remember that this discomfort is temporary. The important thing is to withstand the feelings of guilt that may arise and not allow them to direct your behavior. Use the guilt as a stimulus to more fully affirm yourself.

With consistency, the discomfort will give way to a profound sweetness of being, of feeling the joy of belonging to yourself. As a woman radiating with the permission to be her full self, you offer a powerful "frequency of possibility" for others. You become the fulfillment of an ancient dream of your foremothers—a woman who is an individual, a woman unto herself . . .

The Mother Wound is a common wound we as women *all* share, and it's a bridge for us all to connect with each other, to heal, to grow, and to emerge from patriarchy and into a new era of collective female power.

Patriarchy is ending, as all eras eventually do. As we heal the Mother Wound, we are creating a new mother line of women, beyond families, beyond time, beyond cultures, a more globally cohesive and growing group consciousness that prioritizes women. And we are creating a group consciousness that questions male authority and their erroneous claim to universal truth. As we center women and actively dismantle patriarchal systems in the world and in ourselves, which healing the Mother Wound allows us to do, we can collectively birth a new era and a new earth.

ACKNOWLEDGMENTS

I'd like to thank the brave women who came before me, writers whose work has come from a commitment to telling the truth about their lives as women: Adrienne Rich, Audre Lorde, Marge Piercy, Andrea Dworkin, Kate Millett, bell hooks, Phyllis Chesler. I'd also like to honor Mary Oliver, Maya Angelou, Alice Walker, Virginia Woolf, and Gerda Lerner. Over the years, their words have inspired me to fully develop my own drive, the drive to grow, to investigate, to lean into my pain, to explore my own inner mysteries, and to share my discoveries with other women.

Thank you to my agents Terra Chalberg and Meg Thompson for your belief in this work and your efforts to bring this book to full fruition. Your wisdom, expertise, and friendship have meant so much. Thank you to my editor, Emma Brodie, for your incredible feedback, guidance, and editorial expertise. I can't thank you enough for talking things through with me, encouraging me, and sharing my enthusiasm and vision for this book. Thank you also to Cassie Jones, Kiele Raymond, Maggie Stephenson, and Trista Hendren.

I'd like to thank Sophia Style, along with Mónica Manso Benedicto and Isabel Villanueva, who were the first to reach out and invite me to come teach my first workshops in Barcelona and introduced me to their network throughout Europe and beyond.

I'd like to thank dear friends old and new: Toko-pa Turner, Karen Sharpe, Heather Kamins, Abigail Hartman, Elizabeth Bridgewater, Pam Parmakian, the Webster family, Tayla Findeisen, Jillian Casadei,

Rachel Smith Cote, Kathleen Fakete, Jim Bauerlein, my B.A.S.I.L. sisters, the Pottern Family.

Thank you to the women I've collaborated with on other projects who have offered their enthusiasm, wisdom, and support: Lourdes Viado, Karly Randolph Pitman, Lucy Pearce, Layla Saad, Erica Mather, Emmeline Chang, Katarzyna Majak, Anna Chan, Rachel Ricketts, and Jeannie Zandi.

To Lise Weil, Kim Chernin, Cynthia Rich, thank you for your conversations and stories. To Karna Nau, Sandra Derksen, Ali Brown, Eleanor Beaton, thank you for your expertise and feedback.

I'd also like to thank all my clients, students, and readers from around the world who have shared their stories with me through my courses, workshops, and retreats. Thank you for your courage to do this deep work and for giving me feedback on how this work has transformed your lives and continues to do so. It's such a joy, honor, and privilege to witness and support you on this path.

I'd like to thank J., in whose presence I have healed, grown, and transformed, and whose loving encouragement, patience, and support were vital in helping this book come together.

And finally, I'd like to thank my therapist, Nicole Ditz, whose steady, unwavering support and brilliant expertise over the past twenty-two years has helped me heal, grieve, and thrive to the uttermost. Since I was nineteen years old you have been by my side through it all. Words can't describe the depth of my gratitude for how you have, through your unwavering motherly love, helped me realize that I am lovable and to slowly develop and internalize that loving mother within myself; something that can never be destroyed or taken away from me, and that will be with me forever.

APPENDIX

Topics in this book touch on subjects like brain functioning and complex developmental trauma. Due to the fact that I am a coach and not a psychotherapist or trauma specialist, I have asked my therapist, Nicole Ditz, to provide this appendix below with information for those who want to learn more. A list of clinical resources follows this appendix for further exploration.

Nicole Ann Ditz

Integrative depth psychotherapist specializing for over twenty years in the long-term intensive treatment of complex developmental trauma in adults. www.holisticdepththerapy.com

Disclaimer: The emerging field of developmental complex trauma encompasses vastly comprehensive and multidisciplinary fields that contribute to wide-ranging scientific investigations, theoretical knowledge, and innumerable treatment modalities. These include, but are certainly not limited to, the brain sciences, interpersonal neurobiology, developmental psychology, attachment research and practice, cognitive sciences, contemporary relational psychoanalysis, models of characterological development, as well as myriad experiential, somatic, affective/emotional, component-based, and relational schools of treatment. Given this complexity and the limited space allocated in this appendix, I am only able to provide cursory explanations here. You can check out my website and the resources below if you are interested in exploring this complex field further.

My style of therapy includes numerous practices, modalities, and theories. These practices have included but are not limited to CBT,

DBT and learning distress tolerance skills, Gestalt role-plays, psychodynamic object relations work on ways one internalizes the bad mother introject, Jungian practices, dreamwork, the expressive arts/inner process journaling, voice dialogue working with inner parts/critic, solution-focused therapy when problems of living arose, Internal Family Systems, memory reconsolidation, traumatic transference work, traumatic reenactment and repair work, working with internal structural dissociation of inner parts, emotional regulation trauma techniques, transpersonal work, and depth couples work.

- **Complex Developmental Trauma** is often the result of persistent physical and emotional abuse and/or neglect as well as threatening, rejecting, invalidating, invasive, and chronic emotional misattunements that generally began in early childhood and that occurred within the vulnerable child's primary attachment caregiving system. Parents are sometimes quite well-intentioned but, due to their own psychological problems and unprocessed traumas, simply unable to care for and nurture their children in healthy ways. Developmental trauma can lead to varying levels of widespread and multifaceted disruption and disorganization of both the rapidly developing brain's neural and structural architecture as well as the autonomic nervous system, inclusive of the sympathetic and parasympathetic branches. These branches are responsible for fight/flight/freeze/collapse/shut down reactions secondary to major threats like trauma. The traumatized brain is marked by a lack of robust integration between the top executive prefrontal brain region and the more primitive emotional and survival-oriented limbic midbrain and brain stem. Secondarily, trauma can diminish the rich synaptic connectivity between the horizontal right and left brain regions and cause cross-hemispheric disorganization. The right subcortical hemisphere, among its innumerable other functions, is responsible more for storing prelinguistic implicit emotional trauma memories and somatic trauma-related sensations, whereas the left hemisphere is more oriented toward conscious logical, analytical, verbal, and cognitive abstract understanding. Since a good portion of relational childhood trauma is stored in preverbal unconscious neural brain networks, a therapy based predominately on cognitive verbal analysis is of limited usefulness in promoting healing. A competent trauma therapist must spend much time connecting with the adult's primitive subcortical emotional right brain through deep attachment-based processes and experiential work.

Complex Developmental Trauma and its deleterious impact on brain and nervous system organization leads to widespread damaging brain alterations in consciousness, arousal, emotional, cognitive, perceptual, and relational/attachment systems, as well as internal working brain models of self, others, and the world. This can lead to ongoing emotional dysregulation; dissociative symptoms; damage in the formation of a robust sense of self with often heavy shame-based identifications; feelings of pervasive isolation/ aloneness; occasional overwhelming spontaneous eruptive affects of terror, horror, or despair; as well as varying levels of chronic anxiety, agitation, depression, and/or anger. Interpersonal symptoms may include, for example, distrust of others, social anxiety, and insecure primary attachment styles such as anxious/preoccupied, avoidant/ dismissive, and disorganized attachment. A pervasive and distorted negative worldview can form based on the way the child was treated within the traumatic familial environment. Complex subconscious projections may constellate around a nebulous sense of external threat, general unease, and fear of known and unknown others who may harm, invade, or criticize the fragile self. Conversely, another traumatic worldview based on an unconscious childhood history of emotional deprivation may instead unconsciously search for an idealized savior mother or father figure in relationships, institutions, social groups, religious/spiritual organizations, and so on.

Trauma becomes deeply embedded in the child's (and later adult's) neural brain pathways and nervous system. Thus traumatic symptoms are reexperienced repetitively in the adult's present embodied subjectivity via painful sensations, emotions, perceptual distortions, and oscillating states of sympathetic hyperarousal and parasympathetic hypoarousal that lie outside the brain's window of tolerance, a window in which emotions and experiences can be easily integrated. This can leave survivors feeling as though they are on a distressing roller coaster moving between unsafe high sympathetic states of fear/panic/anger and parasympathetic states of numbing/ dissociation/collapse. Neural triggering of trauma-related issues occurs even when cued by very subtle associations in the current environment that remind the brain subconsciously of childhood traumatic events, triggering the firing of these old engrained overreactive neural brain pathways. If others, for example, seem inattentive to a trauma survivor with an emotional neglect history, this could trigger disproportionate feelings of rejection, abandonment, or shame in the survivor. Given this constant experiential brain and nervous system replay of the trauma in the present, much more of my time is spent working with the current manifestations and sequelae of developmental trauma rather than excavating memories from the past. Trauma from the past is not really in the past, but rather lives on powerfully and experientially in the present, unless intensive healing is undertaken. Fortunately, our brains have remarkable neuroplasticity and are able to change throughout life. Research within the past decade in brain imaging, molecular biology, neurobiology, and epigenetics has revealed that long-term psychotherapy can effect changes and modifications in synaptic plasticity, neurotransmitter metabolism, and even gene expression.

- **Characterological False Self–Defensive Organizations:** These are a hallmark of complex relational developmental trauma because the child's brain, sense of self, and personality were formed within the crucible of a traumatizing and threatening family system within which the child had to survive. The false self forms a protective shell over the true self core and gets shaped to accommodate to the caregivers' implicit and explicit demands. These adaptations are attempts to preserve an insecure and fragile attachment bond with the primary caretaker and minimize further abuse and rejection. These characterological adaptations can take myriad forms. In the population of higher-functioning clients with whom I work, the adaptations I see most frequently include pleaser/compliant/over-accommodating types; strong/hero/in-control types; compulsively perfectionistic/successful/productive types; caretaker/mediator/parentified-child types; emotionally detached/cerebrally dominant types; and dreamy/dissociative/spiritual types. These and countless other adaptations are sadly often rewarded and reinforced by society both in childhood and adulthood. Much of my time as a trauma therapist is spent carefully and gently dismantling the constricting excesses of these defensive false personas while at the same time helping clients to grow and develop an exuberant, robust, and free authentic sense of self. (For an interesting descriptive read on trauma, psychological masks, and false/true self issues, I would refer you to my website section "The Invisible Faces of Complex Trauma.")

- **Black Hole:** In contemporary psychoanalysis and trauma theory, the black hole is described as dissociative gaps, breaches, internal voids, unformulated experiences, and missing structures in the formulation of a solid and cohesive sense of self. These deficits or psychological holes in self-structure are a consequence of a person's childhood development occurring within abusive, intrusive, and neglectful families. Authentic solid self structure coalesces and consolidates when a child develops within a generally calm, supportive, safe, protective, and emotionally attuned caregiving environment.

When the environment is traumatizing, the child is not able to rest in and explore her/his intrapsychic experience of self, but rather has to live, in a sense, inside out, hypervigilant to the threats in the external familial environment and defensively trying to anticipate and protect herself/himself from psychological and even sometimes physical harm. This creates traumatic disruptions in the process of self-formation. The holes in self-structure correlate with brain and nervous system disorganization, dysregulation, and internal structural dissociation. This, in turn, allows primitive eruptions of intense overwhelming affects like terror of annihilation, horror, or intense shame to sometimes break through defense structures and flood the child's and later the adult's conscious self. Some clients describe this subjectively as feeling like they might "disappear, dissolve, be destroyed, go crazy, implode, or shatter." Other clients describe these holes phenomenologically as being "empty, dark, cold spaces of nothingness" where they feel completely alone and fear they will cease to exist.

- **The External Womb:** As a deeply integrative and relationally based developmental trauma therapist, I conceive of the long-term corrective therapeutic relationship as being metaphorically a type of reparative therapeutic nest or external womb. The therapeutic relationship/alliance has been empirically found across all theoretical schools of psychology and interpersonal neurobiology to be the central healing agent regardless of what other practices and therapeutic strategies are employed. Within this specialized therapeutic womb, I provide for my clients an ongoing and steady flow of psychological, emotional, cognitive, and relational supplies that were missing during their critical formative childhood years of brain and self-development. This enriched relational growing environment provides millions of micro moments of empathic attunement, compassionate presence, skillful responsiveness, resonance, validation and valuing, emotional holding and regulation, reframing of perceptual distortions, processing of traumatic memories, repair of therapeutic ruptures, psychoeducation, teaching innumerable new psychological skills, and a plethora of experiential opportunities to practice new ways of being an individuated and connected authentic self. The therapeutic womb allows for the growth of a new internalized working model of earned secure attachment. Some academic psychological schools refer to this therapeutic attachment relationship as providing a type of "limited reparenting." The burgeoning fields of brain sciences and neurobiology, along with new technology like fMRIs, are providing more and more evidence that this type of long-term corrective therapeutic relationship actually promotes neuroplastic changes in the brain's processing, integration, and structure.

- **Building an Authentic Sense of Self in Therapy:** A person's sense of self is always formed and deformed within primary caregiving relationships, beginning from birth. When those primary attachment relationships are fraught with traumatizing interactions, billions of healthy relational supplies crucial to the development of authentic self-formation are missing, and the process of developing a solid sense of self is profoundly derailed. However, due to lifelong brain plasticity, integrative relational trauma therapists like myself are able to provide, within a new corrective therapeutic relationship, and over many years, enough of the relational supplies that were missing or distorted at crucial formative periods. This is obviously not the same as receiving these supplies and a secure attachment relationship as a baby and child. Yet it is still so amazing to me how many of my clients are able to grow from being chronically emotionally dysregulated, lost, disconnected from themselves, unaware of their true inner needs/wants, trapped within painful characterological defense styles and unhealthy relationships to becoming significantly more assertive, confident, self-aware, alive, emotionally regulated, secure in their sense of self-worth, and able to form healthy, fulfilling relationships and experience themselves internally as solid and real. This is the hard-won miracle of the slow constellation of true selfhood. It seems to take forever—two steps forward, one step back. Old ways of being, defenses, and wounded patterns are formidable and tenacious. Yet for those with perseverance, fortitude, and courage to stay the course, I have witnessed the growth of an authentic and evolving sense of self in so many people who started off feeling broken, worthless, and hopeless. People are damaged in early traumatizing relationships, but they can also be helped to change, heal, and grow a new sense of self within skillful and emotionally responsive relationships throughout the life span. It is impossible to grow an authentic sense of self alone.

• **Inner Mother, Inner Child, and Internal Bonding:** Inner child parts are considered subpersonalities in a healthy, nontraumatized adult. They carry the developmental imprint in our brain of our formative childhood experiences: explicit and implicit memories, feelings, beliefs, views of ourselves and the world, as well as early primary attachment experiences. In the case of developmental trauma, these formative experiences were rife with deeply distressing emotions such as fear, shame, distrust, and hurt in primary relationships and a basic lack of safety and emotional security. For trauma survivors, these child parts or regressive brain states are often, at least initially, partially dissociated within the self system in order to allow the adult to function in the world. We might metaphorically conceive of these traumatized child parts as appearing in the adult person during dysregulated sympathetic nervous system activity, such as strong fear and anger, or overactive parasympathetic states, such as shame and despair. We can continue to extend this metaphor to the idea of traumatized inner child states as being representational of more primitive, subcortical unconscious brain stem and limbic region activity associated with prelinguistic strong emotions, sensations, survival needs, warped internal working models of insecure attachment relations, as well as traumatic fight/flight/freeze/shut down states.

The metaphorical "inner mother" can be imagined to be associated with bilateral prefrontal executive mature brain regions marked by conscious reason, logic, problem solving, and interoceptive self-reflective skills. This inner mother has the capacity to develop self-system leadership, learning to regulate and self-soothe intense states of distress in the child subparts and translate them into conceptual understanding and effective actions. These inner mother executive brain capacities are learned by internalizing, over a long time, the "mothering" functions of the trauma therapist. Trauma survivors often initially have little capacity for felt insight and emotional self-regulation, as primitive traumatized affective states are very powerful and easily overwhelm the higher regions of the brain. Thus, the therapist must directly attend to providing relational supplies and emotionally attuned care of the adult's child parts for quite some time until the adult grows the capacity to take over these skills for herself.

Over much time, as a secure internal attachment bond forms between inner mother and inner child sub-selves, the brain becomes more vertically and horizontally integrated from the top down and across the right and left hemispheres. This gives the healing survivor a sense of greater calm, harmony, competency, safety, security, emotional regulation, and well-being. Inner child subparts do not disappear, as some believe, but rather grow a felt sense of being emotionally secure and compassionately attended to by the loving presence of an inner mother self. They are slowly integrated within the person's multifaceted sense of self. This internal brain coherence allows the person to navigate the tasks of adult life competently while infused with the vitality, imagination, and aliveness of the healed and held child parts.

If you are interested in reading further, refer to my website sections "Trauma and Treatment of the Inner Child" and "Voices of the Inner Child."

CLINICAL RESOURCES ON COMPLEX DEVELOPMENTAL TRAUMA, PSYCHOTHERAPY, AND THE NEUROSCIENCES

Armstrong, Courtney. *Rethinking Trauma Treatment: Attachment, Memory Reconsolidation, and Resilience.* New York: W. W. Norton & Company, 2019.

Badenoch, Bonnie. *The Heart of Trauma: Healing the Embodied Brain in the Context of Relationships.* New York: W. W. Norton & Company, 2017.

Cozolino, Louis. *The Neuroscience of Psychotherapy: Building and Rebuilding the Human Brain.* New York: W. W. Norton & Company, 2002.

Fisher, Janina. *Healing the Fragmented Selves of Trauma Survivors: Overcoming Internal Self-Alienation.* New York: Routledge, 2017.

Heller, Laurence, and Aline LaPierre. *Healing Developmental Trauma: How Early Trauma Affects Self-Regulation, Self-Image, and the Capacity for Relationships.* Berkeley, CA: North Atlantic Books, 2012.

Pease Banitt, Susan. *Wisdom, Attachment, and Love in Trauma Therapy: Beyond Evidence-Based Practice.* New York: Routledge, 2019.

Schore, Allan N. *Right Brain Psychotherapy.* New York: W. W. Norton & Company, 2019.

Solomon, Marion, and Daniel J. Siegel, eds. *How People Change: Relationships and Neuroplasticity in Psychotherapy.* New York: W. W. Norton & Company, 2017.

Streep, Peg. *Daughter Detox: Recovering from an Unloving Mother and Reclaiming Your Life.* Ile D'Espoir Press, 2017.

Van der Kolk, Bessel. *The Body Keeps the Score: Brain, Mind, and Body in the Healing of Trauma.* New York: Viking, 2014.

BIBLIOGRAPHY

Bargh, John A. *Before You Know It: The Unconscious Reasons We Do What We Do.* New York: Atria Paperback, 2019.

Bowlby, John. *A Secure Base: Parent-Child Attachment and Healthy Human Development.* New York: Basic Books, 1988.

Brach, Tara. *Radical Acceptance: Embracing Your Life with the Heart of a Buddha.* New York: Bantam, 2003.

Bradshaw, John. *Homecoming: Reclaiming and Championing Your Inner Child.* New York: Bantam, 1990.

Cori, Jasmin Lee. *The Emotionally Absent Mother: A Guide to Self-Healing and Getting the Love You Missed.* New York: Experiment, 2010.

Dworkin, Andrea. *Pornography: Men Possessing Women.* New York: Plume, 1989.

Evans, Patricia. *The Verbally Abusive Relationship: How to Recognize It and How to Respond.* Holbrook, MA: Adams Media, 2010.

Friday, Nancy. *My Mother, My Self: The Daughter's Search for Identity.* New York: HarperCollins, 2010.

Gibson, Lindsay C. *Adult Children of Emotionally Immature Parents: How to Heal from Distant, Rejecting, or Self-Involved Parents.* Oakland, CA: New Harbinger, 2015.

Harris, Massimilla. *Into the Heart of the Feminine: An Archetypal Journey to Renew Strength, Love, and Creativity.* Asheville, NC: Daphne Publications, 2014.

Lerner, Gerda. *The Creation of Patriarchy.* New York: Oxford University Press, 1986.

Martinez, Mario E. *The Mindbody Code: How to Change the Beliefs That Limit Your Health, Longevity, and Success.* Boulder, CO: Sounds True, 2016.

Maté, Gabor. *In the Realm of Hungry Ghosts: Close Encounters with Addiction*. Toronto: Vintage Canada, 2018.

Millett, Kate. *Sexual Politics*. New York: Columbia University Press, 2016.

Moffitt, Phillip. "Healing Your Mother (or Father) Wound." 2011. Retrieved from http://dharmawisdom.org/teachings/articles/healing-your-mother-or-father-wound.

Oliver, Mary. *Dream Work*. Boston: Atlantic Monthly Press, 1986.

Penny, L. "Most Women You Know Are Angry—and That's All Right." *Teen Vogue*, August 2, 2017. Retrieved from https://www.teenvogue.com/story/women-angry-anger-laurie-penny.

Piercy, Marge. *Circles on the Water: Selected Poems of Marge Piercy*. New York: Knopf, 2002.

Reuther, Linda. "Homecoming." *In Her Words: An Anthology of Poetry about the Great Goddess*, edited by Burleigh Mutén, 222. Shambala, 1999.

Rich, Adrienne. *On Lies, Secrets, and Silence: Selected Prose, 1966–1978*. New York: W. W. Norton & Company, 1995.

Shaw, George Bernard. *Annajanska, the Bolshevik Empress*. Whitefish, MT: Kessinger Publishing, 2004.

Sieff, D. F. "Confronting Death Mother: An Interview with Marion Woodman." *Spring Journal* 81 (2009): 177–199.

Tolle, Eckhart. *The Power of Now: A Guide to Spiritual Enlightenment*. Vancouver: Namaste Publishing, 2004.

Winnicott, D. W. "Ego Distortion in Terms of True and False Self." In *The Maturational Processes and the Facilitating Environment: Studies in the Theory of Emotional Development*, 140–57. New York: International Universities Press, Inc., 1965.

PERMISSIONS

Pages vi–vii: From *Dream Work,* copyright © 1986 by Mary Oliver. Used by permission of Grove/Atlantic, Inc. and the Charlotte Sheedy Literary Agency. Any third party use of this material, outside of this publication, is prohibited.

Page 9: From *The Power of Now: A Guide to Spiritual Enlightenment.* Copyright © 2004 Eckhart Tolle. Used with permission

Pages 25 and 244: Excerpt from "Husband-Right and Father-Right" and excerpt from "Disloyal to Civilization: Feminism, Racism and Gynephobia" from *On Lies, Secrets and Silence: Selected Prose 1966–1978* by Adrienne Rich. Copyright 1979 by W. W. Norton & company, Inc. Used by permission of W. W.. Norton & Company, Inc.

Pages 32–33, 96–97, 147: Republished with permission of New Harbinger, from *Adult Children of Emotionally Immature Parents: How to Heal from Distant, Rejecting, or Self-Involved Parents* by Lindsay C. Gibson, 2015; permission conveyed through Copyright Clearance Center, Inc.

Pages 93–94: The concept of "The Many Faces of the Good Mother" has been adapted from *The Emotionally Absent Mother,* Updated and Expanded Second Edition, by Jasmin Lee Cori (The Experiment, 2017).

Page 123: From *Pornography: Men Possessing Women* by Andrea Dworkin. Copyright © 1989 with permission of Elaine Markson Literary Agency.

Pages 127–28: From "Healing Your Mother (or Father) Wound" by Phillip Moffitt, https://dharmawisdom.org/teachings/articles/healing-your -mother-or-father-wound. Used with permission.

Page 138: United States and Canada, "Right to life" from *Circles on the Water* by Marge Piercy, copyright © 1982 by Middlemarsh, Inc.

INDEX